WAIVER DISTRIBUTED

AMONG THE DEPARTMENTS

ELECTION, ESTOPPEL, CONTRACT, RELEASE

BY

JOHN S. EWART, K.C., LL.D.

AUTHOR OF *ESTOPPEL BY MISREPRESENTATION* AND OTHER WORKS

WITH A FOREWORD BY

ROSCOE POUND, PH.D., LL.D.

CAMBRIDGE

HARVARD UNIVERSITY PRESS

LONDON: HUMPHREY MILFORD

OXFORD UNIVERSITY PRESS

1917

FOREWORD

By ROSCOE POUND

"Holding to the word," says Jhering, "is one of the phenomena by which an immature mental development is universally characterized. And so it is in law. The history of law might write over its first chapter the motto 'In the beginning was the word.' To all uncultured peoples the word, both the written word and the word solemnly spoken, appears something mysterious. Naïve belief ascribes to it supernatural force. . . . To the old Romans the word is a force. It binds and looses, and it has the power, if not to move mountains, yet certainly to transport fruits to another's field, yes even to draw gods from heaven and to cause them to abandon a besieged city." The attempts to identify law with morals and reliance upon ethical principles rather than upon legal rules, which go by the name of equity or natural law, deliver legal systems for a time from this tyranny of the word and lead to critical differentiation of substance and form, spirit and letter. But the reign of words does not come to an end. When men come to rely upon reason rather than upon arbitrary form to keep down the personal element in the administration of justice, reason has to work with words. Judges and jurists seek to measure conduct by maxims, to put each cause by a logical process into the pigeonhole of the appropriate legal category or to deduce the appropriate solution from a given conception.

Because of their moral flavor and the scope for individualized application afforded by their loose generality, maxims are in much favor in periods of legal growth. In the maturity of law, however, the demand for certainty, for security of acquisitions and security of transactions as the basis of the economic order, push maxims into the background. What were regarded as epigrammatic formulations of universal principles come to be regarded, to use Sir James Stephen's phrase, as "little more than pert headings of chapters." For a season men turn to juristic conceptions and believe that justice may be administered by a rigid logical development of these conceptions. To-day we are not so sure of the all sufficiency of the so-called jurisprudence of conceptions. In a new period of growth we feel acutely the force of Jhering's jibe that juristic conceptions "require a world of their own in which they exist wholly for themselves, free from every connection with life." We come to see that there is much more to be done than to maintain the security of acquisitions and security of transactions and that the social interest in the moral and social life of the individual man is not adequately secured by our method of deduction from traditional conceptions. Nevertheless that method is a permanent acquisition of legal science and is rather to be confined to its proper field than to be discarded.

It remains that we be sure our conceptions are what they purport to be. What Kantorowicz calls a *Wortwissenschaft* is quite as possible in the legitimate field of the method of conceptions as in that part of the administration of justice which calls for a jurisprudence of actualities. The metaphysician, whose chief business is with conceptions, encounters the same difficulty. William James tells us that he seeks the key to things in "some illuminating or power-bringing name. That word names the universe's principle; to possess it is after a fashion to possess the universe itself. 'God,' 'Matter,' 'Reason,' 'the Absolute,' 'Energy,' are so many solving names. You can rest when you have them. You are at the end of your metaphysical quest." Many things that pass for conceptions in the maturity of law, prove on critical examination to be but solving words. They are but substitutes for thought. Indeed what enables them to endure is a convenient elasticity and vagueness of outline that gives a certain play to the judicial instinct while preserving the appearance of rigid logical deduction. Hence the prevalence of these solving words is not a mere matter of mental inertia. Nor are these words by any means so deceptive as to have escaped searching scrutiny in the past, had it been convenient so to scrutinize them. Just as procedural fictions enable the hard and fast procedure of the strict law to achieve justice and dogmatic fictions impart elasticity to inflexible and immutable legal rules, so these pseudo-conceptions are often modes of escape from the inconvenient exigencies of a system of logical water-tight compartments. While jurists have been declaiming against a jurisprudence of conceptions, courts have been quietly, perhaps subconsciously, finding a way by developing soft spots in what appears a hard legal crust, concealed by words and phrases that have the appearance of fixed conceptions yet yield readily to the touch. But such pseudo-conceptions are at best a crude device. As we become able to define the respective provinces of rule and discretion, of logical deduction from conceptions and of individualized adjustment to standards, of analytical application on the one hand and equitable application on the other hand, every reason for the existence of these soft spots will cease. Like fictions, which have done their work, they will be no more than traps to catch the unwary.

We speak of the tyranny of words in jurisprudence, as if these masterful solving words prevented thought. In truth, however, if the solving words of the maturity of law have enslaved some careless thinkers, they have been grossly overworked by many a man of action in the law who sought the ends of justice instinctively with scant regard for the juristic means. Such words and phrases as malice, privity, duty, nuisance, implied, intention of the testator, vested and contingent, should be conceded an eight-hour day.

Having previously looked into the case of that much-enduring word " estoppel " Mr. Ewart now takes up another slippery word worn smooth with overuse and shows us " waiver " as a pseudo-conception. As one reads his acute and convincing exposé of this juristic talisman, one can but feel that the " absence of general conceptions, good or bad," which the past generation took to be a virtue in our legal system, is in part responsible for our excessive recourse to solving words. That simple generalization, the legal transaction (act-in-the-law, *Rechtsgeschäft, acte juridique*), would have served us well where as one of its multifarious activities " waiver " has been striving to stop a gap. The declared will to effect a legal result, given effect by the law, lurks behind much that has been called " waiver." Having no such general conception, but only special conceptions of contract, release, and the like, with special requirements in the way of form or consideration, we have sought to add another special conception of vague content, with what success, Mr. Ewart has well shown.

PREFACE

CRITICISM upon three grounds may possibly be forfended by a few words of explanation.

From a reader's point of view, there is too much repetition of the central thesis, and of insistence upon its validity. Systematic readers, however, will probably be few, whereas the author ventures to hope that many of his profession will consult the pages dealing with subjects in which, from time to time, they may be specially interested; and he believes that each of these men will acknowledge the advantage of a repetition which renders perusal of the whole work unnecessary.

It may be said, also, that while very many of present-day books are little more (sometimes a little less) than well-arranged digests, and that while authors (with a few exceptions) content themselves with transfer to their pages of good, bad, and indifferent judicial opinion, the present writer, in attacking received opinion, errs flagrantly in the other direction. In reply, an assurance and a suggestion are offered: an assurance that the writer, being well aware of his responsibility as well as of his personal limitations, presents what he has to say in no spirit of dogmatic infallibility; and a suggestion that, even as the French, German, and other professions would have much reason to be grateful to anyone who would introduce into their systems the principles of estoppel, so it may be that there are, in our system, some pretensed principles of "waiver" which are rightly unasserted elsewhere. If so, some one ought to attempt their elimination.

As a third criticism, it may be said that, on some occasions, the last case appears to have escaped the attention of the author. But books may have different purposes, namely, to indicate the existing state of the law, or to attempt to improve it. The present work is of the latter class. It is more critical and philosophical than authoritative; and the cases are referred to for purposes of elucidation rather than as conclusive pronouncements. For that purpose, the last of them may have less value than some of its predecessors.

The Hon. Mr. Justice Anglin of the Supreme Court of Canada has been kind enough to peruse the manuscript of the present work, and to him the author is indebted for many valuable suggestions.

JOHN S. EWART.

OTTAWA, CANADA, December, 1916.

CONTENTS

TABLE OF CASES CITED

WAIVER DISTRIBUTED

CHAPTER I

INTRODUCTORY

ABSENCE OF " WAIVER." The explanation of the somewhat curious title of the present volume is that although the author commenced to write a book about " waiver," he very soon ascertained that there was not enough " waiver " to write a book about. Twelve years ago he sketched the work which he had set himself to do in these words:

> Waiver is entangled with estoppel, election, and contract; and the first step towards separation will be taken when it is observed that it is principally in the law of insurance that waiver and estoppel become involved; in the law of landlord and tenant that

> waiver and election seem to blend; and in the law of contracts that waiver is confounded with agreement. Closely studying waiver in these three great departments, comparing and contrasting it there, with estoppel, election, and contract, will enable us to see what there is in it that is special and peculiar to itself. And let our procedure be to assign to these three departments such cases as properly belong to them, and, examining the rest, see what we can make of them.

Proceeding on these lines, the result arrived at was that nearly all cases of supposed " waiver " could very easily be placed in one or other of the three departments above mentioned. Some had to be assigned to release (in one sense a part of contract) leaving only a few stragglers of negligible character. " Waiver " evidently was an empty category, and modification of the title of the book had become necessary.

REAL " WAIVER." This general statement must be qualified by the admission that, in the older law, may be found one case of " waife " (translatable into " waiver ") and one of " waive ":

> (1) Waife is when a theefe hath feloniously stollen goods, and being neerly followed with Hue and Cry, or else overcharged with the burden or trouble of the goods, for his ease sake and more speedy travailing, without Hue and Cry, flyeth away and leaveth the goods or any part of them behinde him, etc. then the King's officer or the Reeve or Baylife to the Lord of the Manor (within whose jurisdiction or circuit they were left) that by prescription, or grant from the King, hath the franchise of Waife, may seize the goods so waived to their Lord's use, who may keep them as his owne proper goods, except that the owner come with fresh suit after the felon, and sue an appeale, or give in evidence against him at his arraignment upon the indictment, and he bee attainted thereof, etc. In which cases the first owner shall have restitution of his goods so stollen and waived.[1]

[1] Termes de Ley, ed. 1642, p. 285; quoted in Stroud's *Jud. Dic.* 2207. Waifs are *bona waviata*: Stephen's *Com.*, 16th ed., vol. II, 653. And see Foxley *v.* Annesley, 1599, Cro. Eliz. 694; 5 Rep. 109, where the word is spelled *waved*.

(2) A woman

> is called " Waive," as left out or forsaken of the law, and not an outlaw as a man is; for women are not sworn in Lutes to the King nor to the law as men are, who therefore are within the law, whereas women are not, and for that cause they cannot be said outlawed, in so much as they never were within it.[1]

These are the only sorts of " waiver " or " waive " that the author knows of; and that is all that he is able to say about them. Had his original purpose remained unchanged, his book would have been finished as soon as commenced.[2]

DISTRIBUTION OF " WAIVER." All else that is usually spoken of as " waiver " is, in the judgment of the author, referable to one or other of the well-defined and well-understood departments of the law, Election, Estoppel, Contract, Release. " Waiver " is, in itself not a department. No one has been able to give it satisfactory definition, or to assign to it explanatory principles. The word is used indefinitely as a cover for vague, uncertain thought. And although, on occasion, it may have helped some judges to do right under an appearance of legal principle, yet, upon the whole, and especially in insurance cases, its presence in our system of jurisprudence has been disastrous not only to clarity of conception, but to the general administration of justice.

In enunciating new doctrine of such apparently fundamental character, the author cannot restrain a feeling of hesitation and doubt, but he takes comfort and courage from various features of the existing situation: (1) Nobody has yet thought that he knew enough about " waiver " to attempt its exposition in a book.[3] (2) Although many

[1] See foot-note 1, page 4.

[2] An owner of property may, if he choose, return it to the common stock, and such action is properly spoken of as abandonment rather than as waiver: Atchison v. McCullough, 1836, 5 Watts (Pa.) 14; Dikes v. Miller, 1859, 24 Tex. 417; Eads v. Brazelton, 1861, 22 Ark. 509; Burke v. Hammond, 1874, 76 Pa. 179; Livermore v. White, 1883, 74 Me. 452.

[3] Publication, since the above was written, of a work by Mr. Renzo D. Bowers

judges and text-writers have indicated views as to some of the elements of "waiver," there is not only no consensus of opinion, but there is the widest diversity and conflict. (3) Nobody appears to know whether "waiver" is unilateral or bilateral; whether it is the same as election, estoppel, contract, release, or some or one of them; and nobody seems to care.

DEFINITIONS OF "WAIVER." The usual definitions of "waiver" are:

"An intentional relinquishment of a known right."[1]

"A voluntary relinquishment of some rights."[2]

"The relinquishment or refusal to accept a right."[3]

"A waiver must be an intentional act with knowledge."[4]

Those are the definitions, but no case can be produced in which a right has been effectively relinquished save by contract, estoppel, or release. And "waiver" appears to be effective only because, being sufficiently loosely defined, it

entitled *A Treatise on the Law of Waiver*, although excellent in some respects, does not compel modification of the text. See post, pp. 21, 2.

[1] Bradfords *v.* Kents, 1862, 43 Pa. 484; Stewart *v.* Crosby, 1863, 50 Me. 134; Kent *v.* Warner, 1866, 12 Allen (Mass.) 563; Shaw *v.* Spencer, 1868, 100 Mass. 395; West *v.* Platt, 1879, 127 Mass. 372; Bennecke *v.* Ins. Co. 1881, 105 U. S. 359; Boynton etc. *v.* Braley, 1881, 54 Vt. 95; Millikin *v.* Welliver, 1882, 37 Ohio St. 466; Dawson *v.* Shillock, 1882, 29 Minn. 191; 12 N. W. 526; Pratt *v.* Douglas, 1884, 38 N. J. Eq. 539; Sill *v.* Sill, 1884, 31 Kan. 248; Burroughs *v.* DeCouts, 1886, 70 Cal. 371; Holdsworth *v.* Tucker, 1887, 143 Mass. 374; 9 N. E. 764; Portland, etc. *v.* Spillman, 1893, 32 Pac. 688; 23 Or. 592; Hecht *v.* Brandus, 1893, 4 Misc. Rep. 61; 23 N. Y. Supp. 865; In re Smith, 1895, 108 Cal. 115; Rice *v.* Fidelity, etc. 1900, 43 C. C. A. 278; 103 Fed., 427; Fairbanks etc. *v.* Baskett, 1903, 71 S. W. 1113; 98 Mo. App. 63; Central Life, etc. *v.* Roberts, 1915, 176 S. W. 1139; 165 Ky. 296. Many other authorities may be found in *Words and Phrases Judicially Noticed* under the word *Waiver*.

[2] Stewart *v.* Crosby, 1863, 50 Me. 134; Dawson *v.* Shillock, 1882, 29 Minn. 191; 12 N. W. 526.

[3] Bouvier. Approved in Hecht *v.* Brandus, 1893, 4 Misc. Rep. 61; 23 N. Y. Supp. 865.

[4] Darnley *v.* London, etc., 1867 L. R., 2 H. L. 43; 36 L. J. Ch. 404; 16 L. T. 217; Hoxie *v.* Home, etc. 1864, 32 Conn. 40; Bennecke *v.* Ins. Co., 1881, 105 U. S. 359; Montague's Adm'r. *v.* Massey, 1882, 76 Va. 314; Findeison *v.* Metropole, etc., 1885, 57 Vt. 524; Holdsworth *v.* Tucker, 1887, 143 Mass. 374; 9 N. E. 764; McKinney *v.* German, etc., 1895, 89 Wis. 658; 62 N. W. 413.

sometimes assumes the garb of one of these and sometimes that of another. "Waiver" is said to have close relations with election also, because when you choose one thing, you are said to "waive" your right to the other — a right that you never had.

Let us take an introductory, and therefore short, view of the alleged affinities of "waiver" to these other subjects:

"WAIVER" AND ELECTION. In his work on Contracts, Mr. Bishop has a chapter with the caption "Election and Waiver," of which the first sentence is as follows:

> The law, in all its departments, is constantly presenting to the choice of people its different paths, so that a person who has elected one has waived another. The doctrines of election and waiver, therefore, belong together. We shall here contemplate so much only of them as pertains to contracts.[1]

If you had a choice between a horse and a mule, and you chose the horse, you would not say that you "waived" the mule. For you did not. You had an election between two animals, and, electing to take one, you could do nothing with reference to the other.[2]

You do not "waive" a right to appeal by acting upon the judgment — as is often said.[3] You elect whether to accept the judgment, or to appeal from it. If you chose to appeal, would you say that you had "waived" your acceptance of the judgment? It is customary to say, that where goods are tortiously taken and sold, the owner may "waive" the tort and sustain an action in assumpsit for money had and received[4]; but nobody would think of saying that the

[1] Ed. 1907, p. 326. And see Warren *v.* Crane, 1883, 15 N. W. 465; 50 Mich. 300; United Firemen's, etc. *v.* Thomas, 1897, 82 Fed. 406; 27 C. C. A. 42; Supreme Lodge, etc. *v.* Quinn, 1901, 29 So. 826; 78 Miss. 525; Cable *v.* U. S. Life, 1901, 111 Fed. 19; 49 C. C. A. 216.

[2] See *infra*, pp. 25, 7.

[3] Videan *v.* Westover, 1897, 29 Ont. R. 6, note.

[4] Dallas *v.* Koehler, 1914, 92 Atl. 356; 86 N. J., Law, 651.

owner might "waive" his action in assumpsit and bring an action in trespass. The owner has a right to elect; he makes his election; he gives up — he "waives" nothing.

The erroneous statement, that by choosing one thing you "waive" the other, has induced the very general effacement of election — that which takes place; and the installation of "waiver" — that which never happens. It has produced the following and much else:

> It is well settled in this court, that upon such forfeiture the policy becomes voidable at the election of the insurance company, not void. And an insurance company cannot sleep upon its intention to avoid the policy, to the prejudice of the insured. The forfeiture may be waived by laches of the insurance company misleading persons interested in the policy to their prejudice.[1]

The first two sentences deal (with sufficient accuracy) with election, and they complete the exposition — the company has a right to elect, and, if it wish to terminate relationship, it must exercise its right promptly. The addition of the third sentence (that the "forfeiture may be waived") can be explained only by the power of the habitual use of erroneous phraseology.

"WAIVER" AND ESTOPPEL. "Election and waiver belong together," but in the *American Digest* estoppel and "waiver" are treated as though they were much the same sort of thing. In the index, under "Waiver," you will find "See Estoppel," or you will be referred to other headings, under which you will read "Estoppel or Waiver in General." Plainly, the gentlemen of the digest do not distinguish between estoppel and "waiver." They are not to be blamed. They must follow the courts; and it is un-

[1] Appleton v. B. A., etc., 1879, 46 Wis. 33. Approved in Cannon v. Home, etc., 1881, 33 Wis. 596; 11 N. W. 11. And see Northern v. Grand View, 1901, 183 U. S. 308; 101 Fed. 27.

fortunately true in the United States, as the text-writers tell us, that

> The terms *waiver* and *estoppel* are ordinarily used both by the courts and text-writers as synonymous in the law of insurance.[1]

"WAIVER" AND CONTRACT. That election and estoppel lie a little out of the best beaten tracks, may afford some apology for their unscientific association with "waiver." For its classification as a contract, no excuse can be admitted; and yet, in the cases, we find such statements as these:

> An express waiver is in the nature of a new contract, modifying, to some extent, the old one.[2]
>
> To constitute a waiver, it must be founded upon a consideration.[3]

According to other authorities, "waiver" is not so much a contract as the product of contract. For example, in Fry on Specific Performance, may be found the expression "waiver by mutual parol agreement"[4] — as though "waiver" were a legal situation arrived at by contract. So also it is said that

> A mutual agreement is necessary to waive a prior contract.[5]

"WAIVER" AND RELEASE. Waiver and election "belong together." Waiver and estoppel are "synonymous in the law of insurance." Waiver is both contract and product of contract. And, once more,

> A waiver is nothing unless it amounts to a release.[6]

"WAIVER," CONTRACT, AND ESTOPPEL. "Waiver" and contract are thus often associated; and "waiver" and

[1] Vance on Ins., 1904, p. 343. To the same effect is Richards on Ins., p. 158.

[2] Kiernan *v.* Dutchess, etc., 1896, 150 N. Y. 194; 44 N. E. 698. Approved in Germania, etc. *v.* Pitcher, 1902, 64 N. E. 921; 160 Ind. 397.

[3] Linwood, etc. *v.* Van Dusen, 58 N. E. 576; 63 Ohio St. 183.

[4] 5th ed., § 1024.

[5] Whittaker *v.* Fox, 1865, 14 W. R. 193; 13 L. T. 588. And see Coss *v.* Lord Nugent, 1833, 5 B. & Ad. 65; 2 L. J., K. B. 127; Sanderson *v.* Graves, 1875, L. R. 10 Ex. 234; 44 L. J. Ex. 210; 33 L. T. 269.

[6] Stackhouse *v.* Barnston, 1805, 10 Ves. 466.

estoppel still more frequently; but combination of the three, with "waiver" resting on the other two, is rare. Mr. Bishop puts the matter in this way:

> The doctrine of waiver rests on one, or other, or on all in combination, of the following three principles, as the special facts and nature of the particular case indicate: namely, the principle of contract by mutual concurrence of the wills; the principle of contracts created by law; and the principle of estoppel.[1]

But why if, in any particular case, you have contract or estoppel, you should wish to build "waiver" upon it, the learned author does not explain.

"WAIVER" AND PERFORMANCE. Difficult as is the acceptance of all these *aliases* and alliances, when thus brought into close juxtaposition, assent to the assertion that "waiver" of a policy-condition by the insurer is really evidence of the performance of it by the insured, is still more difficult. But some authorities so declare. For example, in an action on a policy, the company pleaded failure to furnish proofs; the plaintiff replied that he had furnished them; and, under this reply, was held to be entitled to prove "waiver" of the condition:

> It is merely evidence of a performance. It is not the case of a substitution of a new contract for the old one; it is not an excuse for non-performance by the prevention or discharge of the defendants; but it is evidence of performance.[2]

A New York case distinguished — saying that if no proofs had been delivered, evidence of "waiver" could not be given in support of an allegation of performance, but that it would be admissible in aid of the delivery of defective proofs."[3]

[1] On Contracts, 1907, p. 330. And see Linwood *v.* Van Dusen, 1900, 63 Ohio 198.

[2] St. Louis Ins. Co. *v.* Kyle, 1848, 11 Mo. 292. And see American, etc. *v.* Mahone, 1878, 56 Miss. 189; McCullough *v.* Phœnix, 1892, 113 Mo. 616; James *v.* Mutual, etc., 1898, 148 Mo. 10. *Contra:* Diehl *v.* Adams Co., 1868, 58 Pa. 443.

[3] Meech *v.* Nat., etc., 1900, 50 N. Y. App. 148; 63 N. Y. Supp. 1008.

In another case, a reply of "waiver" to a defence of non-delivery of proofs, was said to be unnecessary, because

> The doctrine of waiver, in this connection, is, in substance, and effect, *estoppel in pais*, and *estoppels in pais*, at common law need not, although they might, be pleaded specially.[1]

"WAIVER" AND LEGISLATION. The word "waiver" and its derivatives have frequently been introduced into legislation; sometimes merely reprehensibly, and sometimes with vitiating effect. Section 16 of the English statute, 45, 6 Vic., c. 61, for example, provides that

> the drawer of a bill, or any indorser, may insert therein an express stipulation . . . waiving as regards himself some or all of the holder's duties —

language which could not have been used had the draughtsman understood that everybody's "duties" are founded upon the terms of the contract (expressed or implied), and that "waiving" some of the duties imposed by one form of contract really means the formation of a contract of different character.[2] Other examples of tainted statutes will be referred to in a later chapter.[3]

UNLIMITED MISAPPLICATION. There appears to be no limit to the ingenious misapplications of the word "waiver." We have seen that Mr. Bishop has said that "the doctrines of election and waiver belong together";[4] that "the doctrine of waiver rests" on contract or estoppel;[5] and this is the curious way in which he indicates that a man need not plead the statute of limitations unless he wants to:

> If the right to sue upon a violated contract is barred by the statute of limitations, the delinquent may waive this defence.[6]

[1] German, etc. *v.* Grunert, 1884, 112 Ill. 76. And see Gans *v.* St. Paul, etc., 1877, 43 Wis. 108; Replogle *v.* Am. Ins. Co., 1892, 132 Ind. 360, 31 N. E. 947.

[2] See *infra*, p. 15. [3] In chapter 7. [4] *Ante*, p. 7. [5] *Ante*, p. 10.

[6] On Contracts, 1907, p. 42. To the same effect is Page on Contracts, vol. iii, § 1677. And see Wright *v.* Fire Ins. Co., etc., 1892, 12 Mont. 478; 31 Pac. 87; Geo. Gifford Co. *v.* Willman, 1915, 173 S. W. 53; 187 Mo. App. 29.

Mr. Bishop introduces " waiver " in still other characters. At one place he says that

> the doctrine of ratification is a branch of that of election and waiver, treated of in a preceding chapter.[1]

In another place, under the heading " Consent or Waiver," he says that

> The doctrine of this sub-title is expressed in the familiar maxim " Volenti non, fit injuria." Waiver is simply a particular form of consent.[2]

And it is certain that Mr. Bishop could not, upon any other subject than " waiver," frame such incoherence as the following:

> We have seen that, to a large extent, the binding effect of waiver proceeds from the doctrine of estoppel, where no consideration is required. Moreover, an executed waiver, even though it was in the nature of an ordinary contract and voluntary, follows the rule of other executed contracts, which are good without a consideration; so that if, in fact, no return for it was made, it was like any other gift, and cannot be recalled.[3]

But " waiver " cannot *proceed* from estoppel (We must avoid, if possible, another *filioque* controversy), and " waiver " cannot be contract.

Still another author speaks of " a waiver of a right to rescind a contract," [4] when what he meant was that an election had been made to continue it. Elsewhere, it was said that a company was not bound by its " waiver," because " there was a non-acceptance of this waiver." [5]

Unilateral and Bilateral Characteristics. It is, of course, quite impossible that " waiver " can be election,

[1] On Contracts, 1907, p. 350.
[2] On Non-Contracts, §§ 49, 53.
[3] On Contracts, 1907, p. 335.
[4] Page on Contracts, vol. i, § 294.
[5] Phœnix, etc. *v.* Spiers, 1888, 87 Ky. 289; 8 S. W. 453.

estoppel, contract, and release. If it were identical with any one of them, it would, for that very reason, have little resemblance to any of the others.

Commencing with "waiver," we may say that (if it is anything) it is (it certainly used to be) of unilateral character. The possessor of some property throws it away. The effect may be that someone else is benefited, but "waiver" has no relation to benefits. A watch is thrown away, and some functionary or finder is so much the richer (if the true owner do not intervene). But the "waiver" is complete although the watch be never found, although it be flung into the ocean.

Election is "waiver's" nearest neighbor, for it, too, is unilateral. But in election, the act has a legal effect upon the relationship between two persons, or upon the legal right of some party. "Waiver" has no such effect. "Waiver" implies that you have something, and that you are throwing it away. Election, upon the other hand, implies that you have a right to get one of two things, or to occupy one of two positions, by choosing between them.

Release comes next in order; but it is bilateral, inasmuch as it requires concurring acceptance by someone else.

Estoppel is also bilateral, and depends, not (as in release) merely upon the concurrence of the estoppel-asserter, but upon his consequential action.

Contract is the furthest removed from "waiver" and unilateralism, for it connotes the equal action of the two interested parties.

"Waiver" cannot be all, or like all, of these. If it be identical with any one of them, let us say so, and we shall understand that we have two names for the one thing. And if it be not identical with any one, let us so declare, and ascertain, if we can, whether it has any separate and independent existence.

This fundamental and widespread confusion affords some justification for an effort at clarification. If any better warrant be needed, it is the fact, as we shall see, that here and there, among judicial *dicta* as to the nature and attributes of "waiver," may be found not a little support for the present writer's views.

USEFULNESS OF THE WORD "WAIVER." Notwithstanding what has been said, "waiver" is a serviceable word, and no sweeping condemnation of it is intended. But observe that it is used in three different ways:

(1) It occurs frequently in general literature and conversation, and, there, its use is entirely unobjectionable. No one would think of disapproving Cowper's line, "She rather waives than will dispute her right." But if we are told that, as a matter of law, she had waived it, our informant might well be asked whether he meant that she had executed a release; and, if not, what had she done?

(2) Technical use of the word as descriptive of a legal situation is indefensible.

(3) Introduction of it into legal discussion, for any purposes, is misleading, and is subversive of general appreciation of correct principle. For lucidity, we must define our terms and use them accurately.

"WAIVER" AND SUCTION. There is no legal situation, no legal concept, which can be properly described by the word "*waiver.*" It bears the same relation to scientific law as the word *suction* bears to physics. For although *suction* is a useful word in general conversation, it describes no natural force. And when men tell you that something happened through suction, the word, although possibly conveying the intended idea, must be translated into atmospheric pressure, muscular action, or some other well-known force before any argument can be based upon it. It is not itself a category. Neither is "waiver."

Confusion through "Waiver." Much confusion would be avoided if the word were altogether excluded from legal proceedings and legal discussion. But, probably, that is too much to hope for; and the admission is necessary that its presence, or the presence of some other such word, is convenient. For example, we say that presentment and protest of a note were "waived," and that is an easy way of saying that the contract was in such form that the endorser was to be liable without presentment or protest. But the evil of the expression is that the whole situation is thereby turned around and completely misunderstood. For it conceals the fact that, if the habit were to write out endorsements in full, in one class of them would be a promise to pay if certain steps were taken by the holder, while in the other class would be a promise to pay without that condition; and that the first of those contracts is now conventionally expressed by mere endorsement, and the second by endorsement and the words "presentment and protest waived."

Better Phraseology. But while we cannot get rid of the word altogether, let us be careful so to confine its use that it may do no unnecessary damage. And let us abandon all such misleading phrases as "waiver by mutual parol agreement" (as though waiver were a legal situation arrived at by means of a contract); "waiver is only another name for the doctrine of estoppel" (for if it is, let us have one name); "estoppel is the ground upon which waiver rests," and "a waiver must be supported by an agreement or by estoppel" (as though agreement and estoppel were useful supports to some other legal situation); "a waiver is nothing unless it amounts to a release" (and then it *is* a release); certain acts "will amount to a waiver . . . and estop the insurer" (as though the insurer had to be twice killed.

"Waiver" in Indiana

Harvard Law Review Article. In 1905, the present writer contributed to the *Harvard Law Review* an article embodying the views now under enunciation. Prior to that time, the decisions of the State of Indiana had proceeded upon traditional lines — breach of condition created a forfeiture, from which the only hope of escape was "waiver" or estoppel — and those methods were undifferentiated.[1]

After the appearance of the *Harvard Law Review* article (possibly *post* rather than *propter hoc*), judicial opinion indicated a change of view, and in one of the cases the court said:

> The misuse of the word "waiver," in this connection, is clearly shown by a recent writer in an illustrative article: *Waiver in Ins. Cases* (Ewart), 18 Harvard Law Rev. 365.[2]

But the application of the principles of election, as advocated in the article, has not been quite consistently adhered to. "Waiver" still retains its phraseological place,[3] and, in some lines of cases, even its determining force. Speaking broadly, "waiver" is thought to apply to defaults after the occurrence of a loss, while election is applied to prior defaults.[4]

[1] Supreme, etc. *v.* Volkert, 1900, 25 Ind. App. 638; 57 N. E. 203; Hanover, etc. *v.* Dole, 1898, 20 Ind. App. 333; 50 N. E. 772; National etc. *v.* McBride, 1904, 162 Ind. 379; 70 N. E. 483; Farmers', etc. *v.* Reavis, 1904, 163 Ind. 321; 70 N. E. 518; Penn, etc. *v.* Norcross, 1904, 163 Ind. 379; 72 N. E. 132; German-Am. *v.* Yeagley, 1904, 163 Ind. 651; 71 N. E. 897. The statement in the text has no reference to cases of election between remedies, or, in pleading, to election between defences; as to which see Germania, etc. *v.* Pitcher, 1902, 160 Ind. 392; 64 N. E. 922.

[2] Mod. Woodmen, etc. *v.* Vincent, 1907, 40 Ind. App. 714; 80 N. E. 427; 82 N. E. 475.

[3] Western, etc. *v.* Ashby, 1913, 102 N. E. 45; 53 Ind. App. 523. Very few of the other cases are quite free of the old phraseology.

[4] The impropriety of this distinction is pointed out in cap. 9.

Ohio Farmers' etc. *v.* Vogel.[1] This case was decided about the date of the Review article above referred to, but evidently was not influenced by it. It applied " waiver " (by denial of liability) to a defence based upon the absence of proofs of loss; while to the defence of a breach of the clause as to the tenement becoming vacant, the court said that the company

> had the right to elect between two inconsistent courses, and having chosen one, it will be excluded from all rights and benefits of the other. In such a case, in the absence of fraud, it will be conclusively presumed that the insurer, while he keeps the premium, waives the inconsistent courses.

" Waiver," it will be observed, is applied to a default subsequent to the loss; and the effect of election, as applied to a default prior to the loss, is not only imperfectly stated, but is supplemented by " waiver."

Glens Falls Ins. Co. *v.* Michael. In the following year (1906) came the important case of Glens Falls Insurance Co. *v.* Michael.[2] The policy stipulated, that " if the interest of the insured be other than unconditional and sole ownership," the policy should be void, and the defence was that the insured was a life-tenant only. The court declared that the company had made no inquiry as to title; that the assured was not guilty of fraud, for he was unaware of the condition; and that the company must be presumed to have been aware of the state of the title. To that very bad law (as the present writer submits) the court added something very much better:

> The same result is obtained, and the replies upheld by another course of reasoning. In our opinion the word "void " is used in the policy in the sense of voidable: Hunt *v.* State Ins. Co. (Neb.) 92 N. W. 921, and cases cited. If a title to the property insured, other than a sole and unconditional fee simple in the insured,

[1] 1905, 166 Ind. 245; 76 N. E. 977. [2] 167 Ind. 659; 79 N. E. 905.

ipso facto rendered the policy void, then it was void as to both parties. It will scarcely be insisted by anyone that the insured, at their option, might have treated the policy as void, and recovered the premium paid, prior to the fire; but the evident meaning of the policy was that, for a breach of its terms, the insurer acting with reasonable diligence, at its option, might avoid the contract. If the appellant could elect to avoid the policy for any reason, it is equally clear that in a case like this, where the insured had an insurable interest, *it could elect not to do so, and treat the policy as valid.*[1] If the stipulations with regard to title made the contract voidable only, then, upon discovery of the true condition of the title, whether before or after the loss, the insurer was required to make its election either to regard the contract as valid or void. A court cannot by its fiat alone render a voidable contract void, but it can only adjudge that the party entitled to avoid it had done so, and that it thereby and for that reason became invalid. If appellant desired to avoid this policy for the reasons pleaded, it was required to act with reasonable promptness after acquiring knowledge of the facts; and thereupon it was its duty to notify appellee of its decision to avoid the policy, and of the reasons therefor, and to return, or tender, or in some appropriate way manifest its willingness and readiness to restore, the unearned premium received. The answers filed do not disclose the time when appellant learned the true state of appellees' title, nor deny knowledge of the same at the time of issuing the policy, but proceed upon the theory that the policy was void *ab initio*, and without any action on the part of the insurer. This theory was wrong, and the averment of facts insufficient. The answers should have pleaded the covenants or conditions relied upon, a breach, and the acts done by appellant in pursuance of its election to avoid the contract.

Comparison of the above official report of the opinion with the report in The Insurance Law Journal[2] appears to indicate the existence, on the part of the court, of conscious rejection of " waiver." For evidently the words above italicized were substituted for others into which, through mental

[1] Italic letters are not in the original.
[2] 34 L. J. N. S. 904.

habit, the writer had lapsed. As first written, the language was:

> If the appellant could elect to avoid the policy for any reason, it is equally clear that . . . *it could waive its right to do so* and treat the policy as valid.

That was improved and now reads as above:

> If the appellant could elect to avoid the policy for any reason, it is equally clear that . . . *it could elect not to do so* and treat the policy as valid.

MODERN WOODMEN, ETC. *v.* VINCENT. In the following year (1907), the doctrine of the case just mentioned was restated in Modern Woodmen, etc. *v.* Vincent,[1] but, unfortunately, not without lapse into the language of forfeiture and "waiver." The action was upon a life policy, and the defence was a misrepresentation as to age. The court said

> The answer under consideration shows, (1) the existence of a warranty (which was immaterial to the risk); and, (2), its breach. It does not contain an allegation of an election by the appellant to avoid said policy, nor any facts tending to show such election. It is based upon the theory that the breach of the warranty *ipso facto* rendered the contract void from the beginning.
>
> The contract was not a nullity from the beginning. It ceases to be binding upon the insurer only after it has elected to avoid it because of the breach of a warranty or condition.
>
> It follows that an answer which seeks to defeat an insurance policy because of a breach of warranty, must not only set up the warranty and the breach, but also an election by the insurer to avoid such policy because of such breach, and this ought certainly to be true where the warranty was in regard to a fact immaterial

[1] 40 Ind. App. 714; 80 N. E. 427; 82 N. E. 475. Followed in Ætna, etc. *v.* Bockting, 1906, 39 Ind. App. 586; 79 N. E. 524; U. S. *v.* Clark, 1907, 41 Ind. App. 351; 83 N. E. 762; Farmer's, etc. *v.* Hill, 1909, 45 Ind. App. 605; 91 N. E. 361; State Life, etc. *v.* Iones, 1911, 48 Ind. App. 186; 92 N. E. 879; Supreme Tribe, etc. *v.* Lennert, 1911, 93 N. E. 869; 98 N. E. 115; 178 Ind. 124; Metropolitan, etc. *v.* Johnson, 1911, 94 N. E. 785; 49 Ind. App. 233.

> to the risk, the breach of which in no way added to the liability or burden to the insurer, and because of which it is improbable that any election to avoid would ever be made.
>
> No doubt the insurer might declare a forfeiture of the policy for breach of warranty, and after it had elected to take advantage of such breach it might waive the right thus secured, but until such election is made there is nothing to waive. If it always treats the policy as valid, such facts constitute, not a waiver, but an election to treat the policy as valid instead of void, a matter which in the first instance rests with the insurer, and in regard to which it must itself elect. The misuse of the word "waiver" in this connection is clearly shown by a recent writer in an illustrative article: *Waiver in Insurance Cases* (Ewart), 18 Harvard Law Rev. 365.
>
> Cases involving questions similar to the one here presented are numerous. Their multiplicity and conflicting logic renders a return to elemental principles not only satisfactory but essential, and the result thus reached is so eminently just and fair as to commend itself.

The "return to elemental principles" is welcomed; but the Review article must not be held responsible for the assertion that if the company

> had elected to take advantage of such breach, it might waive the right thus secured —

that, having terminated the contract, the company could, by "waiver" or any other unilateral act, re-establish the ruptured relationship of the parties.

RETURN TO "WAIVER." Notwithstanding the clear statement of the Glens Falls *v.* Michael case,[1] two subsequent cases proceeded upon the forfeiture and "waiver" idea.[2] In both the defaults occurred after loss, and, probably, the application of election to such defaults was not perceived.[3]

[1] *Ante*, p. 17.

[2] Providence *v.* Wolff, 1907, 168 Ind. 690; 80 N. E. 27; Caywood *v.* Supreme, etc., 1908, 171 Ind. 410; 86 N. E. 482.

[3] See *post*, Cap. 9.

In a later case, Northern, etc. *v.* Carpenter,[1] the defence was, that by the terms of the policy it was not to become effective till certain things were done; and the court not only held that the stipulation might be waived, but referred to the Glens Falls *v.* Michael case as having proceeded upon similar ground.

After a temporary return to election,[2] waiver was placed in full possession of the field in Majestic, etc. *v.* Tuttle.[3]

"WAIVER" ELECTION, AND ESTOPPEL. In a recent case, Supreme Tribe, etc. *v.* Lennert,[4] the court appears to hover between election, "waiver," and estoppel. It said:

> Contracts of insurance, with provision such as the one here with regard to occupation, are not rendered absolutely void, but merely voidable by the insurer upon breach of such provision.
>
> Where an insurance company knows of a breach of a condition of a policy, but receives and retains premiums thereafter, the breach is waived, and the company is estopped to deny its liability for loss under the policy.

BOWERS ON "WAIVER"

Since the foregoing pages were written, there has been published a volume entitled "A Treatise on the Law of Waiver" by Mr. Renzo D. Bowers. The author defines waiver as

> the voluntary abandonment or surrender, by a capable person, of a right known by him to exist, with the intent that such right shall be surrendered and such person forever deprived of its benefit.[5]

And he adds that

> there are four components of a complete and valid waiver, namely: A Person *sui juris;* an Existing Right; Knowledge on

[1] 1912, 52 Ind. App. 432; 94 N. E. 782.

[2] Western, etc. *v.* Ashby, 1913, 53 Ind. App. 518; 102 N. E. 45.

[3] 1914, 58 Ind. App. 98; 107 N. E. 22.

[4] 1913, 178 Ind. 122; 98 N. E. 15.

[5] P. 19.

> the part of the Person of the Existing Right; and an Intention of the Person having such knowledge to surrender the Right.[1]

Waiver, therefore, is a purely unilateral act. One person only takes part in it. It is complete when that person has evinced "an intention . . . to surrender the right." And no co-operation or consequent action by anybody else is necessary.

But almost immediately after making this clear, the learned author adds:

> The doctrine of Waiver has in every case one of three principles for its foundation — the concurrence of the wills of the parties; a contractual relation created by law; or estoppel induced by conduct.[2]

The meaning of these sentences may not be very clear and, unfortunately, is nowhere explained,[3] but they appear to indicate that waiver can *never* be unilateral.

The author speaks of waiving a defence to an action by not pleading it[4] — although not one of his three necessary foundation principles has any application to the absence of the plea. He speaks of "a waiver of the right to redeem" a mortgage;[5] and he says that a mortgagor may "release or waive his equity"—using the two words interchangeably.[6] And so on. Apart from its conformity to conventional phraseology, Mr. Bowers' book is (if the present writer may be permitted to say so) creditable to himself and useful to the profession.

[1] P. 20. [2] Pp. 20, 21.

[3] The idea is taken from Bishop on Contracts (see the extract quoted, *ante*, p. 10) and the alteration of the language is not an improvement.

[4] Pp. 175–177. [5] P. 205. [6] Pp. 209, 211.

CHAPTER II

"WAIVER'S" ALIASES

"WAIVER'S" ALIASES

VERSATILITY OF "WAIVER." The ubiquity and versatility of "waiver" are made possible by the looseness of its definition. For if you are content to say that "waiver" is "An intentional relinquishment of a known right,"[1] you plainly equip it for successful masquerading in very dissimilar departments of the law. Observe the following:

ELECTION. You have a right to elect between two legal situations; and for determination of the limits and methods

[1] *Ante*, p. 6.

of exercise of your right, we send you to the law of election. But "waiver" steps in, saying that when you choose one situation, you intentionally relinquish your right to the other; therefore

> "the doctrines of election and waiver belong together;"[1]

and therefore the doctrine of "waiver" (although there is none) ought to be appealed to.

ESTOPPEL. Upon the faith of your misrepresentation, some one changes his position, prejudicially, and we turn to estoppel for the applicable law. But "waiver" interposes with the assertion that you have intentionally relinquished your known right to allege and prove the facts as they are; and that therefore

> waiver belongs to the family of estoppel, and often they are convertible terms.[2]

CONTRACT. To determine whether you have agreed to the modification of a term of a contract, we appeal to the law of contract. But "waiver" intervenes, telling us that modification of a term of a contract is an intentional relinquishment of your right to adhere to the contract as it is; declaring that

> "an express waiver is in the nature of a new contract"[3]

and inviting us to discuss whether consideration is not an essential element of "waiver."[4]

RELEASE. And, finally, "waiver" claims to be identical with release because

> a release is a relinquishment, concession, or giving up of a right, etc.[5]

Let us observe, a little more closely, "waiver's" incursions and pretences.

[1] *Ante*, p. 7. [2] *Infra*, p. 31. [3] *Ante*, p. 9. [4] *Post*, pp. 39, 41.
[5] Coopey *v.* Keady, 1914, 73 Or. 66; 144 Pac. 99.

"Waiver" and Election

Inaccuracy and Confusion. For the simple statement that, upon breach of a policy-condition, the insurance company may elect whether to continue or discontinue its liability, substitute that the company has a right to "waive the forfeiture," and you have made clear reasoning impossible. Policies are usually expressed to be void upon the happening of certain defaults by the insured (that is, the policy is to be void if the insurer so elect); and when a default happens (although no election has taken place) it is assumed that the policy has been forfeited, and the insured endeavors to prove that the insurer has "waived" either the stipulation of the policy, or the breach of it, or the forfeiture — he is not very careful to distinguish in that regard. That is all wrong. The case is purely one of election. The default has not only not caused forfeiture of the policy, but has not in the least affected it. The contract remains as it was, until election is made to cancel it. Then it is at an end. And no "waiver" or other unilateral act of the Company can re-establish it.

Reason for Confusion. Substitution of "waiver" for election appears to have been due to the joint influence of two misconceptions;

1. In dealing with election, the courts frequently say, that when you choose one alternative, you "waive" the other:

> The doctrine of election of remedies applies, that, one having been chosen, all others are deemed waived.[1]

That is inaccurate, for you have no right to both remedies. You have a choice between them. You exercise the choice. And you "waive," or throw away, nothing.[2] But the inaccuracy is very popular, and, as one writer puts it,

[1] Pratt v. Freeman, 1902, 115 Wis. 660; 92 N. W. 368.

[2] *Ante*, p. 7.

> Waiver, equally with its counterpart election, pervades nearly or absolutely every department of law.[1]

2. The second misconception is that above referred to, namely that the breach of a stipulation in a policy (for example) creates a forfeiture.

And the coalescence of these two misconceptions produces the following: (1) A breach of a condition gives to the insurer a right of election; (2) election to continue the policy is a relinquishment of the right to end it; (3) relinquishment of a right is a " waiver " of it; (4) therefore, relinquishment of the right to end the policy is a " waiver " either of the stipulation or of the breach of it; (5) and, therefore, by a *tour de force*, election to continue the policy is a " waiver of the forfeiture " created by the breach. For example, in Porter on Insurance it is said that premiums

> must be so paid or the policy is voidable at the election of the insurers, who may, however, waive the forfeiture.[2]

It may be suggested that we might continue to say that there is " waiver " of the forfeiture when the election is *not* to take advantage of the default. But waiver of what? Not of the breach, for it may still be sued upon.[3] Not of the forfeiture for there is none. And not of the right to elect, for that has been exercised. If you choose to say that election to continue the contract is a " waiver " of your right to determine it, say also that election to determine the contract is a " waiver " of your right to continue it. Then try it, for example, on election between an orange and an apple, and explain that if you choose the orange, you " waive "

[1] Bishop on Contracts, 1907, 329.

[2] 1908, p. 502, and see p. 192.

[3] When a lessor continues a lease notwithstanding default in payment of rent, he may still sue for the rent. He does not " waive " it. And see S. Pearson, etc. *v.* Dublin, 1907, A. C. 351; Webb. *v.* Roberts, 1907, 16 Ont. L. R. 279; Caldwell *v.* Cockshutt, 1913, 30 Ont. L. R. 244; Carrique *v.* Catts, 1914, 32 Ont. L. R. 567.

the apple. When you go to town, you waive your right to stay at home.

EFFECT OF SUBSTITUTION OF ELECTION FOR "WAIVER." That is not only very unreal but very misleading and damaging. It is responsible for endless confusion, and very many erroneous decisions. Observe shortly some of the effects of the elimination of the ideas of forfeiture and "waiver," and the steady application of election:

1. PLEADING. According to the current form of pleading (save in England[1] and the State of Indiana),[2] the insurer, in his defence, alleges (1) the clause in the policy providing that the contract shall be void upon the happening of a certain event, and (2) the occurrence of the event; and the plaintiff replies "waiver" of the clause. But that is clearly wrong. For valid defence, there must be three allegations: (1) the clause in the policy providing that, upon the happening of a certain event, the company should have *a right to elect* to continue, or to terminate, the contract; (2) the occurrence of the event; and (3) that thereupon the company elected to terminate. Without this last, the plea is obviously insufficient.[3] And to such a plea, waiver, as a reply, is, of course, quite inapplicable. The plaintiff joins issue upon the allegation of election.

If the policies read in the way they are construed, no one would think of omitting, from the insurer's defence, the allegation of the fact of election. For example, if the policy provided that, upon default, the "directors may, at their option, annul the policy," a necessary averment would be that the directors did annul the policy.[4] And if, in the

[1] Roberts *v.* Davey, 1833, 4 B. & Ad. 672; 2 L. J. K. B. 141; Deposit, etc. *v.* Ayscough, 1856, 6 E. & B. 763; 26 L. J. Q. B. 29.

[2] *Ante*, pp. 16–21.

[3] See *infra*, Cap. 9.

[4] An allegation that a committee of the directors annulled the policy would be insufficient: Jolliffe *v.* Madison, etc., 1875, 39 Wis. 111.

usual policy, the words *void at the election of the insurer were* substituted for the word *void*, nobody would make a mistake about the form of the insurer's defence.

2. Relevancy of Facts. All the facts which, heretofore, have been appealed to as evidence of "waiver" will be relevant upon the issue of the company's election to terminate. And a great deal of confusion will be got rid of (as we shall see) by dealing with them in that way.

3: Onus of Proof. The onus of proof will be changed. Heretofore the burden of proving "waiver" lay heavily upon the insured.[1] Now the insurer must prove election to cancel. For if there be no such election, the contract remains in force. At present, even when the case is recognized as one of election, the vitiating influence of the words forfeiture and "waiver" induces the idea that "waiver," and not election, must be proved.

4. Proof of Agency. Heretofore the insurer had to prove the authority of the person who is alleged to have "waived" the condition. Many a righteous case has failed because of that requirement. Henceforth, the onus is on the company to establish that the official who is alleged to have made the election had authority sufficient for that purpose.

5. Silence-Strategy. Silence-strategy will be no longer available to the companies. At present some courts say that breach of a condition is a forfeiture of the policy, and that a "waiver" of such forfeiture

> cannot be inferred from mere silence. It (the company) is not obliged to do or say anything to make a forfeiture effectual.[2] It

[1] There is no doubt that, as at present regarded, the onus is on the assured to prove both "waiver" and authority to "waive": Bosworth *v.* Merchants, etc., 1891, 80 Wis. 393; Frank *v.* Sun, etc., 1893, 20 Ont. A. R. 570; 32 Can. S. C. R. 152; Atlas *v.* Brownell, 1899, 29 Can. S. C. R. 544; Northern, etc. *v.* Grand View, etc., 1901, 183 U. S. 361; Hyde *v.* Lefaivre, 1902, 32 Can. S. C. R. 479.

[2] What does that mean?

> may wait until claim is made under the policy, and then in denial thereof, or in defence of a suit commenced therefor, allege a forfeiture.[1]

And these courts are, at all events, consistent in thus holding. For if we assume that breach of a condition has, in reality, " forfeited," in the sense of terminated, the policy, there can be no reason why the company should send notification of any sort to the insured. He knows of the breach as well as the company does (and usually better), and he knows, too, that his contract is at an end. Then why tell him anything?

Other courts are less consistent, but more nearly correct, when they declare that

> If the company contemplated the forfeiture of the policy because of the non-payment of the premium, it should at once have so declared, plainly and unconditionally.[2]

Such language (notwithstanding the misuse of the word "forfeiture") rightly assumes that the breach has no effect upon the policy; and that its termination is the result of the company's election. That being so, the necessity for a declaration by the company is obvious. If the breach ended the policy, then, as we have said, the company could have nothing to communicate to the assured, for he knew of the breach and of its legal effect. But if it be the election of the company that is the important factor, then the com-

[1] Titus *v.* Glenn Falls, etc., 1880, 81 N. Y. 419; 8 Abb. N. C. 315. Approved in Cannon *v.* Home, etc., 1881, 53 Wis. 594; 11 N. W. 11. And see Phœnix, etc. *v.* Stevenson, 1879, 78 Ky. 161; 8 Ins. L. J. 927; Smith *v.* St. Paul, etc., 1882, 3 Dak. 82; 13 N. W. 355; Schimp *v.* Cedar Rapids, etc., 1888, 124 Ill. 357; 16 N. E. 229; Queen, etc. *v.* Young, 1888, 86 Ala. 431; 5 So. 116; Armstrong *v.* Agricultural, etc., 1892, 130 N. Y. 564; 29 N. E. 991; Petit *v.* German, etc., 1898, 98 Fed. 803; Banholzer *v.* New York, etc., 1898, 74 Minn. 395; 77 N. W. 295; Parker *v.* Bankers, etc., 1899, 86 Ill. App. 326; Manhattan, etc., *v.* Savage's Adm'r., 1901, 23 Ky. 483; 63 S. W. 279.

[2] U. S. *v.* Lesser, 1899, 126 Ala. 585; 28 So. 646; Pollock *v.* German, etc., 1901, 127 Mich. 460, 86 N. W. 1017.

pany *has* something to communicate, something of great importance to the assured, and something of which he can have no knowledge unless it is communicated to him by the company.

The effect, then, of the change from "waiver" to election is that silence-strategy will be as obsolete as flint muskets, and that the law last quoted will be upheld, rather than that which supports the contrary view. If the company wants to cancel the policy, it must so elect. It cannot have a live policy for premium-catching and a dead one for loss-dodging.[1]

SUPPORTING AUTHORITY. As already indicated, some authorities can be cited in support of the views here enunciated; but even these are not always couched in language beyond the reach of criticism. The following are among the best:

> The common expression "waiving a forfeiture" though sufficiently correct for most purposes, is not strictly accurate. When a lessee commits a breach of covenant on which the lessor has the right of re-entry, he may elect to avoid or not to avoid the lease . . . In strictness therefore the question in such cases is, has the lessor, having notice of the breach, elected not to avoid the lease, or has he elected to avoid it? Or has he made no election.[2]

> What is called a waiver is not, so properly, a forgiveness or a condonation or release of a breach of covenant, as an election to take one estate instead of another.[3]

> Waiver is a voluntary act, and implies an election by the party to dispense with something of value, or to forego some advantage which he might at his option have demanded or insisted on.[4]

[1] Mutchmoor *v.* New Zealand, etc. 1901, 64 Pac. 814; 39 Or. 342; Phœnix, etc. *v.* Lansing, 1884, 15 Neb. 497.

[2] Bramwell B. in Croft *v.* Lumley, 1858, 6 H. L. C. 705; 27 L. J. Q. B. 321. Approved in Clough *v.* London & N. W. Ry. 1871, L. R. 7 Ex. 35; 41 L. J. Ex. 17: 25 L. T. 708, in a judgment which was really written by Blackburn J., see Scarf *v.* Jardine, 1882, 7 App. Cas. p. 360: 51 L. J. Q. B. 612: 47 L. T. 258.

[3] Croft *v.* Lumley, 1858, 6 H. L. C. 713, per Crompton J.

[4] Warren *v.* Crane, 1883, 50 Mich. 301; 15 N. W. 465. And see Cowanhoven *v.* Ball, 1890, 118 N. Y. 234; 23 N. E. 470; Decker *v.* Sexton, 1896, 19 Misc. Rep. 59; 43 N. Y. Supp. 167; United Firemen's Ins. Co. *v.* Thomas, 1897, 27 C. C. A.

A waiver of the right to rescind, or an election not to rescind, is either a matter of express declaration, or, as is more frequently the case, arises as a matter of necessary inference from the acts or conduct of the person against whom it is asserted.[1]

A waiver of conditions in a fire policy is in fact an election not to take advantage of a technical defence in the nature of a forfeiture, and should be looked upon with liberality rather than strictness.[2]

Further extracts may be found in the chapter on Insurance.

"Waiver" and Estoppel

Authority Contradictions. The confusion and contradiction exhibited by the following quotations amply justify the present attempt to elucidate the subject:

The doctrine of waiver rests upon estoppel.[3]

It is well settled in this state that estoppel is not the basis of the rules of law as to waiver of forfeiture.[4]

We use the terms interchangeably.[5]

The terms "estoppel" and "waiver," though not technically identical, are so nearly allied, and, as applied in the law of insurance, so like in the consequences which follow their successful application, that they are used indiscriminately by the courts.[6]

Waiver belongs to the family of estoppel, and often they are convertible terms.[7]

42; 82 Fed. 406; French v. Seamans, 1897, 21 Misc. Rep. 722; 48 N. Y. Supp. 9; Supreme, etc. v. Quinn, 1900, 78 Miss. 525; 29 So. 826; Cable v. United States Life Ins. Co., 1901, 49 C. C. A. 216; 111 Fed. 19; Liverpool, L. & G. Ins. Co. v. T. M. Richardson Lumber Co., 1902, 11 Okl. 585; 69 Pac. 938; Cedar Rapids Water Co. v. City of Cedar Rapids, 1902, 117 Iowa, 250; 90 N. W. 746.

1 Hallahan v. Webber, 1895, 15 Misc. Rep. 330; 37 N. Y. Supp. 613.

2 Corson v. Anchor Mut. Fire Ins. Co., 1901, 113 Iowa, 641; 85 N. W. 806.

3 Ervay v. Fire Assce., etc., 1903, 119 Iowa 308; 93 N. W. 290.

4 Modern, etc. v. Lane, 1901, 62 Neb. 96; 86 N. W. 943; Frasier v. New Zealand, etc., 1901, 39 Or. 347; 64 P. 814.

5 Montreal, etc. v. Walker, 1915, 173 S. W. 802; 163 Ky. 346.

6 May on Insurance, 1900, p. 1203; § 505.

7 Maloney v. N. W. Masonic Aid Assn., 1896, 8 N. Y. App. 579; 40 N. Y. Supp. 921.

The doctrine of waiver, as asserted against insurance companies to avoid the strict enforcement of conditions contained in their policies, is only another name for the doctrine of estoppel.[1]

Waiver is the giving up, relinquishing, or surrendering some known right, and may be found to exist if one acts in such a way that his conduct implies that he has waived his right, and amounts to a bar or obstruction only when established, and may be said to be an estoppel.[2]

Though a waiver may be in the nature of an estoppel, and maintained on similar principles, they are not convertible terms.[3]

The principle upon which the waiver of a forfeiture has been maintained in such cases is undoubtedly similar to that of estoppel.[4]

It would be an estoppel, which is the true ground upon which the doctrine of waiver in such cases rest.[5]

While a waiver of forfeiture need not be based upon a technical estoppel, yet in the absence of an express waiver some of the elements of an estoppel must exist.[6]

[1] Insurance Co. *v.* Wolff, 1877, 95 U. S. 333; Bigelow on Estoppel, 6th ed. 730. Cases too numerous for beneficial citation accept this view, or at all events refer to estoppel as identical with waiver. Among them are, Blake *v.* Exchange, 1858, 12 Gray, 271; Hoxie *v.* Home, etc., 1864, 32 Conn. 40; Ripley *v.* Aetna, etc., 1864, 30 N. Y. 164; Diehl *v.* Adams, etc., 1868, 58 Pa. 452; Elliott *v.* Lycoming, etc., 1870, 66 Pa. 26; Jewett *v.* Home, etc., 1870, 29 Iowa, 565; Security, etc. *v.* Fay, 1871, 22 Mich. 473; Lewis *v.* Phœnix, etc., 1876, 44 Conn. 91; Abbott *v.* Johnson, 1879, 47 Wis. 243; 2 N. W. 332; Mobile, etc. *v.* Pruett, 1883, 74 Ala. 498; Northwestern, etc. *v.* American, 1887, 119 Ill. 336; 10 N. E. 225; Niagara Ins. Co. *v.* Miller, 1888, 120 Pa. 517; 14 Atl. 385; Redmond *v.* Canadian, etc., 1891, 18 Ont. A. R. 342; Atlas Ins. Co. *v.* Brownell, 1899, 29 Can. S. C. R. 544; Traders, etc. *v.* Cassell, 1900, 24 Ind. App. 241; 56 N. E. 259; Rice *v.* Fidelity, etc., 1900, 42 C. C. A. 278; 103 Fed. 427; Fairbanks, etc. *v.* Baskett, 1903, 98 Mo. App. 65; 71 S. W. 1113; Central Life, etc. *v.* Roberts, 1915, 176 S. W. 1139; 165 Ky. 296.

[2] Croswell *v.* Conn. Indemnity Assn., 1897, 51 S. C., U. S. 478; 29 S. E. 236. And see Hennessy *v.* Met. Life Ins. Co., 1902, 74 Conn. 706; 52 Atl. 490.

[3] Queen Ins. Co. *v.* Young, 1888, 86 Ala., 430; 5 So. 116. And see Mee *v.* Banker's, etc., 1897, 69 Minn. 217; 72 N. W. 74.

[4] Hollis *v.* State, etc., 1884, 65 Iowa, 459; 21 N. W. 774. Approved in Home, etc. *v.* Kennedy, 1896, 47 Neb. 138; 66 N. W. 278. And see Weidert *v.* State, etc., 1890, 19 Or. 261; 24 Pac. 242; Billings *v.* German, etc., 1892, 34 Neb. 502; 52 N. W. 397; Frasier *v.* New Zealand, etc., 1901, 39 Or. 347; 64 Pac. p. 814.

[5] Elliott *v.* Lycoming, etc., 1870, 66 Pa. 22.

[6] Holt on Insurance, 623; Armstrong *v.* Agricultural, etc., 1892, 130 N. Y. 565; 29 N. E. 991.

The contention that a waiver must have the elements of an estoppel in cases of this kind cannot be sustained.[1]

Waiver need not combine the elements of estoppel.[2]

The doctrines of waiver and estoppel, as applied to insurance contracts, cannot be profitably treated separately, since the same circumstances that will raise an estoppel will usually also afford sufficient evidence of an implied waiver.[3]

There should be something in the nature of an estoppel in order to constitute a waiver of such conditions in the policy.[4]

Where such waiver distinctly appears . . . the party will be estopped.[5]

The distinction between waiver and estoppel, as applied to the law of insurance, is not in all respects clearly defined.[6]

Was there ever such confusion?

1. " Waiver " rests upon estoppel. But estoppel is not the basis of " waiver."

2. " Waiver " and estoppel may be used indiscriminately and interchangeably; the one is only another name for the other. But " waiver " and estoppel are not convertible terms.

3. " Waiver " must have some of the elements of estoppel. But " waiver need not combine the elements of estoppel."

4. There ought to be " something in the nature of an estoppel in order to constitute a waiver." But there is not.

5. Where " waiver " is proved, " the party will be estopped." But the distinction between them " is not in all respects clearly defined."

THE TEXT-WRITERS. The text-writers are as unsatisfactory as the courts. One of them says that:

[1] Modern, etc. *v.* Lane, 1901, 62 Neb. 96; 86 N. W. 943; Frasier *v.* New Zealand, etc., 1901, 39 Or. 347; 64 Pac. 814.

[2] Fink *v.* Lancashire, etc., 1894, 60 Mo. App. 673.

[3] Vance on Insurance, 1904, p. 343.

[4] Grigsby *v.* German, etc., 1890, 40 Mo. App. 276.

[5] Queen, etc. *v.* Young, 1888, 86 Ala. 430; 5 So. 116.

[6] Kiernan *v.* Dutchess, etc., 1896, 150 N. Y. 195; 44 N. E. 698. Approved in Germania, etc. *v.* Pitcher, 1902, 160 Ind. 392; 64 N. E. 921.

An estoppel exists when the insurer has brought about, or allowed, such conditions as make it inequitable for him to claim a right to which he would otherwise be entitled. A waiver is recognized to give effect to the intention of the party waiving, while an estoppel is enforced in order to defeat the fraudulent intention of the party estopped.[1]

Estoppel here loses its distinctive features. And all the help we can get as to " waiver " is equal to the light which might be thrown upon contract by the statement that " contract is recognized to give effect to the intentions of the parties contracting."

Quite as luminously, another text-writer distinguishes in this way:

The doctrines of waiver and estoppel are so commingled in the cases that underlying distinctions are frequently disregarded. Waiver implies an intention not to assert a known right, by one who has full knowledge of the circumstances. It is the result of a mental conclusion arrived at by the party; while an estoppel is a conclusion drawn by the law from something said or done by a party upon which another has relied to his prejudice. Estoppel may thus exist where there is no technical waiver. It is often said that a party waived certain rights, and, therefore, is estopped from thereafter asserting them.[2]

Waiver is " the result of a mental conclusion," but so also is the making of a will. Estoppel, surely, is rather an exclusion of the truth, than " a conclusion drawn by the law." What is " technical waiver? " And why, when a man has " waived " something, ought we to say that he is " estopped "? If he were " estopped," could we properly say that he had " waived " the thing? What do the words mean?

The latest of the text-writers[3] gives us no more help than

[1] Vance on Ins., 1904, p. 343.

[2] Elliott on Ins., 1907, p. 148. And much to same effect, is May on Ins., 1900, p. 1182, § 497.

[3] Richards on Ins., 1909.

his predecessors. For, after suggesting some unreal distinction between "waiver" and estoppel, he says that

> the words waiver and estoppel, however, are often used interchangeably by the courts;[1]

and he proceeds, throughout three chapters, bearing the joint title "Waiver and Estoppel,"[2] in very much the same way as the courts. For example:

> Nevertheless, all the courts recognize that there exists in the law of insurance an equitable doctrine of waiver and estoppel, but when and how to apply it is the perplexing problem.[3]

Occasionally, in these three chapters separation is made between "waiver" and estoppel, but such references only serve to make more confusing what has been previously declared. For example, at one place the author says:

> In case, however, there is no element of estoppel or of new consideration, then, by the weight of reason and authority, the act of waiver, unless it is evidenced by an executed written statement or agreement, is not binding upon the insurer.[4]

Why, if there be "no element of estoppel or new consideration," an effective act of waiver must be in writing, the author does not explain. He refers to no statutory requirement of a writing. He also says:

> I admit, of course, that there is a sound doctrine of parol waiver, which I contend must always be based upon estoppel or new consideration.[5]

Clearly, either estoppel or new consideration (that is, contract) is sufficient in itself. And if so, why base "waiver" upon them? Would any advocate know how to build up a

[1] Richards on Ins., 1909, p. 158.
[2] The author proceeds in the same way in his *Cases on Insurance*, pp. 132–155.
[3] Richards on Ins., p. 165. Observe the word "it."
[4] Richards on Ins., 1909, p. 160; Richards, Cases on Insurance, p. 138.
[5] 13 Columbia Law Rev., 1913, p. 55.

case of " waiver " upon either of them? Would it be of any value? And what would the thing look like?

Upon some occasions the author makes approach to election:

> If with knowledge of the forfeiture, the insurer elects to revive the contract, and evinces his election by an unequivocal and positive act of confirmation, or by conduct amounting to an estoppel, he cannot thereafter insist upon the past breach.[1]

The sentence occurs in the middle of the author's treatment of the whole subject, and is not preceded by any reference to election. That the author did not appreciate the significance of the election to which he refers, is shown by the fact that he speaks of an election " to revive the contract," whereas the insurer's election has the effect of *continuing* the existence of a policy which has never been affected.

Confusion is complete when, as in the following sentences, " waiver," estoppel, and election are jumbled together:

> Again, where the policy during its life, whether before or after loss, becomes voidable at the option and to the knowledge of the insurers, words or acts of the insurers, confirmatory of the validity of the contract, ought to be taken as good evidence of the exercise of this option to condone the default, if otherwise their effect would be to mislead the insured to his prejudice. To this last proposition substantially all the authorities agree, provided the representative of the insurer, acting on its behalf, has sufficient power to waive.[2]

Election in the first part of the first sentence; estoppel in the latter part of it; and waiver in the second sentence. Another paragraph is open to the same criticism:

> Any unequivocal and positive act by the insurers, recognizing the policy as valid, and inconsistent with the notion that the company proposes to avail itself of a breach — as, for example, the acceptance of a premium or assessment, the delivery of a

[1] Richards on Ins., p. 159.

[2] *Ibid.*, p. 163.

policy or a renewal receipt, or the levying of an assessment, or the endorsement of any permit on the policy — constitutes a waiver of all known grounds of forfeiture, and the company is said to be estopped from setting them up in defense, provided the insured can show that by such an act he has been misled to his injury.[1]

Here we have it that an indication of an *election* (an indication of what the company "proposes" to do) is a *waiver* and *estops* the company, if the assured has been misled. This appears to be building estoppel upon "waiver" and "waiver" upon election, whereas the same author has assured us, inversely, that parol waivers "must always be based upon estoppel or new consideration."[2]

DISTINCTION BY CYC. A notable attempt at distinction between "waiver" and estoppel is to be found in 40 Cyc., p. 255.[3]

While "waiver" belongs to the family of estoppel, and the doctrine of "estoppel" lies at the foundation of the law of waiver, they are nevertheless distinguishable terms. It is difficult to make a distinction between "waiver" and "estoppel" which will give to each a clear legal significance and scope, separate from and independent of the other, as they are frequently used in the cases as convertible terms, especially as applied to the law of contracts and in the avoidance of forfeitures.

That is not very hopeful, but the writer proceeds:

There are, however, several essential differences between the two doctrines. Waiver is the voluntary surrender of a right; estoppel is the inhibition to assert it from the mischief that has followed. Waiver involves both knowledge and intention; and estoppel may arise where there is no intent to mislead. Waiver depends upon what one himself intends to do estoppel depends rather upon what he causes his adversary to do. Waiver involves the acts and conduct of only one of the parties; estoppel

[1] 13 Columbia Law Rev., 1913, p. 171. [2] *Ante*, p. 35

[3] Quoted at length in Central Life *v.* Roberts, 1915, 176 S. W. 1139; 165 Ky. 296.

> involves the conduct of both. A waiver does not necessarily imply that one has been misled to his prejudice or into an altered position; an estoppel always involves this element. Estoppel results from an act which may operate to the injury of the other party; waiver may affect the opposite party beneficially. Estoppel may carry the implication of fraud, waiver does not. Estoppel may arise as between consistent remedies; for waiver by election to operate as a bar, the remedy must be inconsistent. A waiver may be created by acts, conduct, or declarations insufficient to create a technical estoppel. The most general distinction lies in the fact that the term "waiver," besides implying an intention on the part of a party to relinquish a right which is not present in estoppel, refers only to the act or consequences of the act of the party against whom the waiver is sought to be enforced, regardless of the attitude assumed by the other party; whereas estoppel arises where, by the fault of one party, another has been induced, ignorantly or innocently, to change his position for the worse in such manner that it would operate as a virtual fraud upon him to allow the party by whom he has been misled to assert the right of controversy.

If this be all true, the writer's reference to the difficulty of making distinction between "waiver" and estoppel appears to be unwarranted. That the explanation is not quite satisfactory even to the writer himself, appears from the sentence with which he follows those just quoted:

> The distinction is more easily preserved in dealing only with express waiver, but where the waiver relied upon is constructive, or merely implied from the conduct of a party, irrespective of what his actual intention may have been, it is at least questionable if there are not present some of the elements of estoppel.

Waiver, then, does not necessarily involve intention, and does not depend "upon what one himself intends to do." Closer examination would convince the writer that he is dealing with contract, election, and release on the one hand, and estoppel on the other, and that he can find no case of "waiver" which cannot be placed under one or other of these heads.

"WAIVER" AND CONTRACT

AUTHORITY CONTRADICTIONS. Of contract we know the definition; of "waiver" the alleged definition is "an intentional relinquishment of a known right;" and whether these are the same or are totally dissimilar, appears to be a reasonably simple question. But if so, how are we to account for the following contradictory statements?

An express waiver is in the nature of a new contract, modifying, to some extent, the old one.[1]

Waiver is necessarily a matter of mutual intention between the contracting parties, in the nature of a new contract between them.[2]

A waiver may be evidenced by express agreement.[3]

To constitute a waiver, it must be founded on a consideration.[4]

The waiver or dispensation is not in the nature of a contract which requires the support of a consideration, but rather of an estoppel.[5]

A waiver, being merely a voluntary relinquishment of a right, cannot be regarded as a contract, and does not require a new consideration to support it.[6]

There may be a valid waiver of rights of a certain kind (that is formal as distinguished from substantial rights) without consideration; showing that waiver differs from contract. A landlord may waive the forfeiture of a term for non-payment of rent, the maker of a note may waive demand and notice of protest, a party may waive the statute of limitations of frauds, without consideration. But where substantial rights are involved, we apprehend that a waiver must be supported by a consideration to be valid.[7]

[1] Kiernan *v.* Dutchess, etc., 1896, 150 N. Y. 195; 44 N. E. 698. Approved in Germania *v.* Pitcher, 1902, 160 Ind. 392; 64 N. E. 921.

[2] Order of United Commercial, etc. *v.* Boaz, 1915, 150 Pac. 822; 27 Colo. App. 423.

[3] Smith *v.* Snyder, 1895, 168 Pa. 543; 32 Atl. 64.

[4] Linwood Park Co. *v.* Van Dusen, 1900, 63 Ohio, St. 198; 58 N. E. 576; Terrell *v.* Proctor, 1915, 172 S. W. 996.

[5] Viele *v.* Germania, etc., 1868, 26 Iowa 56.

[6] Schwartz *v.* Wilmer, 1899, 90 Md. 144; 44 Atl. 1059.

[7] Fairbanks, etc. *v.* Baskett, 1902, 98 Mo. App. 64; 71 S. W. 1113.

A waiver, to be operative, must be supported by an agreement founded on valuable consideration, or the act relied on as a waiver must be such as to estop the party from insisting on performance of a contract or forfeiture of the condition.[1]

Waiver need not be based upon any new agreement or estoppel.[2]

In Titus *v.* Glenn Falls Ins. Co. 81 N. Y. 410, it was held that an effective waiver need not be based on either a new agreement or an estoppel. Substantially the same holding was made in Hollis *v.* State Ins. Co., 65 Ia. 454; and such is now the settled doctrine of this court.[3]

As already said, the doctrine of waiver is to relieve against forfeiture; it requires no consideration for a waiver, nor any prejudice or injury to the other party.[4]

This confusion equals that just dealt with under the heading " Waiver and Estoppel." For the assertions are as follows

1. " Waiver " is " in the nature of a new contract." But " waiver or dispensation is not in the nature of a contract." And " waiver " may be evidenced by contract.

2. " Waiver must be founded on a consideration." But " waiver does not require a new consideration to support it."

3. " Waiver " of formal rights does not require consideration. But " waiver " of substantial rights does require

1 Ripley *v.* Aetna Life Ins. Co., 1864, 30 N. Y. 164. And see New York, etc. *v.* Watson, 1871, 23 Mich. 486; McFarland *v.* Peabody, etc., 1873, 6 W. Va. 425; Underwood *v.* Farmer's, etc., 1874, 57 N. Y. 500; Merchant's, etc. *v.* Lacroix, 1876, 45 Tex. 158; Belknap *v.* Bender, 1878, 75 N. Y. 446; 31 Am. Rep. 476; Texas, etc. *v.* Hutchins, 1880, 53 Tex. 61; Northwestern *v.* American, 1887, 119 Ill. 329; 10 N. E. 225; Lantz *v.* Vermont, 1891, 139 Pa. 546; 21 Atl. 80; Decker *v.* Sexton, 1896, 19 Misc. Rep. 59; 43 N. Y. Supp. 167;

2 Titus *v.* Glens Falls etc., 1880, 81 N. Y. 419; 8 Abb. N. C. 315; Mee *v.* Bankers, etc., 1897, 69 Minn. 210; 72 N. W. 74; Corson *v.* Anchor, etc., 1901, 113 Iowa 641; 85 N. W. 806; Modern, etc., *v.* Lane, 1901, 62 Neb. 89: 86 N. W. 943; Supreme, etc., *v.* Hall, 1901, 24 Ind. App. 316; 56 N. E. 780; Johnston *v.* Phelps, etc., 1901, 63 Neb. 21; 88 N. W. 142; Hartford *v.* Landfare, etc., 1902, 63 Neb. 559; 88 N. W. 779; Cassimus *v.* Scottish, etc., 1902, 135 Ala. 256; 33 So. 163.

3 Modern, etc. *v.* Lane, 1901, 62 Neb. 96; 86 N. W. 944; Frasier *v.* New Zealand, etc., 1901, 39 Or. 342; 64 Pac. 814; Elliott on Insurance, 1907, pp. 149, 178.

4 Clark *v.* West, 193 N. Y. 349; 86 N. E. 1.

consideration. " Waiver " by a lessor of forfeiture of a lease is " waiver " of a formal right.

4. " Waiver " must be supported either by " an agreement founded on valuable consideration," or by estoppel. But " waiver need not be based upon any agreement or estoppel; " it requires neither consideration, nor prejudice to the other party.

5. We shall have occasion to observe also that a document which bound nobody may, by " waiver " become a contract binding upon a person who took no part in the " waivering." [1]

6. It has been said too, that " non-acceptance " of a waiver will deprive it of efficacy.[2]

EXPLANATION. The explanation of all this confusion emerges when we observe that the cases are dealing, for the most part, with the modification of contracts, and that the word " waiver " is being loosely applied as a method by which parts of contracts can be eliminated. The defence to an action for non-performance of some term in a contract may be:

1. Cancellation of the clause by subsequent agreement.
2. Release from performance.
3. Estoppel to require performance.
4. Accord and satisfaction, or acceptance of substituted performance.

And the idea is that there is, also, the defence of " waiver "? If so, what are its elements? Will " waiver " be established by proof of the emission of a few words — words which do not amount to contract, or release, and words which are not followed by any consequential action. No case known to the present writer so declares. Every well-decided case of modification of contract by " waiver " can be put upon better ground.

[1] *Infra*, cap. 6.

[2] Phœnix, etc. *v.* Spiers, 1888, 8 S. W. 453; 87 Ky. 293.

"Waiver" and Release

Identical or Different? If "waiver" be "an intentional relinquishment of a known right," what is release? Is "waiver" release without a consideration? And is release without consideration of any value? If it is, we may give release its discharge and install "waiver." If, on the other hand, relinquishment without consideration is invalid, we must adhere to release, and deny the efficacy of "waiver." But if "waiver" be unchecked by some attempt at definition, it will probably supersede release; and already the phraseology of the one is being applied to the other.

For the present, however, the language of 1805 will be generally accepted:

> As to waiver, it is difficult to say precisely what is meant by the term with reference to the legal effect. A waiver is nothing unless it amounts to a release. It is by a release or something equivalent only that an equitable demand can be given away. A mere waiver signifies nothing more than an expression of intention not to insist upon the right; which in equity will not, without consideration, bar the right any more than, at law, accord without satisfaction would be a plea.[1]

If "waiver" be release, we ought to use one term only, and so save ourselves from such language as the following:

> Conditions in a contract under seal can be waived by parol, where the waiver is in the nature of a release or discharge.[2]

The only example of what might be called "waiver" as distinguished from release is the renunciation of claim on a bill or note. For that there was the authority of the law merchant, now frequently embodied in statutes.[3]

[1] Stackhouse *v.* Barnston, 1805, 10 Ves. 466. Waiver at law and in equity are the same thing. Commercial, etc. *v.* New Jersey, etc., 1901, 61 N. J. Eq. 446; 49 Atl. 155.

[2] Palmer *v.* Meriden, etc., 1901, 188 Ill. 521; 59 N. E. 247; Starin *v.* Kraft, 1898, 174 Ill. 120; 50 N. E. 1059.

[3] See the English statute of 1882, § 62; Re George, 1890, 44 Ch. D. 627; 59 L. J. Ch. 709; Edwards 1896, 2 Ch. 157; 65 L. J. Ch. 557.

CHAPTER III

VOID AND VOIDABLE

VOID AND FORFEITED. If all misconceptions of the words *void* and *forfeiture* could be eradicated, we should have very little difficulty with " waiver."

A tenant commits some breach of covenant, giving the landlord a right to declare the lease " void," and we say that the lease has been forfeited, and that the forfeiture may be " waived." We use the same phraseology with reference to breaches of stipulations in insurance policies and in other connections. When we say *void*, we mean voidable. When we say *forfeited*, we mean that one of the parties may elect to cancel. And when we say that the forfeiture may be " waived," we mean that the election may be to continue the legal relationship and not to terminate it.

> Matters which are properly voidable are commonly spoken of as void. Technically and legally speaking, they are improperly so called. But the word *void* is so often used by good writers, and even by legal writers, in the sense of invalid, ineffectual or not binding, that it can hardly be said that this is not a correct and legitimate use of the term. Our books are full of the loose and inaccurate use of these words, and many difficult questions have grown out of this circumstance.[1]

Probably we should be wiser if we avoided the " difficult questions " by agreeing that " the loose and inaccurate use of these words " is *not* " correct and legitimate." The " doctrines of waiver " would disappear in a twelvemonth if we were careful of our phraseology.

CATEGORIES OF VOIDANCE CLAUSES. Clauses providing that contracts shall be " void " upon the happening of some event may, for the purposes in hand, be divided as follows:

1. Clauses which mean that, upon the happening of the event, the contract shall be *ipso-facto* void; either
   (1) void *ab initio*, or
   (2) void in the sense of terminated as to operation.

2. Clauses which mean that, upon the happening of the event, the contract shall be voidable at the election of the party for whose benefit the clause was inserted; either
   (1) void *ab initio*, or
   (2) Void, in the sense of terminated as to operation.

For the sake of brevity the two main classes may be referred to, respectively, as *ipso-facto*-void contracts, and voidable contracts. And it is not at all necessary, for present purposes, that we should arrive at agreement as to the principles of construction upon which contracts should be held to be in the one class or in the other. A few explanatory words only will be devoted to that subject. Recognition of the existence of the two classes suffices for present purposes.

[1] State, etc. *v.* Richmond, 1853, 26 N. H. 238.

"VOID" IN LEASES. In a general way readers may be reminded that, for interpretation of the word *void*, they cannot always depend upon the mere language of the contract — that regard must be paid to its nature, and to the presumed intention of the parties.[1] For example, many leases provide that default in the punctual payment of rent renders the lease "void." But that does not mean *ipso-facto* void; for if it did, a tenant could get rid of a burdensome lease by merely refusing to pay his rent. It means, in leases, and in many other documents, void at the election of him for whose benefit the clause was inserted in the document — at the election, in lease cases, of the landlord.[2] It is, of course, quite competent for people to agree that, upon default, the lease shall be *ipso-facto* void. The language must, however, put that intention beyond dispute. The following phraseology was held not to be sufficient for the purpose:

> The lease, as to the term thereby granted shall, in that case be forfeited; and the same term shall cease, determine and be utterly null and void as if the same had never been made; but the covenants . . . shall continue and be in force against him and them, until he or they shall have fully performed them."[3]
>
> The courts will in almost every possible case construe the proviso for forfeiture as making the lease for all purposes only voidable.[4]

"VOID" IN FIRE POLICIES. How ought we to interpret the word *void* when used in fire insurance policies? According to usual practice in fire insurance, the insured pays his premium and receives his policy — good from one to three years — subject to a cloud of conditions, upon the happening of any one of which it is to be "void." What does the word mean? In leases *void* usually means *void* only if the

[1] Sparenburg *v.* Edinburgh, etc., 1912, 1 K. B. 204; 81 L. J., K. B. 299; 106 L. T. 567.

[2] See chapter on Landlord and Tenant.

[3] Bowser *v.* Colby, 1841, 1 Ha. 111.

[4] Smith's L. C., 1915, vol. 1, p. 476.

landlord so desires, and he may or may not wish to terminate the lease. But is it not *always* the interest of an insurance company to get rid of liability as quickly as it can? and why, then, imagine that the parties intended to provide for an exercise of option? Why should not *void* in those cases, mean *ipso-facto* void? Probably, because, as a matter of fact, the companies do *not* usually wish to get rid of their liability. On the contrary they wish it to continue to the due-date of the renewal-premium, and to help them to provide still further renewal-premiums.

> The company does not desire to terminate the contract. Their business is to take risks, to maintain them, and to receive premiums.[1]

The language of some policies undoubtedly warrants the holding that, upon non-payment of the premiums, they become *ipso-facto* void. Other policies provide for suspension of liability during default in payment — an *ipso-facto* suspension operating automatically and quite independently of the election of the insurer.[2] Into questions of interpretation we do not now enter. People may make such agreements as they wish.[3]

"VOID" IN LIFE POLICIES. As life insurance contracts become older, they usually become of greater value to the assured, and the interest of the companies in their avoidance becomes greater. What was the intention of the parties when they used the word "void?"

A policy provides, for example, that it is to be void if any pre-contractual representation is untrue — does that mean

[1] Sears *v.* Agricultural, etc., 1882, 32 U. C. C. P. 595. In Minnesota, it was said not only that policies are, by breach, rendered *ipso-facto* void, but that, with one exception, "the authorities seems to be unanimous to this effect:" Banholzer *v.* New York, etc., 1898, 74 Minn. 394; N. W. And see Betcher *v.* Capital, etc., 1899, 78 Minn. 240; 80 N. W. 971.

[2] Post, p.

[3] Duckett *v.* Williams, 1834, 2 C. & M. 348; 3 L. J., Ex., N. S. 141; Thomson *v.* Weems, 1884, 9 App. Cas. 671.

ipso-facto void? Probably not, for the clause covers both slight and serious misrepresentations, and the company almost certainly wanted merely a right to elect. And clauses which provide for the termination of liability upon the happening of some future event ought to be construed in the same way; for the event might be of trivial importance and might happen very shortly after the issue of the policy — at a time when the company would certainly not wish to terminate its operation.

But it must be observed that there are different sorts of life policies; that it is quite competent for the parties to agree that the policy shall be *ipso-facto* void upon the happening of default; and that the word *void* must always be interpreted according to the intention of the parties. For example a policy may provide that the company shall not be liable at all until the first premium has been paid.[1] In the same way, the parties may agree for similar immunity during default in the payment of any subsequent premium. And a policy issued by a Benefit Society, in which insurance accompanies membership, may afford grounds of argument quite inapplicable to the policies of the regular companies.[2]

Warning must be given also against too ready acceptance of detached *dicta* declaratory of the *ipso-facto*-void character of life policies. For example, it was said with reference to life policies, that

> time is material and of the essence of the contract, and non-payment at the day involves absolute forfeiture, if such be the terms of the contract.[3]

But the learned judge, probably, did not mean to declare that the policies became *ipso-facto* void, for in another of his sentences he said:

[1] Sears *v.* Agricultural, etc., 1882, 32 U. C. C. P. 601.

[2] Parker *v.* Bankers, etc., 1899, 86 Ill. App. 315; Ostman *v.* Supreme, etc., 1913, 88 Atl. 949; Knode *v.* Modern, etc., 1913, 171 Mo. App. 377; 157 S. W. 818.

[3] New York, etc. *v.* Statham, 1876, 93 U. S. 24. Approved in Klein *v.* Ins. Co., 1881, 104 U. S. 90.

> Delinquency cannot be tolerated or redeemed except at the option of the company.

In other words, the policy was voidable at the election of the company.

Solution of Interpretation Unnecessary. It is not necessary for the purposes in hand to insist upon any view of the proper interpretation of the language above referred to. Indeed, it would be quite impossible to argue the points involved without having some particular forms of policy in view. It will be sufficient to observe that:

1. We may well doubt (as has already been said) whether the companies would themselves desire that the *ipso-facto*-void meaning should be attached to the word *void*. The companies (at all events until losses happen) are interested not in destroying their policies, but in keeping them alive, for the sake both of collecting past-due, and of earning future, premiums.

2. If the policy be *ipso-facto* void, the policy-holder, as well as the company, may so allege; and what would the courts say in the following cases?

(*a*) To an action by the company for unpaid premiums, the insured pleads that the policy provided that it should be void if gasoline were brought upon the premises, and that, prior to the maturity of the premium, gasoline had been so brought.

(*b*) To a defence in an action for payment of a loss, upon the ground of the existence of prior insurance in another company, the insured replies that the alleged policy provided that it should be void upon default in payment of any premium, and that prior to the writing of the new insurance default had been made under the old. In such a case, the courts would certainly declare that

> the mere fact of vacancy did not render its policy void, but voidable only.[1]

[1] Germania, etc. *v.* Klewer, 1889, 129 Ill. 599.

Classification of the Authorities. The authorities may be placed in four categories:

1. Those which declare, and intend to declare, that, upon breach, the policy becomes *ipso-facto* void.

2. Those which declare, but do not mean, that the policy becomes *ipso-facto* void.

3. Those which declare that the breach gives, to a company, a right to elect whether to continue or to terminate the policy, but which cloud the declaration with notions of forfeiture and " waiver."

4. Those which proceed clearly upon the view that the company has a right to elect.

1. Ipso-facto-void Contracts

We are not specially interested in cases within the first of these classes. We assume that, usually, in leases and insurance policies, the word *void* means voidable at the election of the landlord or the insurer, respectively. And we propose to pass under review the current methods of dealing cases in that class; to suggest the elimination from them of the phraseology of forfeiture and " waiver "; and to advocate, for their treatment, adoption of the principles of election. It may be advisable, however, to point out that " waiver " has as little application to *ipso-facto* void, as to voidable contracts.

Upon the happening of the specified occurrence, an *ipso-facto*-void contract becomes immediately void (either void *ab initio*, or thenceforth void in the sense of terminated) without the action of either of the parties — indeed, in spite of the wish of either of the parties. And it has ceased to exist, not at the will of one of the parties, but by the original agreement of both of them. No " waiver," therefore, or any other unilateral proceeding can restore that relationship — can create another *vinculum juris*.

2. Ipso-Facto Void — but not so Meant

Many courts have declared that upon the happening of some specified occurrence, the policy becomes *ipso-facto* void. But sometimes that is not what they meant, for they have added that the companies might " waive the forfeiture " and revive the policies.[1] Those courts would not desire to be taken as affirming, baldly, that after a contract had, in pursuance of the agreement of the parties, been terminated — that after the contractual relations had been ended, one of the parties could resuscitate the contract and restore those relations. Nevertheless their language does frequently carry that meaning — the policy has been forfeited, the policy is void, but the forfeiture may, by the company, be waived and the policy, thus, be revived.

> The law plainly is that, when a policy of insurance provides the premium shall be paid on or before a stipulated day or the policy shall become forfeited and void, time becomes of the very essence of the contract, and a failure to so pay the premium determines it, but concurrent with this principle is always the qualification that this is so unless there be a waiver or estoppel. We fully subscribe to the doctrine that in such cases the forfeiture occurs *ipso facto*, and no act of the company need be done either to declare it or enforce it. But of equal force and dignity is the further fundamental principle that a provision for forfeiture for non-payment of premiums when due is for the benefit of the insurer and may be waived by it. No act need be done to declare tne forfeiture, but some act may be done that will waive it, is the comprehensive rule wherein both principles are blended and harmonized so that right shall be preserved and hardship may be averted.[2]

By the failure, the policy has become *ipso-facto* void; the legal relationship between the parties is (by the agreement of

[1] As in the elaborately considered case of Northern, etc. *v.* Grand View, 1901, 183 U. S. 308; 101 Fed. 27. See also Appleton, etc. *v.* B. A., etc., 1879, 46 Wis. 33; Cannon *v.* Home, etc., 1881, 53 Wis. 585; 11 N. W. 11; Phœnix, etc. *v.* Spiers, 87 Ky. 293; Iowa, etc. *v.* Lewis, 1902, 187 U. S. 335, 348, 353.

[2] Equitable, etc. *v.* Ellis, 1913, 105 Tex. 536; 147 S. W. 1152.

the parties) at an end; and by "waiver" of one of the parties, the contract is restored to force. That cannot be right, but it is a good example of the language of scores of cases.

> By the very terms of the policy, the policy ceased and determined by the non-payment of the premium within the time stipulated in the policy. It could then be revived or continued in life, only in one of three ways: by a new agreement, by the operation of an estoppel, or of a waiver.[1]

If the words "ceased and determined" are to be taken absolutely then the second sentence contradicts the first; for if the agreement between the parties has really ceased to exist — if the legal relationship between the parties has been completely severed — no amount of "waiver" (if by that is meant some sort of an unilateral act) can either revive or continue it.

In a standard text-book is the following:

> If, after the policy has been forfeited by non-observance of a condition annexed to it, the insurers or their agent continue to receive the premiums with full knowledge of the breach of the condition, they will be deemed to have waived the forfeiture, and will not be permitted to avoid the policy.[2]

The learned author indicates that the policy has been forfeited (terminated?) by the insured, but that the insurer will not, afterwards, be permitted to avoid (terminate?) it; and that although the insured did forfeit (terminate?) the policy, yet that the insurer can, by waiver, set it up again. Neither of those assertions can be right. If it be said that by "forfeited" the author did not mean terminated, the reply is that, in that case, there is nothing to "waive," for the policy still exists. The breach has not, in any way, affected it. The insurer has acquired a right to

[1] Robertson *v.* Mct. Life, etc., 1882, 88 N. Y. 544. See also New York, etc. *v.* Watson, 1871, 23 Mich. 487; Frank Moreland *v.* Union, etc., 1898, 104 Ky. 129; 46 S. W. 516; Tilton *v.* Farmer's, etc., 1913, 143 N. Y. Sup. 107; 82 Misc. 129.

[2] Addison on Contracts, 11th ed., pp. 1231, 2.

elect between continuing and termination. That is all that has happened. There has been no forfeiture; and, if there had, no " waiver " could restore it.

The same confusion is to be found in the books on Landlord and Tenant:

> Though an acceptance of rent or other act of waiver may make a voidable lease good, it cannot make valid a deed or a lease which was actually void at first.[1]

— the implication being that the " voidable lease " has, by some breach, been invalidated, and that it may be made " good " by waiver; whereas, until exercise of the lessor's election to terminate the lease, nothing has happened to it.

3. Election, but Confused.

A minority of the cases introduce the principle of election, but very few of this minority keep clear of confusion with forfeiture and " waiver." The following is an example of very many:

> The policy did not become void when the conditions in question were broken. The breach of the conditions merely afforded ground for forfeiture at the option of the insurer. If the insurer, with knowledge of the facts by reason whereof he is entitled to insist upon forfeiture, continues to recognize the policy as in force . . . the forfeiture is waived, and may not be relied upon thereafter.[2]

But if the breach " merely afforded ground for forfeiture at the option of the insurer," there would be no forfeiture until the option had been exercised, and, consequently, no room for " waiver " of the forfeiture. The insurer had a right to elect to continue or determine the contract; by continuing " to recognize the policy as in force," he elected to continue it. There was no forfeiture, and no " waiver."

[1] Woodfall, 19th ed., p. 378.

[2] Hunt *v.* State, etc., 1902, 66 Neb. 127; 92 N. W. 921.

In a Connecticut case it was said that the policy

> was only voidable at their election, and that it was, therefore, competent for them to waive a strict compliance with it after the time stipulated for the payment of such premium; and that, in case of such waiver, the policy would be revived and continue obligatory on the defendants on its original terms.[1]

But if the policy was "only voidable at their election", and if they never so elected, the policy never ceased to exist; was never in the least affected; and there could, therefore, have been no revivor of it.

In a Wisconsin case the court said that

> Upon breach of such a condition, the contract of insurance does not become absolutely void, but voidable only. That is to say, it becomes void at the election of the insurer and not otherwise.

But, spoiling that, the court also said

> that the breach, by the insured, of a condition in the policy, the effect of which, by the terms of the policy, was to render the same void, may be waived by the insurer.[2]

An Ohio court, after declaring that a policy was voidable only, added:

> We then cannot consider that the company exercised their option to forfeit, and their failure to do so was a waiver of such forfeiture.[3]

That word *forfeiture* has made a lot of trouble. In a New York case the court said:

> The policy is to be regarded rather as voidable at the election of the company, than as absolutely void whether they choose to so regard it or not.[4]

[1] Bouton *v.* American, etc., 1857, 25 Conn. 551. See also Continental, etc. *v.* Chew, 1894, 11 Ind. App. 330; 38 N. E. 417.

[2] Webster *v.* Phoenix, 1874, 36 Wis. 71.

[3] Mutual, etc. *v.* French, 1876, 30 Ohio, 240.

[4] Huntley *v.* Perry, 1860, 38 Barb. 572.

But notwithstanding that clear expression, the court referred to the policy as "capable of being made valid" — as though the breach had terminated it.

In an Iowa case, the court said:

> It simply means that the underwriters, upon the violation of his covenants by the assured, shall cease to be bound by their covenants in the policy. . . . The policy does not cease to have a legal existence, it is the only competent evidence of the contract it embodies, and in truth is not void except so far as the underwriters are no longer bound thereby.[1]

That appears to be quite sufficiently void. But in an accompanying note, the court is interpreted as meaning:

> that on the happening of a breach, the contract, so far as it imposes obligations on the party for whose protection the condition is intended, becomes void only on the election of such party so to treat it.[2]

In a Kentucky case, the court said:

> The term "void" as used in the policy is to be regarded as meaning that the insurer may at his exclusive option treat it so, and not that the contract becomes an absolute nullity as to either party. The insurer may therefore by his conduct waive his right of forfeiture, and estop himself from insisting upon it.[3]

In a very recent case, the same court said that

> this right of election should be so exercised as not to subject the insured to unnecessary expense and trouble. And so, if the company is in possession of facts that operate to work a forfeiture, and it intends to rely on these facts to defeat any recovery, it should not be allowed to put the insured to unnecessary expense and trouble by letting him rest under the belief that it does not intend to rely on the forfeiture. In other words, it will be treated as having made the election it had the right to make, not to rely on the forfeiture.[4]

[1] Viele *v.* Germania, etc., 1868, 26 Iowa 51.

[2] *Ibid.*, p. 69.

[3] Phoenix, etc. *v.* Spiers, 1888, 8 S. W. 453; 87 Ky. 293.

[4] Mutual, etc. *v.* Walker, 1915, 173 S. W. 802; 163 Ky. 346.

The implication seems to be, that an election which did not "put the insured to unnecessary expense," etc. would not be an election. If the court had not been bothered with forfeiture and "waiver," it would not have fallen into that mistake.

The text-writers speak in the same unsatisfactory way:

> Where it is stipulated that premiums shall be paid by a certain date, they must be so paid or the policy is voidable at the election of the insurers, who may, however, waive the forfeiture, but are under no equitable obligation to do so, upon tender of the premiums due.[1]
>
> Non-performance of a condition contained in a policy makes the policy voidable at the election of the insurers. They may waive the forfeiture, or, by their conduct after notice of the breach, estop themselves from setting it up. The word "void" in a private instrument can rarely, if ever, exclude the possibility of confirmation.[2]

The use of the word *confirmation* in this connection is novel.

Criticism of the following will make clear the view of the present writer:

> The consequence of a default in the payment of the premium is defined in the policy itself. It declares that, if not paid on the days named, and in the lifetime of the insured, the policy should "cease and determine." By this I understand that it is suspended; it ceases to bind the company and to protect the assured, and this without any act or declaration on the part of the former. It does not require a formal forfeiture. This term is often used, and I think, inaccurately, in such cases. Nor, is the policy void in the general sense of that term. It is voidable at the election of the company, and that election can be exercised without notice to the assured, for the reason that the policy itself is notice that his rights cease with the non-payment of the premium. As to him it is a dead policy. It is true it may be restored to life, by the subsequent payment of the premium and its acceptance by the company. This, however, is a new contract by which the

[1] Porter on Ins., 1908, p. 502.

[2] *Ibid.*, p. 192.

company agrees, in consideration of the premium, to continue in force a policy which had previously expired; in other words, it is a new assurance though under the former policy. Want *v.* Blunt, 12 East, 183.[1]

1. It is true that the word *forfeiture* is often used inaccurately.

2. It is true that the policy " is voidable at the election of the company; " or, in other words, that non-payment has no effect upon the policy, beyond giving to the company an option to continue or to terminate it.

3. Therefore, we cannot say that the insured's " rights cease with the non-payment." They cease after election only.

4. Nor, for the same reason, can we say " that the policy itself is notice that his rights cease with the non-payment" ; for they do not.

5. Nor can we say that the policy is " suspended," or is " as to him a dead policy; " for it is not.

6. Prior to election, the policy has not been affected; and, therefore, it cannot be " restored to life."

7. The last sentence might apply to a case of a policy which had been terminated by election; but not to one in which no election had taken place.

4. Election, Unclouded

Very few cases dealing with the subject in hand apply the principles of election, unclouded by notions of forfeiture and " waiver." The state of Indiana has, as already noted,[2] made some advance but, even there, the courts tend to recur to their former phraseology.

Confusion in an English Statute. The uncertainties and contradictions above referred to have affected the

[1] Lantz *v.* Vermont, etc., 1891, 139 Pa. St. 560, 1; 21 Atl. 80.

[2] *Ante*, pp. 16–21.

phraseology of British legislation.[1] Section 33 of 6 Ed. VII, c. 41, after defining a warranty as including an undertaking "that some particular thing shall or shall not be done," provides as follows:

> A warranty, as above defined, is a condition which must be exactly complied with, whether it be material to the risk or not. If it be not complied with, then, subject to any express provision in the policy, the insurer is discharged from liability as from the date of the breach of warranty, but without prejudice to any liability incurred by him before that date.

In other words, the contract is *ipso-facto* void. But section 34, sub-section 3 provides that

> "A breach of warranty may be waived by the insurer."

That is to say, although by the agreement of both parties, the contract has been terminated, becomes *ipso-facto* void, yet by the subsequent action of one of them, it may be restored to life. According to the contract, it terminated on the 1st of July; and by the waiver of the assured it resumed vitality on the 29th, and covered risks between those dates. The legal relationship between the parties, by the agreement of the parties, ceased; and in spite of agreement to the contrary, was restored, four weeks afterwards, by the "waiver" of one of them.

The draughtsman meant to say that, upon breach, the insurer had a right to elect to continue or to terminate the policy. Section 36, sub-section 2 of the statute itself so indicates, for it provides that if a loss happen through breach of a certain specified warranty "the assured may avoid the contract." A subsequent section (42) provides that upon breach of another specified condition "the insurer may avoid the contract", and then proceeds to declare that the

[1] Other instances than that above specified are referred to in Chapters V and VII.

> condition may be negatived . . . by showing that he (the insurer) waived the condition.

The election idea is correct, but one hesitates at the suggestion of *negativing* a condition of a contract by proving that one of the parties " waived it." [1]

[1] See the chapter on Contracts, *post*, p.

CHAPTER IV

FORFEITURE

REAL PROPERTY LAW. Forfeiture in the law of real property was defined by Blackstone as follows:

> Forfeiture is a punishment annexed by law to some illegal act or negligence in the owner of lands, tenements or hereditaments; whereby he loses all his interest therein, and they go to the party injured, as a recompense for the wrong which either he alone or the public together with himself hath sustained.[1]

At another place he said:

> Upon the same principle proceeded all those forfeitures of estates which resulted from acts done by the tenant incompatible with his estate — e. g. if a tenant for life or for years enfeoffed a stranger in fee simple, that, by the common law, was a forfeiture of his estate.[2]

It will be observed that the effect necessarily follows the act. The feoffment is made, and the feoffer's estate is gone. The forfeiture is automatically accomplished. The feoffer has effected a forfeiture, he has not merely *incurred liability* to forfeiture. By his act, *ipso facto* and *eo instanti*, his estate has left him and vested elsewhere.

[1] Stephens Bl., 16th ed., vol. 1, p. 342. [2] *Ibid.*, p. 191.

SECONDARY MEANING. Retaining this meaning of the word forfeiture, the dictionaries add another, namely, not the deprivation of an estate, but the

> *becoming liable* to deprivation of an estate, goods . . . in consequence of a . . . breach of an agreement.[1]

The result of attaching this secondary meaning to the word, in legal phraseology, is that it is used to describe two quite different legal situations, namely (1) a perfectly accomplished forfeiture (the estate has passed); and (2) an act done, which may or may not, by reason of some further act, eventually result in forfeiture. A lessee commits a breach of some covenant; that act has no effect whatever upon the lease or the term; its only effect (apart from supplying a cause of action for damages) is to give to the lessor, a right to elect whether or not he will terminate the lease. Nevertheless the breach is generally, and quite improperly, spoken of as a forfeiture — even although nothing further happens.

EFFECT OF DUPLICATION. — This duplication of meaning has led to very diversified confusion. It is almost entirely responsible for the presence of " waiver " in cases in which the word *forfeiture* is applied to a breach of a stipulation which may, or may not, result in forfeiture. For, underlying the phraseology in these cases, may be detected the idea that the breach has (as in the first class of cases above referred to) really affected the lease; that there has been a real forfeiture of the lease; that that forfeiture has terminated the lease; and that it can be saved or reinstated by " waiver."

No one would think of applying " waiver " to a case of the first class — to a case in which forfeiture, having *really* been accomplished, the estate has passed. For every one would recognize that if the estate had *really* been forfeited, no " waiver " could replace it in its previous position. Nothing but a new conveyance could do that. But where there

[1] Murray's Dic.

has been no real forfeiture, where something has happened which may, or may not, result in forfeiture, " waiver " is introduced. A policy-holder does something which gives to the insurer a right to elect to terminate the contract; the courts treat the policy as forfeited although no election is alleged; and the insured tries to prove " waiver." In other words, where there is real forfeiture, " waiver " is admitted to be inapplicable. And where there has been no real forfeiture, the case is treated as though it had actually occurred, and could be cured by " waiver." Observe the following:

> The difficulty suggested by the cases cited arises from the ambiguous meaning of the word " forfeiture," which is sometimes employed to express the act of the tenant by which the forfeiture is incurred, and sometimes the act of the landlord availing himself of such forfeiture. In the former case the effect of the act may be waived by an act in *pais*, but there is no case showing that in the latter sense a forfeiture can be " waived ".[1]

That is a most striking example of the misleading power of a word, even if you are perfectly aware of its ambiguity. The court speaks of " the act of the tenant by which the forfeiture is incurred," and says that " the effect of the act may be waived; " but the act does not create a forfeiture; the act has no effect whatever upon the lease; and there is therefore nothing to " waive." The court, of course, meant simply that the landlord, having a right, because of the act of the tenant, to elect to continue or to determine the lease, might choose to continue it. To declare that the lease had been forfeited, and that the forfeiture had been " waived," is to postulate (1) a fictitious legal situation, and (2) an impossible rectification of it by an inverted bit of mentality.

DISTINCTIONS. If we are to make much progress in the understanding of " waiver," we must keep well separated the various customary applications of the word *forfeiture*,

[1] Bailey *v.* Mason, 1852, 2 Ir. C. L. R. 585.

and, for that purpose, it may be well (under protest) to supply distinguishing adjectives:

1. Real Forfeiture, namely, forfeiture which operates automatically. For example, a tenant enfeoffs a stranger, and, by virtue of the agreement, the term, *ipso facto*, merges in the reversion. Or an estate is granted upon conditional limitation, and it terminates in accordance with the stipulation. This we may call *real forfeiture.*

2. Completed-elective Forfeiture, namely, forfeiture accomplished by the exercise of the will of one of the parties interested. A lease, by its terms, is to be void (meaning voidable) upon breach of certain covenants; the breach happens; the lessor elects to terminate the lease; and it terminates. The election has completed the forfeiture.

3. Potential-elective Forfeiture, namely, a situation out of which forfeiture may or may not be accomplished. For example, the lease situation just referred to, prior to any exercise of the lessor's election. The forfeiture is potential only.

Application of the Word Forfeiture. The first of these cases is the only one to which the word *forfeiture* ought to be applied. And we have trouble about " waiver " (1) because *forfeiture* is wrongly applied to the other two, and (2) because the distinction between these other two is not sufficiently observed. Remembering this, observe its effect upon current ideas of " waiver."

1. No one imagines that " waiver " can have any effect in a case of real forfeiture — a case in which forfeiture necessarily, and *ipso facto*, follows upon the happening of the stipulated occurrence.

2. No one ought to imagine that " waiver " can have any effect in a case of a completed-elective forfeiture — a case in which, for example, a lessor has a right of election to continue, or to terminate the lease, and he has elected to ter-

minate it. For, by the agreement of the parties, the lease is at an end, and " waiver " is powerless.

3. We see, therefore, that any operation which " waiver " may be supposed to have, must be confined to cases of potential-elective forfeiture, that is to cases in which there is a right of election, and in which the right has not yet been exercised. But there is no opportunity for " waiver " in that kind of case, for there is no forfeiture to " waive."

Extrusion of " Waiver." By bearing these points in mind, we shall completely get rid of the idea that " waiver " (whatever it may be) can have any effect upon a case of real forfeiture; (2) we shall see that what we have to deal with is, not real or accomplished forfeiture, but its potentiality only; (3) we shall recognize that this potentiality consists in the existence of a right of some one to elect whether to continue the *status quo* or to terminate it; and (4) we shall see that the elector never " waives " that potentiality or surrenders that right — that all he does is to exercise it. Risk of mistake would be much reduced if the word *forfeiture* were confined to the one class of cases. And it must be added that, in suggesting the various adjectives the present writer does not approve the improper use of the noun; he makes concession only, for the purpose of exposition.

Restatement. What has been said is worth putting in another way. No objection need be made to the expressions " by this act he forfeited his life," " by remarriage she forfeited her annuity." In such cases the implication is that there is some law, or some testamentary or other proviso, by which loss of life or loss of annuity is a necessary consequence of the act. We do not mean that the act has given some other person *a choice* as to the continuation or determination of the life or annuity. We mean that the act itself has caused the loss; not that the option of some other person may possibly impose it. And when a tenant has committed a breach of his lease we ought not to say that he has forfeited the lease, because forfeiture is not a necessary consequence of the act, which, at the most, exposes him to the possibility that, at some future time, the landlord will so elect as to terminate the lease. It is not terminated, observe, by the act of the tenant, nor at the time of his act, but by the election of another person, and at a future time (although with relation back).

> I have spoken of the right of re-entry of a landlord as a "forfeiture" of the lease, but the use of the word "forfeiture" in cases of this kind is somewhat misleading. This is not like a condition in a will, non-compliance with which causes a forfeiture. It is a contract between landlord and tenant that if the latter does, or omits to do, certain specific acts, then the landlord may re-enter.[1]

If when a tenant commits a breach of his lease and gives to the landlord an election to cancel, you say that the tenant has forfeited his lease, you have in mind the loss which the tenant will suffer by the exercise of the landlord's right to cancel a valuable lease.

> A forfeit, in the legal meaning of the term, is a loss suffered by way of penalty for some misdeed or negligence.[2]

For observe that you would certainly not use the word *forfeiture* if the lease were one of burdensome character — if you had in mind that the landlord would certainly not terminate it, and that the tenant would lose nothing if he did. You would use the word in the one case and not in the other, merely because in the one case the tenant would, and in the other he would not, suffer. A proper word would fit both cases. If you insist upon using the word *forfeiture*, prior to the exercise of the landlord's election, you should introduce the adverb *potentially*, and so demonstrate that introduction of "waiver" is indefensible.

[1] Barrow *v.* Isaacs, 1891, 1 Q. B. 417; 60 L. J., Q. B. 179; 64 L. T. 686.

[2] Warville on Vendors and Purchasers, 2d ed., p. 951.

WILL CASES. Observe the effect of using the word "forfeiture" in cases of election arising under will cases in which a devisee is given the choice of taking under the will or of retaining some of his own property which the testator has assumed to deal with. It used to be said in such cases that the devisee "forfeited" the gift, if he refused to give up his property.[1] That was quite wrong for he forfeited nothing, and never had anything to forfeit. He had an election between two things and he chose one. If he had elected to take under the will, ought we to say that he "forfeited" his own property? And the mischief of the erroneous phraseology was to divert attention from the proper solution (as subsequently decided) namely that by retention of his property, the devisee does not "forfeit" anything — does not preclude himself from accepting the gift — but must make compensation, only, to the other beneficiary for his disappointment.[2]

CONCLUSION. The present writer believes that the administration of justice will be simplified and improved by directing inquiry not to forfeitures which either have never happened or are irremediable, and not to "waivers," but to election and evidences of election.

[1] The language is still sometimes used: Pomeroy's Eq. Jur. § 462.

[2] Gretton *v.* Howard, 1818, 1 Sw. 409, 432; Rogers *v.* Jones, 1876, 3 Ch. D. 688; Pickersjill *v.* Rodger, 1876, 5 Ch. D. 163; Cavendish *v.* Dacre, 1886, 31 Ch. D. 466; Pomeroy's Eq. Jur. 467, 468 note. Re Chesham, 1886, 30 Ch. D. 466; 54 L. T. 154.

CHAPTER V

ELECTION

One of the purposes of the present work being the substitution, in certain cases, of election for " waiver," some discussion of the principles of election appears to be indispensable. No exhaustive treatment of the subject is necessary.

DISTINCTIONS. Distinguish, so far as may be necessary, between three sorts of election:

1. Election between two properties;

2. Election (part of the substantive law) between termination and continuation of contractual relations; in other words, election between two legal situations.

3. Election (part of the adjective law) between two or more remedies.

1. ELECTION BETWEEN PROPERTIES. The doctrine of election applies to cases (for example) in which, by will,

certain property is bestowed upon A, and A's property is given to B. Under such circumstances A must elect. If he accept the gift, he must surrender his property. And if he retain his property, he must renounce the gift, to the extent of B's disappointment. He may not have full benefit of both.[1]

Mr. Pomeroy bases this doctrine upon the maxim "He who seeks equity must do equity.[2] But title by devise is a legal, and not an equitable title, and the devisee in claiming the estate, is not seeking equity; nor is he seeking equity when continuing his ownership of his own property. The maxim, therefore, cannot be the foundation of the doctrine.[3] At another place, Mr. Pomeroy indicates that the doctrine of election "depends upon the principle of compensation." [4] But all that he meant was that, in case of election against the will, the disappointed beneficiary receives compensation for his disappointment.

Attachment of a tacit condition to the gift, is a satisfactory basis for the rules of election.[5] Mr. Pomeroy objects to it,

[1] If he take under the will and refuse to give up his own property, he must compensate B for his disappointment, to the extent of the value of the less valuable of the two properties: In re Chesham, 1886, 31 Ch. Div. 466; 55 L. J. Ch. 401; 54 L. T. 154.

[2] Eq. Jur., 3d ed., §§ 395, 461, 466.

[3] Indeed the doctrine cannot be said to be peculiar to a court of equity. The remedy by sequestration was not available at law, but, so far as consistent with the system of the common law courts (by way of defence, for example) the validity of the doctrine was acknowledged: Birmingham *v.* Kirwan, 1805, 2 Sch. & L. 450. "The principle of these cases is very clear. The application is more frequent here: but it is recognized in Courts of law every day. You cannot act, you cannot come forth to a Court of Justice, claiming in repugnant rights:" per Lord Loughborough in Wilson *v.* Townshend, 1795, 2 Ves. Jun. 695. In a Massachusett's case, it was said: "In this Commonwealth, it has been decided, in accordance with the opinions of Lord Mansfield, Lord Loughborough, and Lord Redesdale, that the rule holds good at law as well as in equity." See also Smith *v.* Smith, 1860, 14 Gray (Mass.), 532; Brown *v.* Brown, 1871, 108 Mass. 395; Hapgood *v.* Houghton, 1839, 22 Pick. (Mass.), 480, 483; Doe dem. Duke of Devonshire *v.* Lord G. H. Cavendish, 1782, 3 Doug. 55; 4 T. R. 743, note; Wilson *v.* Townsend, 1795, 2 Ves. Jr. 696; Watson *v.* Watson, 1880, 128 Mass. 154.

[4] Eq. Jur., 3d ed., vol. i, § 469.

[5] Cooper *v.* Cooper, 1874, L. R. 7 H. L. 63; 44 L. J. Ch. 6; 30 L. T. 409. The word "stipulation" rather than "condition" would better express the idea intended.

as "only stating the doctrine of election in other words."[1] With deference, one might as well discard the idea of implied conditions in a contract, upon the ground that it would be only stating a rule of construction of contracts. And confirmation of the view is to be found in the fact that, after having (as he says) "ascertained the origin and foundation of the doctrine," Mr. Pomeroy indicates that his subsequent

> discussion will consist mainly in determining with accuracy the nature of the tacit condition imposed by the donor upon the gift.[2]

Objectors to the idea of tacit condition may perhaps be better satisfied with the dictum of Lord Redesdale:

> The general rule is that a person cannot accept and reject the same instrument; and this is the foundation of the law of election.[3]

2. Election in the Law of Contracts. Many cases in the law of contracts involve consideration of the principles of election. For example, a landlord usually has (by agreement of the parties contained in the lease) power to determine the tenancy upon breach by the tenant of some condition. That is to say, he has, upon the happening of the breach, a right to elect whether the tenancy is to continue or to end. And apart from modern statutes, he gets that right by contract. An insurance company, too, has frequently power to terminate the policy or to continue it; and it is by the contract that that option is acquired.

3. Election between Remedies. Election between two or more remedies, part of the adjective law, requires a little elucidation. The following, for example, may be passed:

> Before a case can arise for the application of the principle of election, there must be (1) two co-existing remedies, and (2) those

1 Eq. Jur., 3d ed., vol. i., § 464.

2 *Ibid.*, § 466.

3 Birmingham *v.* Kirwan, 1805, 2 Sch. & L. 449. And see *In re* Chesham, 1886, 31 Ch. Div. 466; 55 L. J. Ch. 401; 54 L. T. 154; Codrington *v.* Codrington 1875, L. R. 7 H. L. 854, 861; 45 L. J., Ch. 660; 34 L. T. 221.

> remedies must be so inconsistent that a party cannot logically choose one without renouncing the other.[1]

But protest must be made against the further statement that " apt illustration " of this principle is found in cases

> in which it is held that one who has sued on the theory that an unauthorized act done in his name has been ratified, cannot afterwards maintain an action on the theory that such act, and the assumed agency of the person by whom it was performed, have been repudiated;

for that is a case of election between two rights, and not between two remedies. It is not a case of choice between different methods of enforcing one ascertained right but a selection of the right to be enforced. It is an option between two legal situations; and, when one of them has been selected, there are not two possible remedies but one only. If the act be ratified there is but one remedy; and if it be repudiated there is another. The two remedies do not coexist. For similar reason it is not correct to say that

> Upon discovering the fraud the plaintiff had his election of two remedies. He could retain his policy, or he could cancel and repudiate it;[2]

For retaining the policy is not a remedy for the fraud. The choice is between two rights — ratification and repudiation.[3]

[1] State *v.* Bank, etc., 1900, 61 Neb. 22; 84 N. W. 406. There must be two remedies in fact, and it is not enough " that he supposes he has two remedies," *Ibid.;* Bunch *v.* Graves, 1887, 111 Ind. 357; 12 N. E. 514; Snow *v.* Alley, 1892, 156 Mass. 195; 30 N. E. 691; and Schrepfer *v.* Rockford, etc., 1899, 77 Minn. 293; 79 N. W. 1005.

[2] Hedden *v.* Griffin, 1884, 136 Mass., 231, 2. And see Driggs *v.* Hendrickson, 1915, 151 N. Y. Sup. 858; 89 Misc. 421.

[3] Warning against another misapprehension may be advisable. Supposing that for a tort committed by a servant you sue and get judgment against a man who was not his master, ought that judgment to interfere with a new action against the real master? The affirmative is asserted; for, it is said, " the plaintiff, by retaining her judgment against Doyle, has elected to treat the wrongful act or omission which occasioned the injury complained of as his, and is not now entitled to insist upon its being the wrongful act or omission of the corporation " (Murphy *v.*

An example of election between remedies is the case of a tortious taking and sale of goods. The owner, it is said, may "waive" the tort and sue for the money.[1] In better language, the owner may elect between his remedies, and having chosen one, he does nothing with the other — does not even "waive" it. If he sued in tort, nobody would say that he "waived" the money.

Another example of election between remedies is the election between action against the joint estate of a partnership, and action against the separate estate of the individual, which the law gives to a person defrauded by one of the partners for the benefit of the firm.[2]

Scope of the Inquiry. Dealing, as we shall, primarily with the law of contract, it will not be necessary to treat comprehensively of election between estates, or election between remedies; although, in considering the requisites and indicia of election, we may, from time to time, derive some help from analogies supplied by these two subjects.

For the situation, in all classes of cases is, to this extent, the same: One person is possessed of a right of choice (between two properties, between continuation and termination of a contract, between two remedies), and some other person's interest will be affected by the choice. So far there is identity; but it may very well be that, for the proper adjustment of rights, different rules may be found to be necessary for the different classes of cases. We shall have to con-

Ottawa, 1887, 13 Ont. R. 341). See a similarly erroneous assumption in Keating v. Graham, 1895, 26 Ont. R. 361. The case is destitute of the first requisite of election, namely the existence of two rights or two remedies. Judgment on a note against a man not a party to it, cannot be a defence by the maker of it. Scarf v. Jardine, 1882, 7 A. C. 345. An article in 16 L. Q. Rev. p. 160, may usefully be considered.

[1] Moore v. Richardson, 1903, 68 N. J. Law, 305; 53 Atl. 1032; Lipscombe v. Citizens, etc., 1903, 66 Kan. 243; 71 P. 583.

[2] Ex. P. Adamson, Re Collier, 1878, 8 Ch. D. 806; 47 L. J. Bk. 103; 38 L. T. 917.

sider this for ourselves as we proceed; for the authorities, in dealing with these rules, take little note of the distinction between the three classes.

CLASSIFICATION. The terms of a contract are ascertained (1) by observation of what the parties signed, or said, or did; and (2) by observation of the implications attaching to what was signed, or said, or done. For this reason contracts are usually classified as (1) expressed, and (2) implied. Rather than apply to the law of election similar classification,[1] it may be better to say that election may be evidenced in the following ways:

1. By declaration, either written or oral.
2. By indicative action, whether accompanied, or unaccompanied, by intention to elect.
3. By indicative inaction, whether accompanied, or unaccompanied, by intention to elect.

Before treating, however, of the circumstances which may he held to be evidence of election, it will be convenient to discuss some of the conditions necessary to election, and some of its effects and characteristics, under the following headings:

1. Knowledge in relation to election.
2. Necessity for intention to elect.
3. Necessity for communication of election.
4. Conditional election.
5. Contradictory elections.
6. Irreversibility of election.
7. Time for election.

KNOWLEDGE IN RELATION TO ELECTION

CLASSIFICATION. The necessity for knowledge as an element in election may be treated under the following headings:

1. Knowledge as to the existence of a right to elect.

[1] Pomeroy: Eq. Jur., §§ 514, 515.

2. Knowledge as to the happening of the circumstances which warrant the exercise of the right.

3. Knowledge as to the existence of circumstances which would affect the choice.

Subject to certain qualifications, we may say that knowledge of all three kinds is a necessary prerequisite of conclusive election between two estates, but that in the law of contracts, election is irreversible although knowledge of the first and third kinds was absent. The reason for such divergence will be stated below.

ELECTION BETWEEN ESTATES. The English law is most indulgent towards a person who has been required to make choice between the acceptance of a benefit given to him (say) by a will, and the retention of some property of his own, which the testator has assumed to dispose of.

> In order that a person who is put to his election should be concluded by it, two things are necessary. First, a full knowledge of the nature of the inconsistent rights, and of the necessity of electing between them. Second, an intention to elect, manifested, either expressly, or by acts which imply choice and acquiescence.[1]

In the United States, a Massachusett's court has said

> If a person, though knowing the facts, has acted in misapprehension of his legal rights, and in ignorance of his obligation to make an election, no intention to elect, and consequently no election, can be presumed. This has been settled in England by a long series of authorities.[2]

And Mr. Pomeroy's summation of the law may be accepted:

[1] Spread *v.* Morgan, 1865, 11 H. L. C. 615; 13 L. T. 164. And see Dillon *v.* Parker, 1818, 1 Sw. 381 (note); Edwards *v.* Morgan, 1824, McClel. 541; 13 Price, 782; 1 Bli. N. S. 401; Kidney *v.* Coussmaker, 1806, 12 Ves. 136; Worthington *v.* Wiginton, 1855, 20 Beav. 67; 24 L. J. Ch. 773; Sopwith *v.* Maughan, 1861, 30 Beav. 235; Wilson *v.* Thornbury, 1875, 10 Ch. App. 239; 44 L. J. Ch. 242; 32 L. T. 350; Serrell: *The Equitable Doctrine of Election*, p. 119.

[2] Watson *v.* Watson, 1880, 128 Mass. 155. And see Bradfords *v.* Kents, 1862, 43 Pa. 474; Worthington *v.* Wiginton, 1855, 20 Beav. 67; 24 L. J. Ch. 773.

> Where an election has been made in ignorance or under a mistake as to the real condition and value of the properties, or under a mistake as to the real nature and extent of the party's own rights, such a mistake is regarded as one of fact rather than law; the election itself is not binding, and a court of equitable powers will permit it to be revoked, unless the rights of third persons have intervened which would be interfered with by the revocation.[1]

These considerations need not be pursued further. Short reference to them could not properly have been omitted; but they are of but incidental, and illustrative value in the exposition attempted in the present work.

Election in the Law of Contracts. Passing from election as between two estates to election as between two legal relationships, we are at once conscious of a complete change of atmosphere. We find ourselves among cases in which the leading principle is finality and irreversibility. And the reason for the distinction is obvious. Election between estates does not, of itself, produce any consequential effect — that is to say, it does not pass an estate, or change any existing legal relationship; and if it be reversed, nothing else has to be undone. If, indeed, it has been followed by consequential action, it may, for that reason, have become irreversible.

In contract, other considerations supervene, for there election affects the legal relationship between parties. It terminates the contract, or (in case of election to continue) puts it beyond liability to termination. And the election is irreversible because revocation would alter those rela-

[1] Eq. Jur., 3d ed., § 512. And see Anderson's Appeal, 1860, 36 Pa. 496; Cox *v.* Rogers, 1874, 77 Pa. 160; Watson *v.* Watson, 1880, 128 Mass. 155; Burroughs *v.* De Couts, 1886, 70 Cal. 371; 11 Pac. 734; Sill *v.* Sill, 1884, 31 Kan. 248; 1 Pac. 556; 13 Halsbury, 125. In later times, some disposition has been shown towards adoption of stricter rule; Dewar *v.* Maitland, 1866, L. R. 2 Eq. 838; 14 L. T. 853. Compare Sopwith *v.* Maughan, 1861, 30 Beav. 235, with Gillam *v.* Gillam, 1881, 29 Gr. 379.

tions. It must be observed that election is effective, because the parties have, in their contract, so agreed. If they have not also agreed that the elector may undo what he has done, he has no power to vary or reverse it. In other words, the right of election in the law of contracts is created by the agreement of the parties; the elector has the power given to him by the agreement; and the relationships between the parties can be affected only in the manner, and to the extent, provided for in the agreement.

1. Knowledge of Existence of a Right to Elect. Remembering the three classes of knowledge above referred to, we may take as illustrative of the first of them (knowledge of the existence of a right to elect) the case of a landlord who knew that a sub-lease had been executed but was unaware that, for that reason, he had a right to elect to terminate the lease. If under those circumstances he should receive, or demand, or distrain for rent subsequently falling due, he would be held to have elected to continue the tenancy; and his election would be irreversible notwithstanding his lack of knowledge.[1]

2. Knowledge of Fact Warranting Exercise of Right to Elect. But the result would be otherwise in the second class of cases; for example, where the landlord was well aware of his legal right to elect, but was unaware of the happening of the act which gave him opportunity for the exercise of his right — for example that the tenant had sub-let. Under those circumstances, we may say (in "waiver" phraseology) tentatively, and subject to what may be said as to the effect of partial knowledge, that:

> One cannot be held to have waived something, of the existence of which he was ignorant.[2]

[1] See the chapter on Landlord and Tenant.

[2] United, etc. v. Freeman, 1900, 111 Ga. 355; 36 S. E. 764. And see German Am. etc. v. Waters, 1895, 10 Tex. Civ. App. 368; 30 S. W. 576; Hoxie v. Home, etc., 1864, 32 Conn. 40; Boynton, etc. v. Braley, 1881, 54 Vt. 92.

3. KNOWLEDGE OF EXISTENCE OF INFLUENCING FACTS. Of the correctness of the two foregoing conclusions, there can be little question, and it is only in connection with the third class of cases (ignorance of influencing facts) that disagreement arises. For example, a premium upon a life policy falls due and is not paid; the company elects to continue the policy, and demands payment of the premium; afterwards it discovers that, at the moment of the demand, the insured was dead — under those circumstances can the company reverse its election because of its ignorance of a fact which would have produced a contrary election? In one such case, an Ontario court said:

> If there was an intention on the defendants' part to elect not to avoid the policy, the intention was not communicated to him, the election was never complete, and the case is simply one of the insured dying while in default.[1]

But observe the confusion: Knowledge of the breach put the company to its election to continue or to terminate the policy; the company elected to continue (for it asked payment of a premium which would not be payable unless it had so elected); and yet the court said, "if there was an intention to elect." *Ex hypothesi*, intention to elect had culminated in election, and the only question was, Could the election be recalled?

In a similar case, an Illinois court said that:

> the application for payment of the past-due premium made after the death (although without knowledge thereof) is satisfactory proof that the company had elected, at the time of the death not to forfeit the policy.[2]

That is substantially accurate, although the words "at the time of the death" ought to have been omitted.

[1] McGeachie *v.* N. Am., etc., 1893, 20 Ont. A. R. 194. And see Manufacturer's, etc. *v.* Gordon; *Ibid.*, 330.

[2] Chicago, etc. *v.* Warner, 1875, 80 Ill. 410. And see Illinois, etc. *v.* Wells, 1902, 200 Ill. 445; 65 N. E. 1072.

Other cases upon this subject make use of the language of estoppel and waiver — the policy is supposed to have been forfeited, and the question is whether, in the absence of knowledge of influencing facts, a " waiver " of the forfeiture is binding upon the company. The Supreme Court of the United States, in a life-insurance case, said:

> To a just application of this doctrine it is essential that the company, sought to be estopped from denying the waiver claimed, should be apprised of all the facts: of those which create the forfeiture, and of those which will necessarily influence its judgment in consenting to waive it.[1]

But the decision is itself a contradiction of the latter of these statements. There had been two breaches of the conditions of the policy: (1) residence in a prohibited area, and (2) default in payment of a premium. After both breaches, but in ignorance of the first of them, the company received a premium on the very day of the death of the insured. Holding that the breach as to residence had not been waived (because the company was not aware of its existence) the court nevertheless held that the breach by non-payment had been waived, although the company was not aware of the illness and death of the insured.[2] Knowledge of the breach was necessary. But ignorance of influencing fact was immaterial.

Knowledge in Ratification Cases. We have seen that knowledge of everything is usually necessary to an irreversible election between estates; and that the only knowledge that is necessary in contracts is knowledge of the existence of the fact which affords an opportunity for the exercise of

[1] Ins. Co. *v.* Wolff, 1887, 95 U. S. 333; 24 L. Ed. 387.

[2] Deciding a similar point in the same way, a Kansas court discussed the Supreme Court decision, and observed the point noticed in the text: Bingler *v.* Mutual, etc., 1900, 10 Kan. App. 6; 61 Pac. 673. And see Mee *v.* Bankers, etc., 1897, 69 Minn. 210; 72 N. W. 74. A Nebraska court, misled by " waiver " phraseology, delivered an opinion contrary to that of the Supreme Court. Hamilton *v.* Home, etc., 1894, 42 Neb. 883; 61 N. W. 93.

election. What is to be said (as a matter of analogy) about knowledge in relation to ratification? There appear to be two distinct classes of cases:

1. Ratification of an act done during infancy; and
2. Ratification of an unauthorized act of an agent.

Authority as to the first of these classes indicates that ignorance of the contents of a document which the infant has signed, and ignorance of the law permitting repudiation, will not afford ground for disavowal of an election to ratify the document.[1]

> The argument sought to liken this case to the case of acquiescence, or waiver, or election, in each of which, before the person can be said to be bound by acquiescence or waiver, or to be put to his election, it has been held again and again he must be aware of the facts and of his rights. I disagree entirely with the attempt to apply that doctrine to a case of repudiation by an infant after he attains twenty-one. I do not believe any authority can be found in which that doctrine has been applied to the right of repudiation by an infant.[2]

Authority as to ratification of an unauthorized act is as follows:

> The general rule is perfectly well settled that a ratification of the unauthorized acts of an agent, in order to be effectual and binding on the principal, must have been made with a full knowledge of all material facts; and the ignorance, mistake, or misapprehension, of any of the essential circumstances relating to the particular transaction alleged to have been ratified, will absolve the principal from all liability by reason of any supposed adoption of, or assent to, the previously unauthorized acts of the agent.[3]

[1] An infant's act (capable of ratification) is not a void but only a voidable act (Carter *v.* Silber, 1892, 2 Ch. 278; 61 L. J. Ch. 401; 66 L. T. 473; S. C. sub nom. Edwards *v.* Carter, 1893, A. C. 365; 63 L. J. Ch. 100; 69 L. T. 153); whereas the unauthorized act of an agent (if there can be such an act) is said to be ineffective until ratified. Whether that makes any real difference with reference to the subject in hand, the present writer is unable to say.

[2] *Ibid.*, per Kay, L. J.

[3] Owings *v.* Hull, 34 U. S. 629. And see LaBanque Jacques Cartier *v.* LaBanque

The present writer has never understood ratification. If an infant's marriage contract (when beneficial) be binding upon him until repudiated, then we may take it that the other parties to the contract (knowing of the non-age) have agreed that it shall be revocable at the will of the infant, within a reasonable time after he comes of age. That is intelligible; but it is not ratification. If the other parties do not know of the non-age — if they believe that they are executing a binding contract, how can they be held bound by that which turns out (months or years afterwards) not to have been obligatory except at the option of the infant. Indeed their plight is worse than that, for, during the nonage, they cannot ascertain (save perhaps by legal proceedings), and the infant cannot declare, whether or not the document is to become a binding transaction. The position is somewhat the same as if A should execute what purports to be a contract between himself and B, but which is not binding upon B because the person who assumed to act for him had no authority; for in that case, too, it is said that the document may be treated by B as an option; that he has a reasonable time within which to make up his mind what he will do about it; and that if he determine to "ratify," he may afterwards repudiate upon the ground that he had not "a full knowledge of all material facts." Surely there was, or was not, a contract originally binding upon both, or upon neither.[1]

PARTIAL KNOWLEDGE. The only knowledge necessary to an irreversible election, in cases of contract, being knowledge of the existence of the fact giving occasion for the exercise of election, the question arises as to the effect of

d'Epargne, 1888, 13 A. C. 118; Williams *v.* Bartholomew, 1798, 1 Bos. & P. 326; Wilmott *v.* Barber, 1880, 15 Ch. D. 96; Moxon *v.* Payne, 1873, L. R. 8 Ch. 885; Atkinson *v.* Burland, 1901, 14 Man. 215; Butterworth *v.* Shannon, 1885, 11 Ont. App. 86.

[1] See also *infra*, p. 124, Chap. on Contract.

partial or incomplete knowledge of that fact. Upon this point there are but few authorities, and probably best service will be rendered by suggesting some distinctions.

But, first, how can the question of partial or incomplete knowledge be material? Is not the only question whether an election has, or has not, been made? If it has been made after partial knowledge of a fact, it will not be affected by subsequent complete knowledge of the same fact. And if it has not been made, it may be made subsequently. That is quite true; but lapse of a reasonable time after knowledge, without election to terminate, is evidence of election to continue the *status quo*. And the question is, Does reasonable time count from the date of partial knowledge of the fact, or only from the time of complete knowledge?

Distinguish between:

1. Partial or incomplete knowledge of the existence of a fact — suspicion rather than knowledge of it;[1] and

2. Partial or incomplete knowledge of all the incidents connected with a known fact. For example the courts have held that if a defrauded person become aware of the fact of the fraud and elect to affirm the transaction, he does not acquire a right to a new election (to repudiate) by the receipt of information as to some incidents of the fraud of which he was formerly not aware.[2]

Distinguish secondly between:

1. Partial or incomplete knowledge as to the existence of one fact; and

2. Complete ignorance of some other fact of the same kind.[3]

[1] See Halsbury's Laws of England, xx, 749, note (b); Carrique *v.* Catts, 1914, 32 Ont. L. R. 561.

[2] Campbell *v.* Fleming, 1834, 1 A. & E. 40; 3 L. J. K. B. 136; Taylor *v.* Short, 1891, 107 Mo. 384; 17 S. W. 970; Doll *v.* Howard, 1897, 11 Man. 577; Halsbury's Laws of England XX, 750; Carrique *v.* Catts, 1914, 32 Ont. L. R. 561.

[3] See Halsbury, Laws of England, xx, 750.

For example, if a tenant have committed two breaches of covenant, and the landlord, being aware of one only, receive subsequent rent, that is not a case of partial knowledge of one breach; it is complete ignorance of the other breach.

If, in dealing with such a question as this last, we use the language of forfeiture and "waiver," we shall probably become involved in some perplexity. Fixing attention upon the forfeiture, we say that, by the breaches (how many immaterial), the lease was forfeited; that the landlord, knowing of the forfeiture, "waived" it; that having "waived" the forfeiture (not the breaches nor any particular breach), he cannot afterwards insist upon it; and we logically conclude that subsequent information as to the existence of breaches, other than those known at the time of the "waiver," cannot enable the landlord to terminate the lease. All the breaches were merged, so to speak, in the forfeiture, and it is the forfeiture that has been "waived."

That conclusion, however, is wrong; and the only alternative statement (still using "waiver" phraseology) is that the landlord "waived," not the forfeiture at all, but only the breach that he knew of; and that he may act freely upon receipt of subsequent knowledge of another breach. But, although this conclusion is right, the statement that the landlord "waived" the breach that he knew of is wrong; for he may, if he so wish, sue upon it.

If it be suggested that there is a third view, namely, that the landlord "waived" neither the forfeiture nor the known breach, but the right to declare a forfeiture, the answer is, that the landlord had a right of choice between continuing the lease and terminating it, and that he did not "waive" that right of choice — he exercised it.

Using the language of election, all ambiguity disappears. We say merely that each breach gives to the landlord, at the time he hears of it, a right of election to terminate, or to continue, the lease. The landlord becomes aware of one breach, and elects to continue the lease. He hears of another (whether it occurred prior, or subsequent, to his previous election is immaterial), and he exercises his election, unembarrassed by what he had done in the other case.

Distinguish, lastly, between:

1. Partial or incomplete knowledge of a fact; and
2. Mistake with reference to a known fact.

For example, the difference between (1) the partial knowledge of an insurance company as to the presence of explosives upon the property insured; and (2) the mistake of the company in overlooking the fact that a premium had not been received by it.

With those distinctions in mind, we return to the question, From what period must we count reasonable time — from complete, or from partial, knowledge of the fact giving occasion for the exercise of a right of election?

Duty to Inquire. Probably the matter is one for decision according to the special circumstances of each case, and the olny point of principle involved is as to the existence of a duty to prosecute inquiry.[1] If a landlord suspect the existence of a sub-lease, or if an insurance company suspect the existence of further insurance, is it bound to ascertain the truth? Ought we to apply the rule that

> No one is held to have waived his rights until it be shewn that he has done so with knowledge of them, or where it was his bounden duty to know them.[2]

Is there in such cases a duty to investigate? May we not rather say that it is the duty of the tenant, and of the insured, to observe the terms of their agreements; and, if they commit breaches of them and apprehend embarrass-

[1] The subject is referred to in Chapter IX, p. 192.

[2] Finley *v.* Lycoming, etc. 1858, 30 Pa. 311.

ment because of delay in the declaration of election, that they may relieve themselves by frank disclosure of the facts. Where a man has a right of election between two estates, and the election is unduly postponed, an action may be brought to compel exercise of the option.[1] In contract cases, election may be required by mere notification of the fact that an occasion for its exercise has arisen.

The cases with reference to the period from which the statute of limitations runs, when the existence of the cause of action has been concealed (for example, underground pilferings of coal) may afford some analogy,[2] although the differences between the two lines of cases are obvious. Discussion of the existence of duty under varying circumstances may be found in the present writer's work on Estoppel.[3]

MISTAKE. Knowledge of the happening of the occurrence giving occasion for the exercise of a right to elect may be partial, because the man who committed some breach of covenant or condition did not convey full knowledge of it to the person who was entitled, upon its happening, to make an election. Mistake, on the other hand, is usually chargeable to the elector himself. Is his election reversible if based upon his own mistake? Upon principle, we should answer in the negative. For observe that the right to elect comes from contract, and that its effect is prescribed by contract. If in pursuance of the contract between the parties, one of them by his election, terminates it, how can it be re-established without the consent of both parties? The elector may regret that he made a mistake; but how can he restore ruptured relations? He pleads that he ought not to be

[1] Butricke *v.* Broadhurst, 1790, 1 Ves. Jr. 172.

[2] Wilson *v.* Thornbury, 1875, L. R., 10 Ch. 248; 44 L. J. Ch. 242; 32 L. T. 350; Booth *v.* Lord Warrington, 1714, 4 Bro. P. C. 163; Blair *v.* Bromley, 1846, 5 Ha. 531; 2 Ph. 354; Gibbs *v.* Guild, 1881, 8 Q. B. 296; 9 Q. B. 59; Powell *v.* Twyford, 1915, S. C. Can. Not yet reported.

[3] Pp. 28–67.

bound by what he did; but meanwhile he has bound the other party; and what he is claiming is not that his mistake has nullified his election, but that, because of his mistake, he is to have a right to nullify his action — that he is to have a second option. The contract gave him only one. Some of the cases declare for irreversibility, but the decisions are not based upon the reasoning here suggested.[1]

Must Election be Intentional?

The Authorities. Probably the most familiar and generally accepted assertion with reference to " waiver " is that it must be intentional. It is " an intentional relinquishment of a known right."[2] " A waiver must be an intentional act with knowledge.[3] Study of the cases, however, induces a distinction between intention to choose, and intention to do the act or say the word, which the courts hold to be a choice.

> Ordinarily when the act which constitutes a waiver is intentionally done, and is unequivocal in significance, it is as matter of law a waiver irrespective of the intention of the parties.[4]

For example, where, after default by a tenant in payment of his rent, the landlord distrained for it, the court said that

> there could be no question of intention left to the jury, as the taking a distress was an act not to be qualified, and an express confirmation of the tenancy.[5]

In the same sense, the House of Lords declared that acceptance of rent " affirmeth the lease to have a continuance," and consequently

[1] Rice *v.* New England, etc., 1888, 146 Mass. 252; 15 N. E. 624; Tobin *v.* Western, etc., 1887, 72 Ia. 264; 32 N. W. 663; Modern, etc. *v.* Lane, 1901, 62 Neb. 95; 86 N. W. 943. But see Robertson *v.* Metropolitan, etc., 1882, 88 N. Y. 545.

[2] *Ante*, p. 6.

[3] *Ante*, p. 6.

[4] Cooper *v.* Ins. Co., 1897, 96 Wis. 366; 71 N. W. 606.

[5] Zouch *v.* Willingale, 1790, 1 H. Bl. 312.

the right of entry is waived or barred, and his intention and desire not to waive it is immaterial.[1]

Cases in the United States are to the same effect:

> To the contention that a waiver or forfeiture necessarily involves an intention to waive, and that from the evidence of the secretary it conclusively appeared that the defendant did not intend to waive this forfeiture, it may be said that such a rule would allow a secret intention to defeat the legal effect of unequivocal and deliberate acts.[2]

MODIFICATION NECESSARY. These considerations make clear the necessity for modification of the assertion that " waiver " must be intentional. What are we to say about our substitute — election? Election means choice. Can there be a choice without an intention to choose? For example, when a person had been defrauded by a member of a partnership, under such circumstances as gave him a right to elect between action against the joint estate of the firm and action against the individual estates, and the defrauded party, in ignorance of his right to elect, proved his claim against the joint estate, ought he to have been permitted to withdraw his proof and proceed against the individuals? Was the court right in saying as follows?

> It is quite clear that Mr. Adamson never dreamt of electing, never knew anything about electing, and never knew that he had the rights between which he is deemed and adjudged to have elected. To say that such a man has elected is to say the thing that is not, and it is no more open to a court or a judge to say the thing which is not than it is to other men; and the question then really is not whether he had elected, but whether he is estopped from asserting one of two rights which he says he had, by reason of his having successfully asserted the other of them.[3]

[1] Croft v. Lumley, 1858, 6 H. L. C. 720; 27 L. J. Q. B. 321.

[2] Mee v. Banker's, etc., 1897, 69 Minn. 217; 72 N. W. 74. Approved in Modern, etc. v. Lane, 1901, 62 Neb. 97; 86 N. W. 943.

[3] Ex. p. Adamson, re Collier, 1878, 8 Ch. D. 806; 47 L. J. Bk. 103; 38 L. T. 917.

Notwithstanding the *a-priori* acceptability of this view, the authorities place beyond dispute the assertion that

> Whether he intended it or not, if he has done an unequivocal act — I mean an act which would be justifiable if he has elected one way, and would not be justifiable if he had elected the other way, the fact of his having done that unequivocal act to the knowledge of the persons concerned is an election.[1]

PROTEST. Not only is the absence of intention to elect immaterial, but a repudiation and denial of intention will not deprive an unequivocal act of its elective character. For example, if, after breach of some condition giving a landlord a right to re-enter, he should receive subsequent rent with

> a protest that it was received conditionally, and without prejudice to the right to deal with the lands as forfeited,

he has, notwithstanding his protest, elected to continue the tenancy.[2] His intention was, no doubt, to reserve his right — not to exercise it. Nevertheless he has elected, not merely without intention to do so, but actually contrary to his intention.

> The legal consequences of such an act must follow, however much he may repudiate them.[3]

SUGGESTED SOLUTIONS. Inasmuch as election without intention to elect appears to be a contradiction in terms, and yet the courts declare that there may be election without

[1] Scarf *v.* Jardine, 1882, 7 App. Cas. 361; 51 L. J., Q. B. 612; 47 L. T. 258. The words "to the knowledge of the persons concerned" might be omitted. See *post*, pp. 88–95.

[2] Davenport *v.* The Queen, 1877, 3 App. Cas. 131; 47 L. J. P. C. 8; 37 L. T. 727; Mathews *v.* Smallwood, 1910, 1 Ch. 786; 79 L. J. Ch. 322; 102 L. T. 228; Manufacturer's, etc. *v.* Gordon, 1892; 20 Ont. A. R. 314; Strong *v.* Stringer, 1889, 61 L. T. 472; Gulf, etc. *v.* Settegast, 1891, 79 Tex. 263; 15 S. W. 228.

[3] Croft *v.* Lumley, 1858, 6 H. L. C. 725; 27 L. J., Q. B. 321, per Williams, J. And see Worthington *v.* Wiginton, 1855, 20 Beav. 74; 24 L. J. Ch. 773; Upton *v.* Sturbridge, 1873, 111 Mass. 453; West *v.* Platt, 1879, 127 Mass. 372; Modern, etc. *v.* Lane, 1901, 62 Neb. 97; 86 N. W. 943.

intention, some conciliation appears to be necessary. The following suggestions are offered:

Consensus ad idem is necessary to contract, but there may be contract without *consensus*, and the parties to a contract are bound by what they sign, although they had different views as to the effect of the document. Why? Not because *consensus* is unnecessary, but because the parties are precluded from denying its absence. And so if a man do some act, which he could rightfully do only if he had made a certain election, he will not be permitted to disparage his act. He is estopped.

A second suggestion (to be found in the cases) is that intention must be gathered from what a man does rather than from what he says.

> *Non quod dicet, sed quod factum est inspicitur.*
> His act would be taken to be right and bind him, rather than his words make his act wrong.[1]

Even with that aid, however, the courts will sometimes be unable to declare that intention to elect really existed. And for such cases, application of the principles of estoppel may be necessary.

INTENT SOMETIMES IMPORTANT. Questions of intention may be important where the act done is of equivocal character. But of consequence only for the purpose of ascertaining its real import. For example, suppose that a landlord has a right, upon default in payment of rent, to give fourteen days' notice to quit; rent falls due and is unpaid; notice to terminate is given; next day the rent is paid and received, but the right to possession is specifically reserved.

> If the landlord received such rent without protest or notice of any sort, it might be inferred from his silent acceptance of the rent in arrear that the cause of his notice being removed, it

[1] Croft *v.* Lumley, 1858, 6 H. L. C. 706; 27 L. J., Q. B. 321.

> was his intent to revoke it, and waive his right to terminate the lease.[1]

We should rather say, that inasmuch as the landlord had no power to revoke his notice (and thus, of his own motion, to re-establish a lease which had been terminated), the notice prevented the inference that the parties had agreed to the re-establishment of the lease, or the creation of a new tenancy.

Necessity for Communication of Election

Election is in itself a mental state. Must that mental state be notified or communicated to anyone before it becomes operative? A landlord has an option to terminate his lease upon the happening of some event; the event happens; and he elects to terminate — has termination taken place, or is notification a necessary part of the election?

It may be admitted that proof of the existence of an uncommunicated mental state, by any person but him whose election is in question, is frequently impossible; but that difficulty must not lead us to say that, if proved, it is not operative. The elector may prove it, or he may have made some uncommunicated record by which its existence may be sufficiently evidenced.

Election between Estates. In the cases relating to election between estates, there appears to be no suggestion that communication is necessary to the effective exercise of an election. Mr. Serrell sums the law in this way:

> And generally, any act will constitute election by which the person liable to elect treats himself as owner of the property devised or given to him, or otherwise exercises over it a dominion which, unless on the basis of its having been given to him and his having accepted it, he has no right to exercise.[2]

[1] Kimball *v.* Rowland, 1856, 6 Gray (Mass.) 224. Observe that the landlord had a right both to the rent and to the possession; and that his acceptance of the rent therefore was not, necessarily, an affirmation of a continuation of the tenancy. If it had been, his protest would have been unavailing.

[2] The Eq. Doc. of Election, p. 132.

If the devisee sold the property devised to him, his election to take under the will would clearly be complete, although those interested had heard nothing of the sale.

Election in the Law of Contract. In the law of contracts there is some authority that election is incomplete unless communicated. One of the best of English judges has said:

> The reason I take it, running through all the cases, as to what is an election, is this, that where a party in his own mind has thought that he would choose one of two remedies, even though he has written it down on a memorandum, or has indicated it in some other way, that alone will not bind him; but so soon as he has not only determined to follow one of his remedies but has communicated it to the other side in such a way as to lead the opposite party to believe that he has made that choice, he has completed his election and can go no further.[1]

Some analogy may seem to support the view that communication is necessary to election. Mr. Justice Brett, on one occasion, said that a contract is complete when there is an acceptance of an offer "in his own mind . . . before that acceptance is intimated to the proposer," but he was overruled because,

> Having it in your mind is nothing, for it is trite law that the thought of man is not triable, for even the devil does not know what the thought of man is.[2]

There is no true analogy, however, in this respect, between acceptance of an offer and an election. Contract is necessarily bilateral, and is

> the expression by two or more persons of a common intention to affect their legal relations.[3]

[1] Per Blackburn J. in Scarf v. Jardine, 1882, 7 A. C. 360; 51 L. J., Q. B. 612; 47 L. T. 258.

[2] Brogden v. Metropolitan, etc., 1877, 2 App. Cas. 692.

[3] Anson on Contracts, 1913, p. 3.

An offer is nothing unless communicated, or rather there is no such thing as an uncommunicated offer. And there is no such thing as an uncommunicated acceptance. Election, on the other hand, is a purely unilateral act (although affecting another person). It requires no *consensus* and no concurrent act. To say that communication is an essential ingredient in election, would appear to be adding something to the meaning of the word.

TEST CASES. If an insurance company, by resolution of its board, elected to continue a risk, notwithstanding some breach of the policy by the assured, there would, surely be an effective election although its existence had not been communicated to the assured. On a previous page[1] reference was made to a case in which, after default in payment of a premium on a life policy, the company, in ignorance of the death of the insured, sent to him a request for payment of the premium. The request, of course, never reached the insured, but, nevertheless, the court said that the application for payment of the premium was proof of the fact of the company's election to continue the policy. It is difficult to see how any other conclusion could have been reached.

So far from communication of election to continue the *status quo* being necessary, we shall see (when we come to deal with evidence of election) that the very opposite of it, namely, silence, is often ample evidence of election,[2] And generally, it may be said that any conduct indicative of an election is evidence of an election, whether such conduct be known to the persons affected or not.

ELECTION TO TERMINATE. We now seem to have sufficient reason for saying that communication is not necessary to election, but let us see exactly what classes of cases there are, and whether any distinction demands further consideration:

[1] *Ante*, p. 76. [2] *Post*, pp. 115–122.

1. An election between estates is made, but is not communicated to anybody having any interest in the matter; and the election is nevertheless complete and irreversible. That is a case of election between properties. The election in no way affects contractual relations with any one from whom it might evoke responsive action; and upon that ground it may be said not to require communication.[1]

2. Other cases are from the department of contracts, and are of two kinds. Some (including all those in which election is the result of passivity) are cases in which election is to continue the existing relations; that is an election against rescission, or cancellation, or interruption of the *status quo*. And we may take it that in such cases there may be election without communication. In these, too, no responsive action on the part of any other person is necessitated.

3. But if the election be to terminate a contract, ought not that fact to be communicated to the other party, so that he may govern himself accordingly? — so that he may, for example, substitute new insurance for the policy which the election has cancelled? May the company leave the assured in ignorance of its election to cancel, and disclose it only if, and when, a loss has happened — when it is too late for the assured to protect himself by other insurance? Are we, by these considerations, driven to say that although communication is not necessary to an election when, by it, the existing situation is continued, yet that it is necessary to an election if the choice involve interruption, or reversal of the *status quo*?

Interpretation of the Contract. Reply to these questions is to be found in the interpretation of the contract. The parties may have agreed either one way or the other. The usual form being that, upon default, the contract shall

[1] But see Roux *v.* Salvador, 1836, 3 Bing. N. C. 286; 7 L. J. Ex. 328.

be void, meaning voidable at the election of one of the parties — what does that mean? Does it mean that the mere exercise of the election shall terminate the contract? If so, communication is unnecessary. Or does it mean that one of the parties may elect to terminate the contract, leaving unspecified, but implied, what he must do in order to terminate?

Frequently contracts provide the method by which an election to terminate shall be made effective — by giving a notice within a certain time. But in the absence of any such provision, does not the distinction between election to terminate and termination appear well founded? Dropping the word *elect* (as not essential to correct interpretation) does not the clause mean that the party may, if he so desire, terminate the contract? And if so, is not notice to the other party the accepted method by which that object may be accomplished?

For example, some policies provide that the assured may cancel the policy at any time. Contention that that could be done without advising the company was unsuccessful, upon the ground that cancellation must be the act of the company.[1] While the reasoning may not be convincing, the conclusion that one party cannot terminate a contract (unless so agreed) except by a notification to that effect to the other party — that as there is no such thing as an uncommunicated offer or acceptance, so there is no such thing as an uncommunicated rescission or termination — appears to be correct.

Election to Continue and Election to Terminate. This reasoning, however, produces the apparently anomalous conclusion above referred to, namely, that communication is not necessary to an election when, by it, the existing

[1] Colby *v.* Cedar Rapids, etc., 1885, 66 Iowa 577; 24 N. W. 54. The existence of a statute deprives the case of general value.

situation is continued, but that it is necessary if the choice involve its termination. But is not that in accordance with the agreement between the parties, namely, that a contract for a certain period may, upon the happening of some event, be sooner terminated? To continue the contract, after the happening of the event, no action is necessary. It continues unless stopped.[1] Termination requires conformity with the terms of the enabling clause.

OTHER SUGGESTED SOLUTIONS. If the foregoing reasoning be unacceptable, and if it be thought that, for effective termination of such a contract as we have been considering, no communication of an election to terminate is necessary, the following suggestions are submitted.

1. It may be urged that the ouns of proving an election to determine a contract is upon the party alleging termination, that is to say, upon the insurance company; that proof of a real election fails, if the company prove only that it went through the form of a concealed election — an election of which it could take advantage if a loss happened, and otherwise could suppress. Very frequently secret conveyances are, because of this optional and reversible character, held to be simulated and not real.

2. Some courts declare that return of the unearned premium is an essential part of an effective election to rescind a policy of insurance, and they decline to permit the company to escape payment of the loss in the absence of a tender of such return. Discussing the point in a subsequent chapter, the present writer has been unable to accept that view; but he does think that compaines have no right (apart from special contract) to retain premiums which they do not earn, and that, therefore, failure to return a premium may afford some evidence of election to continue the policy — strong enough probably, in many cases, to displace the alleged reality of an asserted election to cancel.

[1] Potter *v.* Ontario, etc., 1843, 5 Hill (N. Y.) 151.

3. It may be urged, in accordance with many analogous cases, that the company was under legal duty to communicate its election to any party prejudicially affected by it, and that, because of the neglect, the company is estopped from alleging its election to terminate. The range of legal duty is constantly and rapidly expanding, and it would be no enlargement of its present limits to posit duty in such a case as that under discussion. For example, when a member of a firm retires from it, he is under duty to give notice of that fact to those accustomed to deal with the firm, in order that they may govern themselves accordingly.[1] And in insurance cases it has been said that:

> When the assured has notified a company that he has procured additional insurance, it is the duty of the company, if it does not intend to be further bound or to continue the risk, to express its dissent, and not allow the party to repose in fancied security to be victimized in case of loss. It is unconscientious to retain the premium and affirm the validity of the contract, whilst no risk is imminent, but, the very moment that a loss occurs, to repudiate all liability and claim a forfeiture.[2]

Many other illustrations could be given of the validity of the rule which, in social life, requires the observance of

> an appropriate measure of prudence to avoid causing harm to others;[3]

and of the rule formulated by Mr. Cababé:

> When a person perceives that, in a matter of interest to himself, another person is acting or about to act, or likely to act, in a mode in which as a reasonable man, he would not act or be likely to act if he knew the real facts, a duty arises on the part of the

[1] Scarf *v.* Jardine, 1882, 7 A. C. 357; 51 L. J., Q. B. 612; 47 L. T. 258.

[2] Pelkington *v.* National, etc., 1874, 55 Mo. 172. Approved in Patterson *v.* American, etc., 1912, 164 Mo. App. 164; 148 S. W. 448. And see Potter *v.* Ontario, etc., 1843, 5 Hill (N. Y.), 151; Mutual, etc. *v.* French, 1876, 30 Ohio 240; Walsh *v.* Hartford, etc., 1876, 16 N. Y. 423; Pollock *v.* German, etc., 1901, 127 Mich. 460; 86 N. W. 1017.

[3] Pollock on Torts, 5th ed., p. 22; Ewart on Estoppel, pp. 28–67.

> former, to inform the latter of such real facts, if he is aware of them, and if the relative position in which the two parties stand toward one another is such that the latter might reasonably expect the former to tell him the real facts if the former were aware of them.[1]

The subject has been fully discussed by the present writer in his work on Estoppel.[2]

CONCLUSIONS. Upon the whole, probably, we may say (1) that a voidable contract continues in force until terminated in pursuance of an election to terminate; (2) that communication of election to continue is unnecessary; (3) that communication of election to terminate is necessary to termination; (4) that if communication to terminate be unnecessary, allegations of uncommunicated election to terminate will be closely scrutinized in cases in which lack of communication would involve an undue advantage to the party asserting it, or a detriment to the party affected by it; and that such lack of communication may estop the elector from assertion of his election.

"WAIVER." We have been assuming that the principles of election are those applicable to a policy containing a clause providing that it shall be void upon the happening of some event. Suppose, now, that we are wrong — suppose that, to use current phraseology, upon the happening of the event, the policy is forfeited and that the forfeiture may be "waived" — what are we to say about the necessity for communication? Evidently this: that the company has nothing to communicate. The policy has been forfeited (terminated) by the act, not of the company but of the policy-holder, and he knows that fact. The company knows, of course, whether it has "waived" the forfeiture, but it is

[1] On Estoppel, p. 86. Perhaps the rule ought to be limited to cases of persons "having a right, and seeing another person about to commit, or in the course of committing, an act infringing upon that right": De Busche *v.* Alt, 8 Ch. D. 314.

[2] Pp. 28–67.

communication of the decease of the policy, not of its resurrection, that we are discussing. How "waiver" breeds confusion even where election is recognized may be seen in the statement that the risk

> commenced running and would have continued to run until the loss occurred but for the breach of its conditions by the assured, which rendered it void at the election of the company, and it is not claimed that there was any waiver of such breach until after the commencement of the present suit. The insurer is not required in such case to formally declare the forfeiture. It is sufficient to set it up by way of defence when sued for the loss.[1]

There was no forfeiture to declare; the plea would not be a declaration of any forfeiture; the only defence would have been an election to terminate; and that was not available, for there was none.

Conditional Election

Can a man make a conditional election — an election to be effective upon the happening of some condition? Suppose, for example, that a landlord were to say to his tenant "I have a right to terminate the tenancy for non-repair, and I notify you that I elect to do so unless the repairs are made within a month;" and that the tenant made no reply? In one case it is said that the notification would be conditionally valid, and that (using the language of forfeiture and "waiver")

> to make the waiver effective, the terms upon which it is tendered ought to be complied with; and he who accepts the offer must in every respect fulfil the conditions by which it is accompanied.[2]

That is to say the landlord offers that, if the repairs are made within a month, the forfeiture will be "waived"; but if

[1] Schimp *v.* Cedar Rapids, etc., 1888, 124 Ill. 354.

[2] Townley *v.* Bond, 1843, 4 Dr. and War. 262. And see Stewart *v.* Smith, 1847, 6 Ha. 223, note.

not, then the tenancy is to terminate without further action or notice.

Such language is inappropriate. It assumes that there has been some forfeiture, and refers to an offer to " waive " the forfeiture — that is to re-establish the *status quo ante.* But as there has been no disarrangement of previous relations, there can be no offer of re-establishment. The default has given to the landlord a right to elect to continue, or to determine, the tenancy; and until election there is no change of position. The question then is: What is the effect of a notification of election to terminate if so-and-so be not done?

In one case a creditor elected to call in the whole debt, because of failure in payment of a single installment, but accompanied his notification of election by the statement: " I will waive the collection, if the installment is paid at once"; the installment was forthwith paid; and the creditor was not permitted afterwards to insist upon payment of the rest of the debt.[1] But this is not a case of a conditional election but rather of an election *plus* an offer: " I elect now to do so-and-so; but I offer upon certain conditions to restore the *status quo ante.*" The election is unconditional and immediately effective; and the language which was used was applicable not to the election but to the offer.

Nearly all the cases may, perhaps, be resolved into the same elements — election and offer. At all events there is no authority (known to the present writer) indicating that an election may be made *in futuro.* Where there is not a present election (with or without an offer of reinstatement), but a declaration that, upon the happening or non-happening of some future contingency, election will follow in prescribed fashion, there is not an election but a prophecy, a forecast of the prophet's action, a contemplated and not a completed act.

[1] Lasher *v.* Union, etc., 1901, 88 N. W. 375; 115 Ia. 231.

Where upon a breach by one party of a condition or stipulation in a contract, the other party thereto has the option to declare the contract forfeited, and thus relieve himself from liability upon it, and seeks to exercise such option, he must do so unconditionally and in plain, positive, and unmistakable terms.[1]

Contradictory Elections

Effect of Contradictions. What is the effect of simultaneous contradictory elections — election to continue, and election to terminate? One reply is that, as the existing situation continues until election to terminate, and as there has been no unequivocal election to terminate, the situation remains unchanged. Under certain circumstances, we might add that the time for election having elapsed, the non-election to terminate was equivalent to election to continue.[2]

Substantially the same result is arrived at by the courts, but not always precisely in the same way. For example, in one case, after default in payment of rent, the landlord gave notice of election to terminate the lease "forthwith," and, at the same time, gave another notice demanding payment of rent up to the next day; the rent having been paid and accepted, the court said that,

> according to the ordinary law relating to landlord and tenant, they must be regarded as having waived or abandoned their equity.[3]

But there was no "equity" in the case. The notice to terminate was authorized by the lease, and the only question was, not one of "waiver" of any equity, but merely whether the election to terminate given by the lease had been well exercised. If it had, payment, and acceptance of the money

[1] Mutual, etc. *v.* French, 1876, 30 Ohio, 254, quoting from Joliffe *v.* Madison, etc., 1875, 39 Wis. 119. See Georgia, etc. *v.* Gibson, 1874, 52 Ga. 640.

[2] Infra, p. 105.

[3] Keith, etc. *v.* National, etc., 1894, 2 Ch. 155; 63 L. J. Ch. 373; 70 L. T. 276.

might be evidence of an agreement to re-establish the old, or to create new, relations; but it could not be a "waiver" of anything.

Better reasoning supports the decision in Evans *v.* Davis.[1] In an action under an agreement for a lease, the proposed landlord claimed damages for breach of a term of the agreement; possession because of the breach, indicative of election to terminate the agreement; and other relief, applicable only to continuation of the tenancy. Held that the lessor had asked

> relief which could only be had in the alternative, and, as the plaintiff did not disclose by the writ which of the two alternatives he desired to pursue, he left the matter open and ambiguous.

There had, therefore, been, by the writ itself, no election either way.

Toleman *v.* Portbury[2] is not so satisfactory. Ejectment was brought by lessor against lessee, based upon a right of re-entry because of two separate breaches of covenant — (1) with reference to the user of the land, and (2) non-payment of rent which fell due after the other breach; and the question was the effect of the second of these claims upon the first. Was the implied assertion that rent accrued after the date of the first breach, evidence of an election to continue the lease notwithstanding that breach? If it was, the right to re-enter under the first claim could not be sustained. Observe that by demanding possession on the basis of the first breach, the landlord appears to be electing to terminate the lease because of it; but by claiming a right to terminate for non-payment of rent (which fell due after the first breach), he is indicating that the lease continued down to the day upon which that rent fell due (rent could not

[1] 1878, 10 Ch. D. 747; 48 L. J. Ch. 223; 39 L. T. 391. See also Moore *v.* Ullcoats, 1908, 1 Ch. 588; 77 L. J. Ch. 282; 97 L. T. 845.

[2] 1871 L. R. 6 Q. B. 243; 40 L. J., Q. B. 125; 24 L. T. 24; L. R. 7 Q. B. 344; 41 L. J., Q. B. 98; 26 L. T. 292.

have fallen due unless the rent had continued to run), and the lessor is, not merely saying that rent was due, but is asking for possession upon the ground of breach of covenant to pay it. Under these circumstances, one should be inclined to say that there had been no election — that the lessor had "left the matter open and ambiguous."

But the court held that the claims in the action were to be taken as (1) an assertion by the lessor of forfeiture because of the user of the land, and, (2), only if he failed in that contention, did he set up the other claim. The word "forfeiture" (as so frequently happens) misled the court. One of the appellate judges said that he could not

> see on what ground it can reasonably be maintained that a landlord by claiming a forfeiture for non-payment of rent, loses the benefit of a previous forfeiture.

Put in that way, it *is* somewhat hard to see. But the point overlooked is that there was no "previous forfeiture" to lose the benefit of. The wrongful user of the land gave, to the lessor, a right to terminate the lease, and the question was, Had he so elected? His claim in the action was ambiguous. It proceeded partly on election to terminate, and partly on election to continue. That is hardly an election to terminate. And without such election, the lease continued.

In cases relating to election between estates, when, by acts of ownership over both estates, there is supplied some evidence of desire to keep both, there is no election at all.[1]

Election Irreversible

Various Cases. In Comyn's Digest we read:

> If a man once determines his election, it shall be determined forever.[2]

Quod semel placuit in electione, amplius displicere non potest.

[1] *Post*, p. 112.

[2] Tit. Election, C. 2. See Bishop on Contracts, 1907, p. 328.

These statements are not so universally true in the department of the law with reference to which they were written (election between properties) as in other branches of the law. Much grace (as we have seen)[1] is extended to beneficiaries under wills, who allege mistake in their first choice. But a landlord can very rarely find a judge who will allow him to elect to terminate a lease after he has once affirmed it. In such cases the courts say:

> Forfeitures are not favored in the law; and when the forfeiture is once waived, the court will not assist it.[2]

Irreversibility is also the rule as between affirming and rescinding a contract induced by fraud;[3] as between various remedies;[4] and Blackburn, J., says that landlord and tenant cases are

> but a branch of the general law that where a man has an election or option to enter into an estate vested in another, or to deprive another of some existing right, before he acts he must elect once for all whether he will do the act or not. He is allowed time to make up his mind, but when once he has determined that he will not consider the estate or lease, whichever it may be, void, he has not any further option to change his mind.[5]

For example, if an insurance company elected to continue contractual relations notwithstanding failure to furnish proofs, it could not, by demanding them, gain a new right of election.[6] And so also, where a vendor elects to rescind the contract because of fraud, he cannot afterwards assert, in bankruptcy of the purchaser, a claim to the purchase money.

[1] *Ante*, pp. 73–74.

[2] Goodright dem. Walter *v.* Davids, 1778, 2 Cowp. 805. And see Monger *v.* Rockingham, etc., 1898, 96 Va. 450; 31 S. E. 609; Farmers', etc. *v.* Kinsey, 1903, 101 Va. 241; 43 S. E. 338; Bleecker *v.* Smith, 1835, 13 Wend. (N. Y.) 536.

[3] Clough *v.* London, etc. Ry. 1871, L. R. 7 Ex. 34; 41 L. J. Ex. 17; 25 L. T. 708.

[4] Scarff *v.* Jardine, 1882, 7 App. Cas. 360; 51 L. J., Q. B. 612; 47 L. T. 258.

[5] Ward *v.* Day, 1863, 4 B. & S. 356. And see Campbell *v.* Fleming, 1834, 1 A. & E. 40; 3 L. J. K. B. 136.

[6] Roberts *v.* Ins. Co., 1902, 94 Mo. App. 151; 72 S. W. 144.

> The contract was at an end, and no act on the part of the plaintiffs alone could revive it.[1]

The right of an elector to rescind his election, upon the ground that he was unaware of some fact which might have influenced his choice, has already been discussed.[2]

WITHDRAWAL OF NOTICE. From the doctrine of the irreversibility of an election must not be implied that notices, of various sorts, may not be withdrawn, or, to use current phraseology, "waived." No one would say, for example, that a notice to produce documents at a trial, or a notice to repair, may not be withdrawn by subsequent notification or conduct. But notices of these sorts are not expressions of election affecting legal relationships. Note the distinction: Suppose that a master properly gives his servant a month's notice to leave; he has thus elected to terminate the hiring; and he has altered the legal position of the servant, who, because of the notice, is entitled (as well as bound) to leave at the time indicated. Such a notice cannot be withdrawn without agreement between the parties. By agreement they may, of course, do anything — contract for a new hiring, or for continuation of the old one.

REVERSAL OF EFFECTS. An election may be irreversible but cannot the effects of election be reversed? Consider various classes of cases:

LEASES. Upon non-payment of rent, a landlord elects to terminate the lease, and commences an action to recover possession; afterwards he accepts subsequent rent; has he not "waived the forfeiture," and restored the lease? Put the question this way: The effect of the landlord's election has been to terminate the tenancy — to end the relationship between the parties, to destroy the *vinculum juris*, *le lien de droit* — can it be restored by "waiver," or anything else

[1] Moller *v.* Tuska, 1881, 87 N. Y. 170.

[2] *Ante*, p. 76.

short of agreement? However frequently disregarded, the law must be

> that receipt of rent after action brought, is no waiver of the forfeiture . . . that no act after action brought could set up the lease again. . . . Where the lease is the ground of the forfeiture and the landlord brings his action upon it, he thereby elects to treat the lease as void; and if anything at all be set up by the waiver, it would not be the lease but it would be a new agreement.[1]

And in a case in which the landlord was anxious, for his own benefit, to change his election from terminating to continuing the lease, the court said that his prior action —

> was an election on his part to forfeit, which could not be retracted by him. And to enable the landlord to get rid of this forfeiture, there must have been a request on the part of the tenants either express or implied to be relieved from the forfeiture.[2]

Rather, we should say, that there must be evidence of a new agreement; and that such evidence may be supplied by the payment and acceptance of rent; for rent implies tenancy. The reason given in Greenwood *v.* Moss[3] for holding that distress for rent, after ejectment proceedings, does not relegate the parties to their previous position as landlord and tenant, is that ejectment is "equivalent to the ancient entry," and the ancient entry put an end to the term. For the same reason, acceptance of rent, after election to terminate, does not, of itself, re-establish a lease — an end has been put to the term. It was because the lease was thus terminated that the English Court of Equity formerly, when relieving a tenant from a "forfeiture" occasioned by non-payment of rent, ordered:

[1] Evans *v.* Wyatt, 1880, 43 L. T., N. S. 176. And see Laxton *v.* Rosenburg, 1886, 11 Ont. R. 199, where it was said that there is no distinction, in this respect, between election upon condition broken, and election under a power to give notice to quit. And see Grimwood *v.* Moss, 1872, L. R. 7 C. P. 360; 41 L. J., C. P. 239; 27 L. T. 268; Morecraft *v.* Meux, 1824, 1 C. & P. 346; reversed on other grounds, 1825, 4 B. & C. 606; Jones *v.* Carter, 1846, 15 M. & W. 718.

[2] Denison *v.* Maitland, 1892, 22 Ont. R. 166.

[3] 1872, L. R. 7 C. P. 360; 41 L. J., C. P. 239; 27 L. T. 268.

> a new lease to be executed similar to the old lease. . . . At law the theory formerly was that the old lease was gone when ejectment was brought, and so the courts of equity required that a new lease should be executed in order to set up the old one.[1]

In England, and some other jurisdictions, legislation has, under certain circumstances, obviated necessity for a new lease.[2] But, in cases to which the statute does not apply, a new agreement must still be made before the relation of landlord and tenant can be re-established. It is not necessary, of course, that there should be an express agreement for a new lease. Payment of rent would be evidence of agreement, as in the case of payment of rent by an overholding tenant. But questions might arise as to whether the new tenancy would be one from year to year (as in the case of an overholding tenant), or one for the remainder of the old term; and whether, in the latter event, the provisions of the Statute of Frauds would not have to be considered.

MORTGAGES. Another example of the principle under consideration is afforded by a mortgage, in which the grant to the mortgagee is expressed to be void upon payment, on certain dates, of certain moneys. If the moneys are promptly paid, the estate reverts to the mortgagor, for the grant is upon a condition subsequent which has been performed. But if payment be made after the due date, the estate does not revert automatically. The mortgagee may "waive" as much as he pleases; but the condition is broken, and the estate remains where the mortgage put it, until it is reconveyed.[3]

ACCEPTANCE OF INTEREST. Agreement not to call in certain principal moneys so long as interest is promptly paid;

[1] Hare *v.* Elmo, 1893, 1 Q. B. 607; 62 L. J., Q. B. 187; 68 L. T. 223; Bowser *v.* Colby, 1841, 1 Hare 130; 11 L. J., Ch. 132.

[2] *Post* in chapter on Landlord and Tenant, at p. 151.

[3] Stewart *v.* Crosby, 1863, 50 Me. 133.

default in payment of interest; notice by the lender to pay the principal; afterwards interest accepted. Here, election having been made, the principal has become due; and the question is, What effect has the subsequent acceptance of the interest? Authority declares that thereby the default was "waived."[1] But why? At the time of the acceptance of the interest, both the principal (by exercise of the election), and the interest (by the terms of the agreement) were payable. The creditor was entitled to them both. Taking one did not require him to leave the other. There was no inconsistency in taking the one and demanding the other. If a landlord terminate a lease because of non-payment of rent, he does not forfeit the rent. Nor does he restore the lease, if he accept what was overdue at the time of his election.

Note, however, that although the principal had become due, its payment could, by agreement, be again postponed; and receipt of the interest without the principal, and without demand for it, or reservation of immediate right to it, might be some evidence of assent to postponement.[2]

Time for Election

Election must be made within a reasonable time. That is to say, in every case there is a certain present situation which may possibly be disturbed by election, and failure to elect within a reasonable time either (1) terminates the right to elect[3] and leaves the situation unaffected or (2) is evidence of election to continue it.[4] For example, a devisee has a choice between a benefit under a will and his own property, and failure to elect within a reasonable time either (1) ends

[1] Langridge *v.* Payne, 1862, 2 J. & H. 423.

[2] See ante, p. 86.

[3] Per Lord Watson in Edwards *v.* Carter, 1893, A. C. 366; 63 L. J., Ch. 100; 69 L. T. 153.

[4] *Post*, p. 119.

his right, or (2) is an election against the will. So also there may be a right to rescind a conveyance or a contract, but if election be not made within a reasonable time, either an election to continue the existing situation may be assumed, or the right to elect to repudiate may be gone. Note however that these remarks do not apply to election between remedies. In such cases there is no "present situation" which will become permanent unless elected agaisnt.

COMMENCEMENT OF TIME. Reasonable time for election has a commencement, as well as a termination, and the starting hour must be determined by the conclusions which ought to be arrived at as to (1) the necessity for complete knowledge of the facts; (2) the duty to ascertain the facts; and (3) the necessity for knowledge of the law. These points have already been discussed.[1]

DURATION OF REASONABLE TIME. Reasonable time is plainly a relative term. Its length varies according to the nature of the case, the position of the parties, and so on. And the courts have been far more indulgent in some lines of cases than in others.

DURATION AS BETWEEN PROPERTIES. Mr. Pomeroy has it that there is no limit of time within which election must be made between properties:

> Unless it can be shewn that injury would result to third persons by delay.[2]

And it has been said that the important question is:

> Has anything been done . . . which cannot be restored or compensated for, or arranged in the settlement.[3]

Another view is that reasonable time continues down to the period for action under the instrument raising the election:

[1] *Ante*, pp. 72–83.
[2] On Eq. Jur., 3d ed., § 513.
[3] Anderson's appeal, 1860, 36 Pa. 496.

> when for the first time, the question arises whether anything is, or is not, to be received . . . under it

no matter how long the anterior lapse may be.[1] And a still further view is that no general rule can be declared:

> I do not find that the Court attempted to define what a reasonable time is, nor do I see how any general rule could be laid down as to what is a reasonable time. A time which might be much more than reasonable in one case, might be quite reasonable in another.[2]

To countervail in some respects this laxity and uncertainty, many of the American States have provided that election by a widow between her dower and benefits under her husband's will must be made within a year after the death, and that, in default, she shall be deemed to have elected to take under the will.[3]

DURATION IN CASES OF INFANTS. An instrument executed by an infant is sometimes voidable and not void; and in such case he may, when coming of age, elect to affirm or to repudiate it. He must do so within a reasonable time. And knowing that he has executed something, he cannot plead, as against delay in electing, that he was unaware of the contents of the document.[4] If a reasonable time elapse without expression of election to repudiate, the infant is bound.[5]

RESCINDING FRAUDULENT TRANSACTION. In a frequently quoted case, in which the owner of goods had been fraudulently induced to sell them to a man who intended to swindle, and not to pay, the court said

[1] *In re* Jones, 1893, 2 Ch. 461; 62 L. J., Ch. 996; 69 L. T. 45.

[2] *Ibid.*

[3] Pomeroy Eq. Jur., 3d ed., § 494; note 1, where the American statutes are collected. See Akin *v.* Kellogg, 1890, 119 N. Y. 441.

[4] Edwards *v.* Carter, 1893, A. C. 367; 63 L. J., Ch. 100; 69 L. T. 153; per Lord Macnaghten.

[5] *Ibid.*, per Lord Watson.

> We think the party defrauded may keep the question open so long as he does nothing to confirm the contract. . . . We think that, so long as he has made no election, he retains the right to determine it either way, subject to this: that if in the interval whilst he is deliberating, an innocent third party has acquired an interest in the property, or if, in consequence of his delay, the position even of the wrong-doer is affected, it will preclude him from exercising his right to rescind. And lapse of time, without rescinding, will furnish evidence that he has determined to affirm the contract; and when the lapse of time is great it probably would in practice be treated as conclusive evidence to shew that he has so determined.[1]

The last sentence of this extract overrules the first, and is believed to be the better law; for, admitting that the defrauder is not entitled to much sympathy, yet his conduct affords little reason for saying that the other party can retain an indefinite option between approbating and reprobating the transaction. The following is more in accord with the present writer's views:

> Unquestionably it is a general rule of law that a party who would rescind a contract, which has been induced or procured by the fraud of the other party thereto, must act promptly and make his election to rescind.[2]
>
> Lapse of time without rescinding will furnish evidence of an intention to affirm the contract. But the cogency of this evidence depends upon the particular circumstances of the case and the nature of the contract in question.[3]

Terminating Policies of Insurance for Breach of Conditions — In this department there is much authority for the statement that the company

[1] Clough *v.* London and N. W., 1871, L. R. 7 Ex. 34, 5; 41 L. J. Ex. 17; 25 L. T. 708.

[2] Paquin *v.* Milliken, 1901, 163 Mo. 101; 63 S. W. 417. And see McCoy *v.* Prince, 1914, 66 So. 950; 11 Ala. App. 388.

[3] Sharpley *v.* Lowth, etc., 1876, 2 Ch. D. 685. Approved in Carrique *v.* Catts, 1914, 32 Ont. L. R. 566.

> may wait until the claim is made under the policy, and then in denial thereof, or in defence of a suit commenced therefor, allege a forfeiture.[1]

But in so holding the courts have been misled by employment of the phraseology of forfeiture and "waiver." They would find difficulty in declaring that an insurance company may postpone its election until a loss happens and an action has been commenced. Using the language of election, the only conclusion is, that

> If they choose to assert their option of forfeiting the policy, they must exercise their option with some degree of promptness.[2]

SUMMARY. Without undertaking a review of the cases, all that can be said about reasonable time for election under contracts is:

1. Lapse of reasonable time will either (1) terminate the right to elect, or (2) supply evidence of election to continue the *status quo*.

2. What is reasonable time has to be ascertained from the nature of the case, the relative position of the parties, and so on.

3. It is not true that a defrauded party may

> keep the question open so long as he does nothing to confirm the contract;

for, as stated in the same case,

> lapse of time, without rescinding, will furnish evidence that he has determined to affirm the contract.[3]

4. The defrauded party must act promptly if he wishes to rescind. He cannot indulge himself with a prolonged option.

[1] Titus *v.* Glens' Falls, etc., 1880, 81 N. Y. 419. Approved in Cannon *v.* Home, etc., 1881, 53 Wis. 594; 11 N. W. 11; Queen Ins. Co. *v.* Young, 1888, 86 Ala. 430; 5 So. 116.

[2] Mutual, etc. *v.* French, 1876, 30 Ohio 247.

[3] *Ante*, p. 108.

5. The same rules govern the election of insurance companies under the power given to them by their policies. They too must act promptly if they would rescind.

FROM WHAT DATE DOES ELECTION OPERATE? If a landlord elect to terminate a lease, from what time is the termination effective — the day of the default, or the day of the election? First impression might lead us to say the day of the election. Default happens today; the tenant remains in possession for two months; and then the landlord elects; was not the tenent a tenant until then? Would not the landlord be entitled to rent until that time? Does not the termination, therefore, date from the election?

Turn to insurance law and see how such a conclusion would work there. Breach by insured (e. g. by introduction of explosives) to-day; fire tomorrow; company hears of breach on the next day; and elects to cancel. If election take effect from its own date, the company will have to pay the loss. That is, probably, not right.

The truth is that as we are dealing with contracts, we cannot, in the absence of documents, give any opinion upon the point, for the parties may have agreed in one way or the other. For example, if in the case of a lease, the agreement is that upon default, the lessor may re-enter, the defeasance will take place not upon the day when the lessor made up his mind to re-enter but upon the day when he did it.[1] And none the less so, because the agreement expressly so provides.[2]

If, on the other hand, a lease or a policy of insurance provide that, upon the happening of a certain occurrence, the agreement shall be void (meaning voidable at the election of the landlord or insurer) then it becomes void as from the

[1] Hartshorne *v.* Watson, 1838, 4 Bing. N. C. 178; 7 L. J. C. P. 138; Selby *v.* Browne, 1845, 7 Q. B. 633; 14 L. J., Q. B. 307.

[2] Hayne *v.* Cummings, 1864, 16 C. B. (N. S.) 421; 10 L. T. 341.

date of the happening if the election be afterward made. The language of the contract must govern.

Somewhat the same point arises in the law of sales. For example a horse was sold with a representation; the contract provided that, if the representation proved to be untrue, the purchaser should have the right to return the horse; the representation was untrue; the purchaser elected to return the horse; and an injury that had happened to him meanwhile was held to be the loss of the vendor and not of the purchaser [1] — the election related back to the transaction.

Election to abandon a wrecked ship to the insurance company is said to be " retrospective, operating from the moment of the casualty." [2]

From what day would the statute of limitations run? The English act provides that

> when the person claiming such land or rent . . . shall have become entitled by reason of any forfeiture or breach of condition, then such right shall be deemed to have first accrued when such forfeiture was incurred or such condition was broken.[3]

Possibly by " condition " was meant conditional limitation, and that, we understand. What was meant by " forfeiture," some court may some day have to make a guess at.

Evidence of Election

Passing over clearly expressed election as needing no elucidation, the present subject may be divided into election as evidenced by (1) activity, and (2) by passivity; and in dealing with these, we must again distinguish between (1) election between properties, and (2) election in the law of contract.

[1] Head *v.* Tattersall, 1871, L. R. 7 Ex. 14; 41 L. J. Ex. 4; 25 L. T. 631.
[2] Arnould: *Marine Insurance*, 1914, § 1205.
[3] 3 and 4 Wm. 4, c. 27, § 3.

Election between Properties. Starting from what would seem to be an assured basis, that

> any decisive act of the party . . . determines his election.[1]

one would think that if a beneficiary took possession of property given him by a will, he would be deemed to have elected to take under the will and consequently be bound to give up any of his own property which might, by the will, have been given to another person, or at all events, to make compensation. No doubt, if, when taking the benefit, he had relinquished possession of his own property, an election would have been made. But it is held that by taking the one and retaining the other (keeping both) he has elected for neither; for the taking indicated election under the will, and the retaining, indicated election against it.[2]

The same idea has been applied to a case in which the beneficiary took possession of the devised property and mortgaged his own.[3] Upon the other hand it is held that making disposition of the devised property "is a clear, deliberate act of election."[4] But where a widow had, during three years, accepted a legacy and an annuity provided by the will, making no claim to her dower, it was thought, in the absence of evidence of her knowledge of the facts, that she had made no election.[5]

It is impossible to extract anything very satisfactory from the cases relating to this subject. The courts, while asserting that an election once made is forever irreversible,

[1] Rockford, etc. *v.* Travelstead, 1888, 29 Ill. App. 659. To same effect, American, etc. *v.* Triumph, etc. 1876, 5 Ins. L. J. 466.

[2] Dillon *v.* Parker, 1818, 1 Sw. 380; Spread *v.* Morgan, 1865, 11 H. L. C. 587; 13 L. T. 164. And see Serrell: *The Eq. Doc. of Election*, pp. 135–9.

[3] Padbury *v.* Clark, 1850, 2 Mac. & G. 298; 2 Hall & Tw. 341; 19 L. J., Ch. 553.

[4] Briscoe *v.* Briscoe, 1844, 1 Jones & LaT. 334; 7 Ir. Eq. R. 123: Worthington *v.* Wiginton, 1855, 20 Beav. 67; 24 L. J., Ch. 773; Rogers *v.* Lane, 1876, 3 Ch. D. 688.

[5] Wake *v.* Wake, 1791, 1 Ves. Jr., 335; 3 Bro. C. C. 255.

are extremely lax in holding parties to their election, and they readily permit change upon allegation of mistake (not only in the facts but as to the law) frequently going so far as to hold that an election is not binding unless it is *shewn* that it was based upon knowledge of both law and facts.[1] We shall have to get away from the cases dealing with election between properties before we shall reach solid ground.

ELECTION IN THE LAW OF CONTRACTS. A good deal of authority may be cited in support of the following:

> To make out a case of abandonment or waiver of a legal right, there must be a clear, unequivocal, and decisive act of the party showing such purpose.[2]
>
> Comme personne n'est facilement présumé renoncer à son droit, les renonciations espresses ou tacites doivent être strictément resserrés dans leurs termes; jamais on ne doit les étendre d'un cas à un autre. Cela résulte de la nature même des choses; tous les auteurs sont d'accord sur ce principe.[3]

On the other hand, scores of cases proceed upon opposite theory, namely that

> Courts will find a waiver upon slight evidence when the equity of the claim made . . . is . . . in favour of the insured.[4]

Degrees of strength, in evidence, ought to bear some relation to probabilities. On the issue whether or not a man has elected one way or another, his interest one way or another ought to be of some importance as indicative of what he would probably have done. It ought to; but very

[1] *Ante*, p. 73.

[2] Ross *v.* Swan, 1881, 7 Lea. (Tenn.) 467.

[3] "As no one is easily presumed to renounce his rights, renunciations, express or tacit, should be strictly confined to their terms; they should never be extended from one case to another. This results from the nature of things; all the authors agree upon this principle." Fav. de Langdale. Repertoire, vo. Renonciation, p. 830.

[4] Lyon *v.* Travellers', etc., 1884, 55 Mich. 146; 20 N. W. 829. Approved in Union, etc. *v.* Bragg, 1901, 63 Kan. 295; 65 Pac. 272, citing Painter *v.* Industrial, etc., 1897, 131 Ind. 68; 30 N. E. 876; Hipwell *v.* Knight, 1835, 1 Y. & C., Ex. 418; 4 L. J. Ex., Eq. 52.

frequently the rule works the other way, and the more clearly you can show that the interest of the elector would naturally have influenced him to terminate the contract, the more strenuously will the court endeavour to find that he elected to continue it.

If, for example, some one alleged that I had elected against acceptance of a large unconditional legacy, he would (because of the bent of my interest) have all sorts of presumptions against him, and my alleged acts of "waiver" would need to be extremely clear and unambiguous. But if he alleged that a landlord had elected to cancel a lease, the greater the value of the tenant's interest, and the greater the probability, therefore, of the landlord's intention to cancel, the more keenly would the courts search for "waiver." The "equity of the claim" makes appeal to the courts, too, in insurance cases. Prove that "forfeiture" of the policy was the company's interest, and the courts will struggle against it.

We are here a long way from the rule that the more improbable proposition must be supported by the stronger evidence. We are operating upon the less rational theory that the courts, being much prejudiced against "forfeitures," will seize upon next to nothing and create "waiver" out of it, for the purpose of preventing the loss of a great deal because of a little fault.

Substituting election for "waiver," we escape the seeming necessity for tricking ourselves into correct conclusion. Noting, for example, that prior to loss, an insurance company is interested in continuation of the risk, whereas after a loss it might desire to escape payment, we give to those facts their proper weight in judging whether or not election has been made by the company. And so, if, after a loss, the company assert that, prior to the loss, it had elected to terminate the policy, its interest in that regard will be taken into account.

With such guidance as we can get from the contradictory rules as to " waiver " and from the reasonableness of the rule as to election, and leaving, unexhausted, consideration of the infinite variety of circumstances which may be held to indicate election of one kind or another,[1] we pass on to examine (as sufficient for the purpose in hand) the evidential value of inactivity and silence; for upon that subject there exists wide diversity of opinion.

Election by Silence

When occasion has arisen for the exercise of a right of election (for example, an insurance company's right to elect to cancel a policy because of some breach of condition), silence, plus the lapse of a reasonable time within which to elect, may be held to be material in one of two ways:

1. It may be regarded as evidencing an election to continue the *status quo ante* — that is, to continue the policy.
2. It may be regarded as terminating the right to elect: with the result that the *status quo ante* is left undisturbed.[2]

In some cases, the first, and in others, the second of these may be the better. But close investigation of them is unnecessary, for we may say that where there is some other evidence of election to continue, the first is the more appropriate, and that, in all other cases, the second, if deemed the better, brings us to the same practical conclusion.

" Waiver." The dicta as to the effect of silence are hopelessly contradictory, the difficulty being that they proceed upon the theory of forfeiture and " waiver of the forfeiture; " that that theory works obvious injustice; and that the courts do not like the conclusion to which they appear to be forced. If we assume that the theory is right — that upon

[1] A number of cases are collected in Halsbury's Laws of England, XX, 749, note (d).

[2] Per Lord Watson in Edwards *v.* Carter, 1893, A. C. 366; 63 L. J., Ch. 100; 69 L. T. 153.

breach of a condition in a policy of insurance the policy is forfeited and can be restored by "waiver" — then no one can doubt the necessary deduction (often quoted) that the company

> is not obliged to do or say anything to make a forfeiture effectual. It may wait until claim is made under the policy, and then, in denial thereof, or in defence of a suit commenced therefor, allege a forfeiture.[1]
>
> The insurer is not required in such case to formally declare a forfeiture. It is sufficient to set it up by way of defence when sued for the loss.[2]
>
> The company is not obliged to do or say anything to make the forfeiture effectual until a claim is made under the policy.[3] It need not do anything shewing an election to avoid it in the lifetime of the insured. If the premium remained unpaid at the time of his death, the policy is void — if they set up the condition. The policy has simply come to an end.[4]

The reason for this is obvious. If the policy be terminated by the breach, then it is the assured himself who has put an end to it; he knows (usually better than the company) that the company is no longer under liability to him; he knows that neither action nor inaction on the part of the company (short of new contract) can re-establish that liability; he does not expect to receive any communication from the company; and the nature of any such communication (short of an offer for re-establishment of the contract) would have no interest for him. Not only is the company "not obliged to do or say anything to make the forfeiture effectual," but nothing

[1] Titus *v.* Glens Falls, etc., 1880, 81 N. Y. 419. Approved in Cannon *v.* Home, etc., 1881, 53 Wis. 594; 11 N. W. 11; Queen Ins. Co. *v.* Young, 1888, 86 Ala. 430; Armstrong *v.* Agricultural, etc., 1892, 130 N. Y. 564; 29 N. E. 991.

[2] Schimp *v.* Cedar Rapids, etc., 1888, 124 Ill. 357; 16 N. E. 229; Parker *v.* Banker's, etc., 1899, 86 Ill. App. 326.

[3] Smith *v.* St. Paul, etc., 1882, 3 Dak. 82; 13 N. W. 355; Phœnix, etc. *v.* Stevenson, 1879, 78 Ky. 157; 8 Ins. L. J. 922; Queen, etc. *v.* Young, 1888, 86 Ala. 431; 5 So. 116.

[4] McGeachie *v.* N. Am. etc., 1893, 20 Ont. A. R. 193.

that the company could do or say would have either precipitating or retarding influence upon it. There is no answer to the argument that:

> The fact that it is the fault and neglect of the insured to pay his premium which avoids the policy must be a matter within his own knowledge; and he cannot reasonably, require the company to inform him of the fact of his own neglect.[1]

And so, in the most recent book on insurance, it is said that:

> Mere silence or inaction on the part of the company after knowledge of a forfeiture by the insured will not in general operate as a waiver. The company has not contracted to search out the insured and advise him as to the legal effect of the provisions of the policy. To hold the contrary is to make a new agreement for the parties.[2]

ELECTION. But if the theory of forfeiture and "waiver" be wrong; if default merely give to the company a right of election; then termination of the policy (if it arrive) is the act of the company, and not of the assured; the assured will not know of the termination unless notified by the company; in the absence of communication, he may assume that it has not been terminated; relying upon that assumption, he may effect no other insurance upon his property; and he may consequently suffer loss. Silence

> had a tendency to lull the insured into a feeling of security, and thus prevent him from protecting himself by getting new insurance.[3]

ILLUSTRATION. — A New York case well illustrates the point in hand. A mortgagee was insured by a policy which provided that if he should commence an action of foreclosure, the policy "shall be null and void." After commencing

[1] Sears *v.* Agricultural, etc., 1882, 32 U. C., C. P. 601.
[2] Richards on Ins., p. 177.
[3] Phœnix *v.* Stevenson, 1879, 78 Ky. 160.

such an action, the mortgagee wrote to the company avowing the fact; alleging that it was done in ignorance of the condition; and asking consent to continuation of the policy. The company remained silent; and eight days afterwards a fire occurred. The court declared that:

> The commencement of the suit rendered the policy from that time void. The plaintiff must have been presumed to know that fact. He deliberately violated the condition and destroyed his contract, and then informed the defendant of his act. It would require some affirmative action on defendant's part, under such circumstances, to indicate that it intended to waive the result of the plaintiff's breach.[1]

That is the result arrived at on the basis of forfeiture and "waiver." Had the court observed that the policy had not been "destroyed"; that nothing had happened to the policy; that "waiver" considerations, therefore, were inappropriate; that the breach had merely given to the company an election to continue or to terminate the policy; and that the question was whether the lapse of eight days did not sufficiently indicate an election to continue it, the decision might (probably would) have been given in favor of the insured. The case is one of very many that may have been decided wrongly, because of current ideas of forfeiture and "waiver."

Confusion. The result arrived at in the following case will meet with general approval, but the opinion of the court contains a curious mixture of forfeiture, waiver, consent, estoppel, and election (The italics are not in the original):

> If notice be given to the company of the additional insurance or increased risk, and no objection be made within a reasonable time, fairness and good faith should *estop* it from insisting upon a *forfeiture* of the policy because its consent was not indorsed upon it according to its literal terms.

[1] Armstrong *v.* Agricultural, etc., 1892, 130 N. Y. 560; 29 N. E. 991.

> The assured has a right to infer therefrom that the company will not insist upon it. It has not spoken as to a matter for its benefit when it could and should have done so to prevent another from being misled to his probable injury. If it had done so, he might have protected himself probably by other insurance. Its silence under such circumstances is *a consent* to the additional insurance.
>
> A *forfeiture* upon this ground is not for fraud. It may cancel the policy by reason of it, but if it does so, it must refund a proper proportion of the premium. It cannot, therefore, remain mute with a knowledge of the existence of a ground of forfeiture, and if there be no loss, retain the entire premium, but, if there be one, rely upon the breach of the contract.
>
> The term "void" as used in the policy, is to be regarded as meaning that the insurer may, *at his exclusive option*, treat it so, and not that the contract becomes an absolute nullity, as to either party. The insurer may, therefore, by his conduct, *waive his right of forfeiture and estop himself* from insisting upon it.[1]

The following will, probably, not be accepted. It is one of the errors induced by the adoption of "waiver" phraseology:

> If the promissory warranty had been a verbal one, the doctrine might be different; but I do not understand . . . that where there is a written and express stipulation upon the face of the policy of insurance, it can be waived by silence, though the insurer knew of its violation.[2]

That is an example of the difficulties induced by what is called "the doctrine of parol waiver"[3] — by the question: "How can a written document be got rid of by a parol waiver?" To which the reply is that there is no necessity for getting rid of it. Construe it properly, and then apply it. And silence may indicate an exercise — not a "waiver" — of the right given by the contract.

SILENCE INDICATES ELECTION TO CONTINUE. We may say, then, that application of the phraseology of forfeiture

[1] Phœnix, etc. *v.* Spiers, 1888, 87 Ky. 293; 8 S. W. 453.

[2] Petit *v.* German, etc., 1898, 98 Fed. 800.

[3] Richards on Ins., p. 162.

and "waiver," to the class of cases under consideration, is wrong. Termination of the policy is the act of the company, and not the act of the assured, and the assured cannot be aware of the termination unless informed of the fact by the company. Under those circumstances, what is the effect of silence by a company after it has knowledge of the happening of some occurrence giving to it a right to elect between continuation and termination of the policy? It is, we say, evidence of an election, but what sort of election does it indicate? If I am speechless when offered an apple or an orange, which have I chosen? Neither, no doubt. But if I have an apple, and am offered an orange in exchange for it, and I remain mute, I am displaying an election to retain my own. And the question, in law, usually arises in similar form. There is a present situation which may be altered by election; and silence naturally indicates continuation, and not termination, of that situation.[1]

For example, in cases arising under wills, when a devisee is put to election between the provisions of the will and the property which he already has apart from the will, silence may be indicative of an election to retain his own property.

If an infant execute a conveyance of his lands, he may elect when he comes of age whether he will affirm or repudiate it. And protracted silence may be sufficient proof of an election to affirm.

Leases usually provide that they shall become void upon the happening of certain breaches of covenant — that is to say, that they shall be voidable at the election of the lessor. And the term will continue, unless the lessor in some way indicates his election to terminate it.

An insured against marine risk gives notice of abandonment, and if the insurer "says nothing and does nothing,"

[1] There is no such "present condition" in cases of election between remedies; and silence has therefore no operation in that department.

the proper conclusion is that he does not accept.[1] The *status quo ante* persists.

A purchaser becomes aware that he had been misled by misrepresentations. He remains silent and his silence indicates election to continue the contract.[2]

That is all reasonably clear, and is in accordance with *a-priori* ideas. A certain state of things exists; a party has a right to end it; he does nothing; and it continues.

There is no difference, in this respect, between contracts of insurance and any other contracts. If the company remain silent, a presumption may arise that it had elected to continue the policy.[3]

ELECTION AND ESTOPPEL. Although election is the applicable principle in the class of cases we have been dealing with, yet, in a class very closely associated, we must pass to estoppel: Within the period provided by a policy for sending to the company proofs of loss, the assured transmits documents which are, in some respects, defective; the company remains silent; and after expiry of the period raises the objection and refuses payment. There is no case for election here. The company could not have declared the policy terminated because of the defects; for the assured had still time in which to perfect them. Still one feels that the company has not acted fairly in postponing its objection until the time had expired, and in such cases it is usual to say that the company had "waived the forfeiture." But that cannot be right for there had been no forfeiture. The true ground for decision against the company is either (1) estoppel — having seen (if, as a matter of fact, it did see) the mis-

[1] Provincial, etc. *v.* Leduc, 1874, L. R. 6 P. C. 237. And see Peele *v.* Merchants, etc., 1822, 3 Mason 27.

[2] Flint *v.* Woodin, 1852, 9 Ha. 622; 22 L. J., Ch. 92; Campbell *v.* Fleming, 1834, 1 A. & E. 40; 3 L. J., K. B. 136; Houston *v.* Brashear, 1913, 158 S. W. 233; Driggs *v.* Hendrickson, 1915, 151 N. Y. Supp. 858; 89 Misc. R. 421.

[3] Teutonia, etc. *v.* Anderson, 1875, 77 Ill. 384; Mutual *v.* French, 1876, 30 Ohio 240; Williamsburg, etc. *v.* Cary, 1876, 83 Ill. 453.

take of the assured, the company was under obligation to advise him of it, or (2) acceptance of the documents as sufficient.

If the proofs are not filed until after the time has expired, there can of course be no estoppel, because the assured cannot change his position upon the faith of the silence. And the Privy Council has held that, in such case, there can be no "waiver" — mere silence, it was said,

> cannot possibly be a waiver of the not sending the proper proofs in, and not sending them in within proper time.[1]

But there may be subsequent election, for the company may, at any time, elect to recognize liability.

LANDLORD AND TENANT. We have been dealing with insurance cases, and it is hoped that the principles upon which they ought to be decided are understood. Let us take those principles into the law of landlord and tenant and see how they will work there. What do we think of the following:

> Mere knowledge and acquiescence in an act constituting a forfeiture does not amount to a waiver; there must be some act affirming the tenancy. . . . It has never yet been held that lying-by would constitute a waiver of a breach of covenant.[2]

That is a good sample of how far wrong notions of forfeiture and "waiver" may lead us astray. Although the courts unanimously acknowledge that the word *void* in leases means *voidable at the election of the landlord*, that fact is here, and often elsewhere, overlooked, and the courts speak as though forfeiture followed breach, and could be cured only by "waiver." The assertion that "there must be some act affirming the tenancy" is obviously erroneous. For until election to terminate, the tenancy remains unaffected — does not need affirmation; and after election to terminate,

[1] Whyte *v.* Western, etc. 1875, 22 L. C. Jur. 220; 7 Rev. Leg. (Que). 114.

[2] Sheppard *v.* Allen, 1810, 3 Taunt 79; Holderness *v.* Lang, 1886, 11 Ont. R. 14.

the tenancy is at an end, and cannot be affirmed (re-established) by the landlord alone.

The extract is also a good example of the benefit of comparative law — in this way: In the department of landlord and tenant, "waiver of forfeiture" usually takes place by acceptance of rent; the periodical payments usually occur at short intervals; silence, after breach and prior to the next rent day usually works no prejudice to the tenant; and usually therefore, the courts are apt, from this single set of instances, to generalize as in the extract. Had they studied the subject as it appears in the law of insurance they could not have said that

> mere knowledge and acquiescence in an act constituting a forfeiture does not amount to a waiver.

They could not have spoken of "waiver of a breach of covenant." And they might even have recalled that, in the case which they had in hand, there was neither "forfeiture" nor "waiver," but a case of very simple election only.[1]

[1] The subject is fully dealt with in the chapter on Landlord and Tenant.

CHAPTER VI

CONTRACT

CURRENT PHRASEOLOGY. It is curious that contract — a subject so well known and so clearly defined — should ever have been confused with "waiver"; and perhaps nothing illustrates so forcibly the vagueness of the conceptions which surround " waiver " as the existence of such confusion. For, so far as "waiver" is anything at all, it is purely unilateral, it is the voluntary relinquishment of something,[1] whereas contract is essentially and necessarily bilateral (sometimes multilateral) — it is an agreement between two or more persons. But notwithstanding this discrepancy, some current phraseology would warrant each of the following inferences:

1. Waiver is, or is very like, contract.
2. Waiver may create contract.
3. Contract may create waiver.
4. Waiver may alter contract.
5. Waiver may terminate contract.
6. Waiver may revive contract after it has been terminated.

1. " Waiver " is, or is very like, Contract

Contradictory Authorities. That " waiver " is, or is very like contract, while asserted by some authorities is contradicted by others. " Waiver " it is said, may be in the nature of contract; or it may not; or it may be something which is evidenced by contract. " Waiver " may need a supporting consideration; or it may not; or " waiver " of some rights may require a consideration, and " waiver " of others need not. " Waiver " must be founded upon contract or estoppel; or it operates freely without adventitious support. All this has already been pointed out.[2]

2. Contract created by " Waiver "

Principal and Agent. Although nobody suggests that " waiver " can supply all the elements of contract, yet the probabilities are that many lawyers would be inclined to accept the decision in the following case: Acting under a

[1] *Ante*, p. 6. [2] *Ante*, pp. 39–41.

power of attorney, A agreed to sell the business of Outram, and stipulated that Outram should not carry on similar business within fifty miles. There being doubt whether the power of attorney warranted the stipulation, the purchaser, during the course of the litigation, offered to waive it; and he asked specific performance of the other parts of the agreement. The trial judge held that

> this offer will not make the agreement binding on Outram, if it was not previously binding.

Upon appeal, it was said — that the waiver of the stipulation

> appears . . . to remove all difficulty, because it is quite obvious that those two clauses are inserted simply and purely for the benefit of the purchaser.[1]

But the first question is, Was there a contract? If not, no amount of "waiver" can make one. And a satisfactory way of answering the question is to consider the rights of Outram, the vendor. Clearly he could not eliminate the unauthorized clause, and (it being deleted) claim that the purchaser was bound by the other parts of the document. If, then, the vendor is not bound by the document as it stands, and if he can do nothing which will bring the purchaser into agreement with him, can the purchaser, by elimination of one of the clauses of the document, make it binding upon the vendor?

In other words has the vendor's pretended agent, when ostensibly making a contract to sell, really given an option to purchase? When the action was commenced by the purchaser, he was insisting upon performance of the document as it stood. But he could not succeed, for the document was not a contract. And so, during the action, he "waived" the stipulation; that is, he claimed to exercise an option to make, for the vendor, a contract out of that which

[1] Hawkesley v. Outram, 1892, 3 Ch. 359; 62 L. J. Ch. 215; 67 L. T. 804.

was not previously binding upon him. The Court held that, by "waiver," the purchaser could do that. It is submitted that the vendor was not bound by what the pretended agent did; that the purchaser could not eliminate a clause, and so create a contract; and that the offer to "waive" the stipulation was, in reality, an offer to make a contract.

RATIFICATION. Consider this case, also: An owner of goods offered to sell them (13 December); A, without sufficient authority, accepted the offer on behalf of B; afterwards the owner withdrew his offer (13 January); afterwards B ratified A's acceptance (28 January). Under these circumstances, the English Court of Appeal held that the owner was bound to carry out the sale.[1] And that appears to be equivalent to holding that the paper which the owner signed as a contract to sell, was really an option to B to purchase (for B might, or might not, as he pleased, have adopted A's act), and an option which the owner could not cancel until after the purchaser had had a reasonable time within which to make his election.

That case does not proceed upon "waiver." It is the converse of the case next above considered. It involves acceptance of the same principle — a principle which, it is submitted, is, when put baldly, quite unsupportable. And the

[1] Bolton *v.* Lambert, 1889, 41 Ch. Div. 295; 58 L. J. Ch. 425; 60 L. T. 685. Although the case has been followed in Re Portuguese, etc., 1890, 45 Ch. D. 17; 63 L. T. 423: and Re Tiedman, 1899, 2 Q. B. 66; 68 L. J., Q. B. 852, 81 L. T. 191, its authority has been shaken by a destructive distinction (Dibbins *v.* Dibbins, 1896, 2 Ch. 348; 65 L. J. Ch. 724; 75 L. T. 137), and by an intimation by one of the judges concerned in it that it ought to be reconsidered (Fleming *v.* Bank New Zealand, 1900, A. C. 577; 69 L. J., P. C. 120; 83 L. T. 1). The case was disapproved in Wright on *Principal and Agent* 81. In Campbell on *Sale of Goods*, 2d ed., 238, 9, an untenable distinction is suggested. Contrary law is clearly stated in Dodge *v.* Hopkins, 1861, 14 Wis. 686; followed in Athe *v.* Bartholomew, 1887, 69 Wis. 43; 33 N. W. 1101. And see Townsend *v.* Corning, 1840, 23 Wend. 435. The subject is treated in Mechem on Agency, 2d ed, vol. 2, p. 514 *et seq.*; 9 Harv. L. Rev. 60; 5 Am. St. Rep. 103; 24 Am. L. R. 580; 5 Law Quarterly Rev. 440.

opinion of the present writer is, (1) that a document signed by some one who professes to be, but is not, a sufficiently authorized agent of A, cannot, at the option of B, be brought within the limits of the real agency by curtailment of its provisions, and so, by "waiver," be turned into a contract; and (2), conversely, that a document which A himself signed as a contract, but which really is not a contract because of the lack of authority of the person assuming to act as B's agent, cannot, at the option of B, be supplemented by ratification, and so turned into a contract.[1]

This volume is not intended as a work upon the law of principal and agent, and the subject cannot here be further dealt with; but the suggestion may be permitted that a constant source of error, in cases of alleged ratification, is the practice of speaking of a document signed by one person on behalf of another, but without his authority, as a *contract* signed by an *agent*; whereas, in truth, there is, under such circumstances, no contract and no agency. In the case just cited, for example, Kekewich, J., led himself astray by saying:

> The contract was with them. . . . The doctrine of ratification is this, that when a principal on whose behalf a contract has been made in the first instance without his authority, adopts it and ratifies it, then . . . the ratification is referred to the date of the original contract, and the contract becomes, as from its inception, as binding on him as if he had been originally a party to it.

The learned judge speaks of the unauthorized act as constituting a "contract," whereas it had no binding effect upon one of the parties to it; he speaks of ratification of "the original contract," while indicating, by his language

[1] On related points, see Prince *v.* Clark, 1823, 1 B. & C. 80; 1 L. J. (O. S.) K. B. 69; Smithurst *v.* Mitchell, 1859, 1 E. & E. 622; 28 L. J., Q. B. 241; Conant *v.* Miall, 1870, 17 Gr. 574; Curtis *v.* Williamson, 1874, L. R. 10 Q. B. 57; 44 L. J., Q. B. 27; 31 L. T. 678; Bridgewater, etc. *v.* Murphy, 1894, 26 Ont. 327; 23 Ont. App. 66; 26 S. C. 447.

that there was no contract until the act of ratification; and he speaks of "a principal on whose behalf a contract was made," whereas, the transaction being unauthorized, there was no principal, no agent, and no contract. It should be observed that the frequently repeated phrase "an agent exceeding his authority" is quite wrong; for an agent, as agent, cannot exceed his authority. What we mean is, merely, that one man wrongfully assumed to act for another man. Misconception would sometimes be avoided if we so spoke. What enlightenment can be expected to be found in a textbook chapter which opens with the following words:

> We now have to consider the doctrine of ratification, whereby the principal may make himself responsible for contracts and acts of his agent outside his authority.[1]

The author did not mean either (1) that contracts require ratification, or (2) that, as agent, a man can do anything outside his authority. But for the misuse of the word *contract*, the following is acceptable:

> Where the plaintiffs are not bound by the contract when it was entered into by one claiming to be their agent, but who in fact was not such agent and had no power to bind them, they cannot afterwards when they find the contract is advantageous to them, affirm the contract made on their behalf by such unauthorized person and compel the other party to perform it on his part.[2]

ESCROWS. It is sometimes supposed that a document executed in escrow may, by a "waiver" of one of the parties, become a delivered obligation. For example, in Vance on Insurance is the following:

[1] The doctrine of ratification will some day be discarded. It rests upon a foolish fiction: Keighly *v.* Durant, 1901, A. C. 240. The observations in Mechem on Agency, 2d ed., § 343 *et seq.* are noteworthy.

[2] Athe *v.* Batholomew, 1887, 33 N. W. 110; 69 Wis. 43.

> Even though the parties may have expressly agreed that the contract shall not be deemed complete until the payment of the premium . . . this stipulation may be waived by the insurer.[1]

In other words, " waiver " by one of the parties can turn into a contract that which both parties have agreed is not to be a contract.

The agreement may be construed in two ways, and in neither of them has " waiver " any application. First, it may be taken to mean precisely what it says, namely that there shall be no contract until the happening of a further event — until one of the parties pays a certain sum of money. In that case, the parties may, if they choose, change their agreement; but, clearly, neither of them can, by his own action, affect it. Secondly, the clause may be forced to mean that the contract shall or shall not be complete without payment, *at the option of the insurer*. In that case, if the insurer so elect, the contract becomes complete, not because of " waiver " of the stipulation, but because the stipulation so provides.

3. " Waiver " created by Contract

The Authorities. Many of the authorities contain such sentences as the following:

1. A mutual agreement is necessary to waive a prior contract.[2]
2. Waiver, by mutual parol agreement, therefore, furnishes a sufficient defence, etc.[3]
3. A contract . . . may, before breach, be waived and abandoned by a new agreement.[4]

[1] P. 178. Approved in Pender *v.* North State, etc., 1913, 163 N. C. 98; 79 S. E. 293. And see Genung, etc. *v.* Mutual, etc., 1901, 60 N. Y. App. 424; 69 N. Y. Supp. 1041; Gordon *v.* U. S., 1899, 54 S. W. 98; Penn, etc., *v.* Norcross 1904, 163 Ind. 379; 72 N. E. 132.

[2] Whittaker *v.* Fox, 1865, 14 W. R. 193; 13 L. T. 588.

[3] Fry on Sp. Perf. 5th ed. § 1024.

[4] Addison on Contracts, 1911, p. 171.

4. The material question is whether the forfeiture was waived, and we see no reason why this may not be done as well by an agreement made for extending the note after its maturity as by one made before.[1]

The fault of the first three of these sentences is that "waiver" is substituted for rescission. The fourth is open to the further objection now well known to the reader. All four are cited in order to call attention to the remarkable versatility of "waiver"—how it may not only be (as already indicated) an important factor in the creation of contract, but, in turn, be itself created by contract.

4. Contract Altered by Waiver

The Authorities. The Supreme Court of the United States has said that:

> A party always has the option to waive a condition or stipulation made in his own favor.[2]

Probably there are few statements which would be more readily accepted; but is it right? Let us examine it.

Non-contract Waiver. There is no doubt that a term of a contract may be extinguished in the same manner as may the whole of the contract, (1) by a new contract,[3] and (2) by a release; and that estoppel is sometimes a good defence against an attempt to enforce it. But the question is, whether there is a still further method whereby a clause of a contract may be rendered imperative. Is there something which one party may say or do which will not amount to a new contract, or to a release; which is not followed by a consequential action of anybody; and yet which will destroy his right to enforce the clause? Is there such a thing as a "non-contract waiver?" A Missouri judge in 1912 said:

[1] Insurance Co. v. Norton, 1877, 96 U. S. 234; 24 L. Ed. 689.

[2] Iowa, etc. v. Lewis, 1902, 187 U. S. 348.

[3] Substituted performance and accord and satisfaction are, for the purposes in hand, sufficiently included in new contract.

> Parties who make a contract have the power to modify it by a subsequent agreement, but there must be a sufficient consideration for the modification to give it contractual force. Since the oral agreement cannot be considered as a contract, may it be regarded as pertinent to the issue of waiver?[1]

The learned judge thought that, in the particular case, it could not be so regarded, because

> It is a logical and legal solecism to speak of a non-contract waiver occurring before the breach has occurred.

In another case, in which the contract provided that the purchaser was to accept or reject the goods on or before the fifth day, and the parties continued after that time to negotiate, the court said:

> It is urged that by the evidence introduced by defendant, and the findings of the court thereon, the written contract between the parties was altered by means of parol testimony. But in our opinion the evidence and finding do not show an alteration of the contract, but only a waiver by the plaintiff of one of its provisions.[2]

Is there, then, such a thing as a non-contract " waiver "? Authority will not satisfactorily answer the question, for the judges and the text-writers hopelessly contradict one another. A few quotations have been brought together upon a previous page, and all that can be gathered from them is that "waiver" is, or is not, new contract; "waiver" must, and need not, have a consideration to support it; " waiver " of some sorts of rights requires consideration, and " waiver " of other sorts does not.[3]

REPUGNANT DECISIONS. It is very curious, that while the courts unanimously concur in holding that a contract can be altered only by a new contract made by both parties, they,

1 Patterson *v.* Am., etc., Ins. Co., 1912, 164 Mo. App. 164; 148 S. W. 448.

2 Fairbanks, etc. *v.* Nelson, 1914, 217 Fed. 218; 133 C. C. A. 212.

3 *Ante*, pp. 39-41.

almost as unanimously, declare that *clauses* of contracts can be eliminated by the action of one of the parties only — namely, by " waiver." The explanation appears to be that, in the latter class of cases, attention is fixed exclusively upon the interest and the action of the party who is said to " waive " the condition. The provision being obviously for the benefit of A, and insistence upon its performance being obviously detrimental to B, the willingness of A to eliminate the condition appears to be the only matter requiring investigation — the concurrence of B is assumed. But the concurrence is none the less necessary. And the statement that a contract cannot be altered without new contract is not more true than that a term of a contract cannot be extinguished by some unilateral act — by " waiver."

" Waiver " and Release. Apply the doctrine that an obligation can be terminated by " waiver " to a release. I am indebted on a bond, and my obligee brings me a release under seal — a complete " waiver," we may say, of an obligation, in the performance of which he is alone interested. Am I bound to accept it? If I do not, has the document, or the gentleman's action, any effect upon the bond? Is there any sort of *ex parte* " waiver " which, against my wish, would efface my obligation under it? And would the answers be different if the release were of one-tenth of the debt, instead of the whole of it? No doubt the holder of the bond cannot be compelled to sue upon it. But no one calls forbearance to sue, a " waiver " of a bond. Even the statute of limitations leaves liability intact, and terminates the right to sue upon it only.

Alteration of Time Limitations. The cases relating to clauses in contracts limiting times for performance, afford the best field for the study of alteration of contracts by " waiver " (1) because there are many such cases, and (2) because we are safe in saying that if a time-limit cannot be got rid of by "waiver," no other sort of stipulation can be ousted in that way.

Current Phraseology. Here, as elsewhere, careless phraseology is responsible for confusion of thought. Take a few examples. In a leading textbook is the following:

> Time, although of the essence of the contract . . . may be enlarged or waived by subsequent agreement.[1]

Waived by agreement! The author meant eliminated. In a well-known case, the court said:

> A mere extension of time is only a waiver to the extent of substituting the extended time for the original time.[2]

What was meant was, not that there had been any "waiver" of anything, but that the contract had been, by agreement, altered in one respect only.

Lord Cranworth, on one occasion, inquired whether the respondent

> had waived that part of the agreement which fixed one month . . . and had agreed to substitute . . . a reasonable time.[3]

But there was no necessity for the first of these inquiries. Answer to the second was all that was necessary. And if Lord Cranworth meant that an agreement to change the clause was a "waiver" of the clause as it stood, further evidence is adduced of the necessity for insistence upon the accurate use of language.

A Test. A good test of current phraseology is afforded by cases in which a purchaser's time to make his payment is not extended but reduced. In these, nobody would say that the vendor, by himself, "had waived that part of the agreement" which fixed one month for payment of the money, and

[1] Dart on V. & P., 6th ed., vol. 1, p. 503.

[2] Barclay *v.* Messenger, 1874, 43 L. J. Ch. 456; 30 L. T. 351. And see Peterson *v.* Queen, 1889, 2 Ex. (Can.) 74.

[3] Darnley *v.* London, etc., 1867, L. R. 2 H. L. 60; 36 L. J. Ch. 404; 16 L. T. 217.

that both parties "had agreed to substitute" one week. Everybody would see that, in that connection, the introduction of "waiver" would be not only gratuitous, but inappropriate, and erroneous. Extension of the time stipulated by contract for performance, like its reduction, is an alteration of one of the terms agreed to, and must be evidenced in the same way as other contracts.[1] Contention that the time had been reduced would require that sort of support, and the principle must be the same in both cases. If, by contract, a builder had six months in which to erect a house, and at the end of three months he was sued for non-completion, upon the allegation that, by "waiver," he had reduced the time by one-half, we should smile at the language; but only because, as applied to such circumstances, our judgments have not been warped by traditionary phraseology. For an appeal to "waiver" would be just as reasonable in that case as in one in which the builder was being sued for non-completion within the contracted six months, and he defended upon the ground of extension, by "waiver," for another six. Habituated by customary, but quite erroneous phraseology, we should see nothing to smile at in extension by "waiver," although quite satisfied that time could not be reduced in the same way.

NEW CONTRACT. In the oft-discussed case of Goss *v.* Lord Nugent, Lord Denman said:

[1] It is said that "waiver" of a written contract, and even of a contract under seal, may be proved by parol: Prudential, etc. *v.* Sullivan, 1901, 27 Ind. App. 36; 59 N. E. 873; Palmer *v.* Meriden, etc., 1900, 188 Ill., 521; 59 N. E. 247. But so far from this being recognized as a distinguishing mark between "waiver" and release, the latter case declares that the parol evidence is competent "where the waiver is in the nature of a release or discharge." A party alleging a variation of time fixed by an agreement must show what the variation was — namely, substitution of some other period, or a reasonable time, or elimination altogether of the time-limitation; and he must show that both parties agreed to the same alteration; Darnley *v.* London, etc., 1867, L. R. 2 H. L. 60; 36 L. J. Ch. 404; 16 L. T. 217; approved in Bennecke *v.* Ins. Co., 1881, 105 U. S. 360; 26 L. Ed. 990.

> By the general rules of the common law, if there be a contract which has been reduced into writing, verbal evidence is not allowed to be given of what has passed between the parties, either before the written instrument was made, or during the time that it was in a state of preparation, so as to add to or subtract from, or in any manner to vary or qualify the written contract; but after the agreement has been reduced into writing, it is competent to the parties, at any time before breach of it, by a new contract not in writing, either altogether to waive, dissolve, or to annul the former agreement, or in any manner to add to, or subtract from, or vary or qualify the terms of it; and thus to make a new contract, which is to be proved, partly by the written agreement, and partly by the subsequent verbal terms engrafted upon what will be thus left of the written agreement.[1]

Apart from the expression " waive " (by which was meant rescind), we are here on firm ground, namely that the parties to a contract may do what they like with it — by a new contract.

Arbitration Agreements. A good illustration may be found in cases of alleged extension of prescribed time for the making of an award. If after expiration of the period, the parties, without protest, continue to attend meetings of the arbitrators, a mutual assent to extension of the time, or to elimination of the time-provision, may well be inferred.[2] But if the period should expire after all the meetings had been held, and one party, without the concurrence of the other, but with knowledge of the expiration of the time, should take up the award and pay the arbitration fees, the incident, being unilateral, could be no evidence of a new contract.

Would it be a " waiver " of the objection? There could hardly be a better example of the confusion introduced with the word. For the apparently inevitable answer is in the affirmative. But the question remains, Can " waiver " by

[1] 1833, 5 B. & Ad., 64; 2 L. J., K. B. 127.

[2] Re Hicks, 1819, 8 Taunt. 694. The language of the judgment is, " They must be taken to have waived this objection."

one party alter a contract made by two parties? Taking up the award would not impose a liability upon the other party — would not, as to him, validate the award. And if the contract be not altered as to one party, how can it have been changed as to the other?[1]

RECEIVING PAYMENT. Take another example of the prevailing confusion:

> The default as to the time may be waived by the conduct of the other party; as, by acts recognizing the contract as subsisting, by receiving payment, or by continuing negotiations.[2]

"Receiving payment" presupposes somebody's making payment; it is the conduct not "of the other party," but of both parties; and it is evidence of new agreement. "Continuing negotiations," too, is mutual, and not unilateral, conduct.

NOTICES. Cannot notices, to which a man is entitled, be "waived"? By the terms of a mortgage, the mortgagee had power to sell after default and service of a certain notice upon the mortgagor; the mortgagee gave the notice prematurely — after two months' default instead of three — and sold the property; could not the defect be removed, and the title made good, by "waiver"? No doubt one period could be substituted for another by agreement between mortgagor and mortgagee. And no doubt, by conduct, the mortgagor might be estopped, as against the purchaser, from raising objection. But is there something which is neither agreement not estoppel which will have those effects? In such a case, "waiver" was urged, but Bowen, L. J., said:

> What is waiver? Delay is not waiver. Inaction is not waiver. Waiver is consent to dispense with notice.[3]

[1] See per Lord Chelmsford in Darnley v. London, etc., 1867, L. R. 2 H. L., p. 57; 36 L. J., Ch. 404; 16 L. T. 217.

[2] 36 Cyc., p. 717. Quoted in McCarty v. Hebbling, 1914, 144 Pac. 499.

[3] Selwyn v. Garfit, 1888, 38 Ch. D. 284; 57 L. J., Ch. 609; 59 L. T. 233.

Consent means agreement; and if that word were substituted for the vagueness associated with "waiver," the English Privy Council could hardly have made such misapplication of Lord Justice Bowen's dictum as to have decided the case of The City of Toronto *v.* Russell [1] as it did.

VENDOR AND PURCHASER OF REAL ESTATE. Is not an instance of "waiver" to be found in a case in which a vendor of real estate delivers his abstract after the period prescribed by the contract, and the purchaser receives it and returns requisitions? Has not the purchaser "waived" the time limit? [2] No: the case is one of election. When the time elapsed, the purchaser had the right to elect (as in so many other cases) whether he would, or would not, proceed with the purchase — the vendor was offering to proceed and the purchaser could agree or decline. If he elected to stop, we would not say that he had "waived" his right to proceed; and when he elects to proceed, why should we say that he "waived" his right to stop? He "waived" — he threw away or relinquished — as truly in one case as in the other. He had a right of election between two positions, and he chose one. He did not "waive" or relinquish the other. He never had it. He had a choice, and he did not "waive" that. He exercised it.

The case is precisely similar, in principle, to that which arises in the case of a contract which permits a vendor to rescind it rather than answer questions of a certain character. When the questions are put, he may elect what he will do. And it is said that

> if the vendors once elect to answer the objections, they are forever thereafter precluded from exercising the option given to them . . . to rescind the contract.[3]

[1] 1908, A. C. 493; 78 L. J., P. C. 1; 99 L. T. 738.

[2] McCarty *v.* Hebbling, 1914, 144 Pac. 499; quoting Waterman on Sp. Perf., § 482.

[3] Tanner *v.* Smith, 1840, 10 Sim. 412. And see Gardom *v.* Lee, 1865, 3 H. & C. 651; 34 L. J. Ex. 113; 12 L. T. 430.

But the phraseology is not quite right, unless it be permissible to say, that by eating your dinner (making your election) you are *precluded* from eating the same dinner (making your election) again. Further discussion of time-limitations may be found in a subsequent chapter.

VENDOR AND PURCHASER OF GOODS. Where a vendor of goods agreed to deliver "on condition of being paid therefor in satisfactory paper at six months," should we not be right in saying that the vendor might "waive" the condition, and that he might deliver the goods without requiring the agreed satisfaction? Many cases can be cited in support of the affirmative. For example, Shaw, C. J. of Massachusetts, in a classic passage, has said:

> The question then . . . was whether the plaintiff had waived the condition of this sale and manifested, by his language or conduct, an intention or a willingness to waive the condition and make the sale absolute without having the satisfactory paper. . . . Waiver is a voluntary relinquishment or renunciation of some right, a foregoing or giving up of some benefit or advantage which, but for such waiver, he would have enjoyed . . . In this case it [the question] was, Did the plaintiff voluntarily deliver the goods, without intending to rely on the condition? [1]

"Waiver" is, it is said, a unilateral act. It is something from which some other person may take benefit, but in which, in other respects, he has no part. "Take benefit!" *Must* he take it? Does it come upon him by force of general law, as an intestate's estate devolves upon the heirs? Or may he accept or refuse it, as he pleases? If the benefit be palpable, there may be little difficulty in proving that he did accept it. But that is not the question. May he refuse, if he so desire? or must he accept? In the case put, must he accept an unconditional delivery, if the vendor so choose?

[1] Farlow *v.* Ellis, 1860, 15 Gray 231.

Observe that the passing of the legal title to the goods depends upon whether the delivery be conditional or unconditional. According to the contract, the delivery is to be conditional, and the title will remain in the vendor until fulfillment of the condition. Can the vendor, without the concurrence of the purchaser, change the effect of the delivery? Can he pass the title to a man who does not accept it? Can he pass it, even as against the wish of the purchaser? Can he, at will, retain or transfer the risk of loss by fire? All this was argued, in the affirmative, in a later Massachusetts case, counsel contending that:

> The waiver of a condition has, in it, no elements of contract, requiring for its efficacy the concurrence of two minds, and, therefore, the purpose of the party receiving the benefit of the waiver is unimportant.[1]

But the Court said:

> It is true that it is entirely at the option of the vendor whether he will waive the condition or not. It requires his voluntary act. But when he voluntarily does the act which, unexplained, constitutes a waiver, he not only may be presumed to intend it, but he changes the relations between himself and the purchaser in respect to the property and the contract of sale. If he would impose any condition upon the purchaser, affecting those new relations, or any obligation not implied from the transfer itself, he should manifest his purpose in some mode, so that the other party may assent or dissent.

"So that the other party may assent or dissent." In another case—one in which the contract provided that title to goods (then delivered by the vendor to the purchaser) should not pass until payment made, the court said:

> The vendor in a conditional sale contract, upon the default of his vendee, may retake the property, or he may treat the sale as absolute and sue for the price, and the assertion of one right

[1] Upton *v.* Sturbridge, 1873, 111 Mass. 453. See also Fishback *v.* Van Dusen, 1885, 33 Minn. 117; 22 N. W. 244.

> is the waiver of the other. The sale became absolute when suit was brought on the notes.[1]

In other words, the vendor may, without the assent of the purchaser, alter the contract; and he may pass title to the goods at a time at which the contract declares that it is not to pass. It is difficult to agree that "waiver" can accomplish all that.

In another case it was said that:

> The plaintiff did not accept the deed, and the defence is, that, although the defendant did not offer to perform the contract according to its terms, yet the plaintiff waived the defect in the offer which was made. As the defect relates to the quantity of land which is to be conveyed the defence is, in effect, that the plaintiff agreed to accept a substituted performance for that which the contract required, and that the defendant offered to perform the contract according to the new agreement; or, if put on the ground of waiver, that the plaintiff relinquished to the defendant the right to require a conveyance of the land.[2]

But is "waiver" sufficient if new agreement fails? In other words, if the plaintiff did *not* agree to pay without receiving a conveyance (as provided by the contract), is he bound to pay? For example, if he had said to the defendant: "You need not convey the land to me," that might mean "and I will pay you all the same;" and there would be evidence of a new contract. But if what was said does not mean that — if, no matter what was said, the contract remains as it was — then the remark could be of no value to the defendant. The learned judge himself said:

> But whether the defence is put upon the ground of waiver or of a new agreement, it is necessary to show an assent to the change on the part of the plaintiff.

But "waiver" (if anything) is unilateral; and "an assent to the change" points to new contract.

[1] Skoog *v.* Mayer, 1913, 122 Minn. 209; 142 N. W. 193. See also Starin *v.* Kraft, 1898, 174 Ill. 123; 50 N. E. 1059.

[2] Holdsworth *v.* Tucker, 1887, 143 Mass. 369; 9 N. E. 764.

Estoppel. While estoppel may under some circumstances afford sufficient reply to a plea of non-compliance with some stipulation, it is, upon other occasions very unnecessarily and inappropriately introduced.[1] For example, a policy provided that the insured goods should not be removed, and that

> anything less than a distinct agreement endorsed on this policy shall not be construed as a waiver of any . . . condition, etc.

The insured informed the president of the company of his intention to remove the goods, and, in reply, the president in effect said:

> Go and remove your goods. You need not bring your policy and have the permission to do so endorsed on it. The insurance shall continue in force without such endorsement.

The court held the company estopped,[2] saying that:

> The principle is that where one party has, by his representations or his conduct, induced the other party to a transaction to give him an advantage which it would be against equity and good conscience for him to assert, he would not be permitted to avail himself of that advantage.

But appeal to estoppel is unnecessary. If (as we must in any case assume) the president had authority to say that "the insurance shall continue in force without such endorsement," the company was bound by the contract evidenced in those words.

Conclusion. The conclusions from the preceding argument are inevitable. One party cannot by "waiver" or any other unilateral proceeding alter a contract made by two or more parties. There is no such thing as "a non-contract waiver." Time for performance of a contract cannot be

[1] Morrow *v.* Lancashire, etc., 1899, 26 Ont. A. R. 179.

[2] Maryland, etc. *v.* Gusdorf, 1875, 43 Md. 513; quoting Ins. Co. *v.* Wilkinson, 1871, 13 Wall (U. S.) 233; 20 L. Ed. 617. And see Pollock *v.* German, etc., 1901, 86 N. W. 1017; 127 Mich. 460.

reduced by "waiver," nor can it, by "waiver," be extended or eliminated. Acceptance of an offer to reduce or to extend is a new agreement; and under certain circumstances, acceptance may, very readily, be inferred. Acts spoken of as "waivers" may, in other cases, be indications of the exercise of a right of election. Estoppel may sometimes be pleaded as a sufficient reason for non-performance of some conditions, but, in some cases, new contract rather than estoppel ought to be asserted.

5. Contract Terminated by Waiver

The Authorities. Many of the authorities contain such sentences as the following:

> A mutual agreement is necessary to waive a prior contract.[1]
>
> Waiver, by mutual parol agreement, therefore, furnishes a sufficient defence to an action for specific performance.[2]
>
> A contract required by statute to be in writing may, before breach, be waived and abandoned by a new agreement not in writing.[3]
>
> A contract may be discharged by agreement between the parties that it shall no longer bind them. This is a waiver, or rescission of the contract.[4]

Confusion. As long as one keeps steadily in mind that "waiver" cannot be the result of contract, and that "waiver" cannot terminate a contract, not much harm can arise from saying that by a new contract you may "waive" an old one. But would it not be better to say simply that contract may be rescinded by contract; for otherwise some students might slip into the idea that "waiver" could have some bearing upon the making of the new contract, and the rescission of the old. For example, apart from the perplexing influence of "waiver," it is probable that the following

[1] Whitaker v. Fox, 1865, 14 W. R. 193; 13 L. T. 588.
[2] Fry on Sp. Perf., 5th ed., § 1024.
[3] Addison on Contracts, 1911, p. 171.
[4] Anson on Contracts, 13th ed., p. 320.

sentence could not have found place in a deservedly popular textbook:

> An agreement to rescind an existing contract must amount to a total abandonment of the whole contract, and not to a partial waiver of some of its terms.[1]

It is difficult to imagine what precisely was the confusion of ideas that appeared to necessitate the warning that "partial waiver" of some of the terms of a contract could not amount to a rescission of the whole contract. The author would never have thought worth his while the statement that rescission of some of the terms of a contract does not amount to rescission of all of its terms. But, for some reason, he did deem it advisable to tell us that "partial waiver" (What is *partial* waiver?) of some of the terms has not that annihilating effect.

"Waiver" might lead us astray, too, in a case in which a policy-holder declined to pay his premium-note, saying that

> he would not have anything more to do with the company, and abandoned the whole thing,

but, after a loss, changed his mind. No doubt he had "waived" as effectively as he could, but he had really done nothing beyond giving to the company a right to elect to treat the policy as cancelled. Not having so elected, the contract remained unaffected.[2]

6. Contract Revived by Waiver

The Authorities. Confusion as to "forfeiture," necessitated the counter-irritant (the word is appropriate) "waiver"; with the logical result that, forfeiture being cured by "waiver," the contract is restored to pristine health.

[1] Fry on Sp. Perf., 5th ed., § 1028.

[2] McAllistor *v.* New England, etc., 1869, 101 Mass. 558.

> By the very terms of the policy, the policy ceased and determined by the non-payment of the premium. . . . It could, then, be revived or continued in life only in one of three ways: by a new agreement, by the operation of an estoppel, or by a waiver.[1]
>
> It became incumbent on the plaintiff to establish, with reasonable clearness, some act of the company to revive the lost liability.[2]
>
> An agent duly authorized may waive the forfeiture, and thereby reinstate the obligation.[3]

Even when it was recognized that the policy was " only voidable at their " (the company's) " election," and therefore not forfeited by breach of condition, the court said that

> it was, therefore, competent for them to waive a strict compliance with it, after the time stipulated for the payment of such premium; and that in case of such waiver, the policy would be revived and continue obligatory on the defendants on its original terms.[4]

One of the standard textbooks has the following

> A policy being forfeited by a violation of some of its conditions, a mere oral waiver of the forfeiture is not sufficient to revive it, unless some new consideration on the part of the assured supervenes, or some transaction takes place between the parties under the contract importing a waiver; such, for instance, as would be equivalent to receiving rent from a tenant for a time posterior to the forfeiture of a lease by non-payment of rent.[5]

Upon which we may observe (1) that a policy is not forfeited by a violation of a condition; (2) that it, therefore, needs no revivification; (3) that if it had been " forfeited " (terminated), it could be revived by new contract, but not by " waiver " (meaning some unilateral act of the company);

[1] Robertson *v.* Met. Life, etc., 1882, 88 N. Y. 544. See also New York, etc. *v.* Watson, 1871, 23 Mich. 487.

[2] McGeachie *v.* North American, etc., 1892, 20 Ont. App. 190.

[3] Cohen *v.* Continental, etc., 1887, 67 Tex. 328; 3 S. W. 296.

[4] Bouton *v.* American, etc., 1857, 25 Conn. 542. See also Continental, etc. *v.* Chew, 1894, 11 Ind. App. 331; 38 N. E. 417; Home, etc. *v.* Karn, 1897, 19 Ky. L. R. 273; 39 S. W. 501.

[5] Phillips on Insurance, 5th ed., vol. 1, pp. 8, 9.

(4) that receiving rent from a tenant is not a revivor of the lease, but is evidence of an election to continue the lease — an election that leaves the lease unaffected.

FORFEITURE AND NEW CONTRACT. The impossibility of reviving a contract by "waiver" is recognized in some of the cases.

> The doctrine of waiver seems applicable properly speaking only during the currency of the contract. . . . After a policy is forfeited, I see not how it could be renewed or revivified except by an express agreement of the insurers.[1]

The court appears to mean that an insurer can "waive" a condition prior to its forfeiture, but that after forfeiture, he can do nothing — there must be a new contract. If it meant that, prior to default, the condition may be "waived," the reply is that a condition cannot be got rid of by "waiver," but by new contract, by release, or by estoppel only.[2] If it meant that, after default, "waiver" cannot revivify the contract, the answer is that default has not affected the contract. But if it meant only, that after *termination* of the contract, "waiver" cannot re-establish it, we may agree.

Somewhat similar criticism must be applied to a case in which, when dealing with a company's defence of non-delivery of a statement of loss, the court said:

> After thirty days had expired without any statement, nothing but the express agreement of the Company could renew or revivify the contract.[3]

For non-delivery of the statement, without consequential election, had not affected the contract. And when election to terminate has been exercised, we ought to say:

[1] Diehl *v.* Anderson, etc., 1868, 58 Pa. 452. And see Home, etc. *v.* Kuhlman, 1899, 58 Neb. 493.

[2] *Ante*, pp. 133–137.

[3] Beatty *v.* Lycoming, etc., 1870, 66 Pa. 9. And see McNeill *v.* Union, etc., 1877, 7 Ont. App. 175; Acey *v.* Fernie, 1840, 7 M. & W. 151.

> Having exercised its rights to cancellation . . . it was not possible for the company by its own declarations to control or limit the effect of the cancellation.[1]

Another erroneous way of stating a possibly correct conclusion is to say that when a landlord brings ejectment based upon breach of some condition

> he thereby elects to treat the lease as void; and if anything at all be set up by the waiver (by the subsequent receipt of rent), it would not be the lease but it would be a new agreement.[2]

Receipt of money as rent, after election to terminate the lease, is not a "waiver" of anything. And "waiver" (a unilateral act) can set up nothing. Payment and receipt of rent is a bilateral transaction, and is evidence of an agreement either (1) to restore the old lease, or (2) to make a new one. May not we say simply that the action of the lessor

> put an end to the tenancy. The right of possession reverted to the landlord . . . and the tenancy being at an end, there could be no new contract except by mutual agreement.[3]

INTERMITTENT REVIVORS. The following may or may not be a logical deduction from the forfeiture and "waiver" *dicta*, but it at least indicates to what curious conclusions the introduction of the ideas may lead:

> Nor is the company bound in case it learns of such vacancy to declare the policy forfeited. It may waive the forfeiture. But such waiver of the right of forfeiture is not a waiver of the condition during the time the breach continued. If the loss occurs while the vacancy continues to exist, the company is not necessarily rendered liable because, knowing the fact, it has not in the meantime forfeited the policy. But if it does not exercise its right in this respect, and the premises are again occupied, and

[1] Commerical, etc. *v.* New Jersey, etc., 1901, 61 N. J. Eq. 453; 49 Atl. 155.
[2] Evans *v.* Wyatt, 1880, 43 L. T. 177.
[3] Nisbet *v.* Hall, 1895, 28 Nova Scotia, 80. See *ante*, cap. 5, p. 352.

> are not vacant or unoccupied when the loss occurs, the liability on the policy would again attach.[1]

Here we have revivor by the insured, as well as by the insurer. The premises become vacant, the policy is forfeited, and for a loss the company is not liable; afterwards the assured retakes possession, the policy is revived, and the company's liability recommences; and so on, according to the choice of residence of the assured. And the insurer has also reviving power: The premises become vacant, the policy is forfeited, and for a loss the company is not liable; afterwards the insurer " waives " the forfeiture, the policy is revived, and the company's liability recommences; and so on, according to the wish of the company.

Observe that the contract is extinguished and re-established at the independent option of both parties; that it terminates (is forfeited) by the act of one party; that either party may resuscitate it; and that, when resuscitated, it commences a new, rather than continues its previous, existence. Nothing of all that appears in the contract. There we find simply, that upon receiving knowledge of the vacancy, the company may elect to continue or to terminate the policy; that if it elect to cancel, the contract ceases; and that if it do not so elect, the contract remains unaffected.

Confusion in an English Statute

The disastrous effects of current phraseology is frequently pointed out in this volume. Perhaps nowhere is it more apparent than in the English Sale of Goods Act.

> Where a contract of sale is subject to any condition to be fulfilled by the seller, the buyer may waive the condition, or may elect to treat the breach of such condition as a breach of warranty and not as a ground for treating the contract as repudiated.[2]

[1] Stephens *v.* Phœnix, etc., 1899, 85 Ill. App. 675. The point is more correctly stated in Home Ins. Co. *v.* Kuhlman, 1899, 58 Neb. 490.

[2] 56 and 57 Vic., c. 71, § 11 (a).

What was intended by this bungle was expressed in Mr. Chalmers' first draft of the clause in this way:

> Where a contract of sale is subject to any condition for the benefit of the seller, the buyer may elect to treat non-performance of such condition as a breach of warranty, and not as a ground for rescinding the contract.[1]

Breach of a condition gives "rise to a right to treat the contract as rescinded;"[2] but the buyer may, if he wish, treat non-performance as a breach of warranty only. That is clear enough. Introduction of the words "waive the condition" made nonsense of the draft. Observe the following:

As a first alternative, the statute provides that the buyer may "waive the condition;" and that means either (1) that he may treat the contract as though the condition were eliminated, or (2) that he may "waive" performance of the condition. In other words, the buyer may upon one of two grounds keep the horse and make no complaint of the breach of the condition.

The second alternative enables the buyer to turn the condition into a warranty, and to sue for damages for breach of it. In other words, he may keep the horse and sue for damages. And thus we find the alternatives of the statute are:

1. The buyer may keep the horse, and not sue for damages; or

2. The buyer may keep the horse and sue for damages.

That was not in the least like the result intended. The purpose was to provide an alternative between (1) enforcing the condition as a condition (treating the contract as rescinded), and (2) treating the condition as a warranty

[1] Chalmers, Sale of Goods, 1st ed., § 14 (1).

[2] Sec. 11 (b). And see § 62. That is the common law; Eversole *v.* Hanna, 1914, 171 S. W. 25; 184 Mo. App. 445; Staver, etc. *v.* Amer. & British, etc., 1914, 188 Ill. App. 634; Winters *v.* Coward, 1915, 174 S. W. 940.

and suing for damages — in other words between (1) returning the horse, and (2) keeping it, plus damages. So intending, the clause should have read:

> the buyer may *enforce* (not, *waive*) the condition, or may elect to treat the breach of such condition as a breach of warranty;

or it might have read:

> the buyer may waive the condition, *and* (not, *or*) may elect to treat the breach of such condition as a breach of warranty;

or, much better, it should have been left as Mr. Chalmers drafted it.

Summary of Chapter

Summarizing the contents of this chapter, its contentions are:

1. "Waiver" neither is, nor does it resemble, contract. So far as it is thought to be anything, it is unilateral, whereas contract is never unilateral.[1]
2. "Waiver" cannot create contract.
3. Contract cannot create "waiver."
4. "Waiver" cannot alter contract.
5. Nor can it terminate contract.
6. Nor can it revive contract.
7. Current employment of the word is prejudicial to clarity of view upon the subjects usually associated with it.

[1] The obligation may be unilateral; but for a contract, there must always be at least two operating parties.

CHAPTER VII

LANDLORD AND TENANT

FORFEITURE AND "WAIVER." The phraseology of forfeiture and " waiver " is responsible for much confusion in the law of landlord and tenant. Unembarrassed by it, we should say that where, by the terms of a lease, the lessor is given power (upon the happening of some event) to terminate the lease (either by re-entry or in any other way) he has a right of election, which he may exercise as he pleases; that if he elect to continue the lease, it continues; that if he elect to terminate it, it ends; that the happening of the event does not, in itself, create a forfeiture of the lease; that it has no effect whatever upon the lease; that as there is no forfeiture by the happening of the event, there can be no " waiver " of the forfeiture; and that, if (wrongly) you choose to say that forfeiture takes place upon the lessor electing to terminate the lease, there can be no " waiver " of that forfeiture, for the lease has been terminated, and nothing but the concurrent action of both parties can re-establish it.

CAUSE OF DIFFICULTY. A leasehold interest is usually of some value, and, therefore, when a tenant does, or omits, something which gives to the landlord a right to elect to terminate the lease, and the probabilities are that the landlord will so elect, it is usually said (prematurely and prophetically) that the lease has been " forfeited; " and, should the landlord " decline to take advantage of the forfeiture," we are apt to say that he " waived " it. That such language is inaccurate and misleading, may at once be seen if we endeavor to apply it to an onerous lease. Forfeiture implies something forfeited, something lost; and when a tenant, under an onerous lease, gives cause for re-entry and we feel certain that the landlord will *not* re-enter, no one would say that the tenant had "forfeited" anything; for if the landlord did terminate the lease, the tenant would be benefited and not damaged. Nor should we, in such case, speak of the landlord "waiving" the tenant's act or default; for the implication would be that the landlord was giving up something ("waiving" some benefit) whereas, in truth, he is insisting upon keeping what he has got — upon the tenant continuing to bear his contracted burden. To keep ourselves clear of fog and difficulty, we must use language that will be applicable to all leases, whether they be profitable, oppressive, or reasonable.

MR. UNDERHILL. It is not quite true, however, that, in the case of an onerous lease, no one would speak of a tenant forfeiting it, for Mr. Underhill has exhibited the evil of the vogue of the popular phraseology by slipping into the following sentence:

> The lessee cannot himself take advantage of a forfeiture, so that, by failing to pay rent, he can put an end to the lease, and thus release himself . . . from liability for the non-payment of future instalments of rent.[1]

Having given to his readers the idea that "a forfeiture" of the lease occurs by default, it was necessary to warn them that "the lessee cannot himself take advantage of it;" for they might very well have thought that if the lease had really been forfeited — completely forfeited — it had actually ceased to exist. If the author, in the above sentence, had substituted for "a forfeiture" the words "his own breach of covenant" (what he really meant) the sentence would have been palpably unnecessary. And if he were to make use of the phraseology of election, no one could imagine him saying (it would be too clearly useless) that which he would have to say if he wished to convey the idea of his sentence:

[1] On Landlord and Tenant, vol. I, p. 641.

> A breach of covenant to pay rent gives to *the lessor* a right of election to continue, or to terminate the lease as he pleases; and *the lessee* cannot exercise the election which has been vested in *the lessor*, and thus release himself from liability for future rent.

The same writer has added to the peculiarities of "forfeiture," when linked with "waiver," this also: that after a forfeiture has been "waived" by the landlord, it may be revived by the tenant:

> Though the receipt of rent may be a waiver of forfeiture created in the past by a failure to pay rent, the tenant is not relieved from paying rent promptly in the future. . . . The default of the tenant, and his refusal to pay after a waiver by the landlord revives the forfeiture, and enables the landlord to recover possession upon a breach of the condition.[1]

In other words, non-payment of rent forfeited the lease; the lessor "waived" the forfeiture; but the forfeiture has not been completely obliterated; for the tenant's subsequent default "revives the forfeiture." In reality, all that has happened is that the first default gave a right of election which was exercised in favor of continuing the lease; and the second default gave another similar right. There was no forfeiture. The lease was not partially obliterated. And it was not revived.

BARON BRAMWELL. In 1858, Bramwell, B., advising the House of Lords used the following language:

> The common expression "waiving a forfeiture," though sufficiently correct for most purposes, is not strictly accurate. When a lessee commits a breach of covenant, on which the lessor has a right of re-entry, he may elect to avoid or not to avoid the lease. . . . In strictness, therefore, the question in such cases is, Has the lessor, having notice of the breach, elected not to avoid the lease? Or has he elected to avoid it? Or has he made no election?[2]

[1] On Landlord and Tenant, vol. I, p. 649.

[2] Croft *v.* Lumley, 1858, 6 H. L. C. 705; 27 L. J., Q. B. 321. Approved in Clough *v.* London, etc., 1871, L. R. 7 Ex. 35; 41 L. J. Ex. 17; 25 L. T. 708, in a

If, instead of admitting that the expression "waiving a forfeiture" was "sufficiently correct for most purposes," the learned judge had said that it was not only absolutely incorrect but very misleading; and if he had himself afterwards refrained from slipping into the looser phraseology, we should probably have been saved from many misconceptions, and not a few erroneous decisions.[1] Contrast the language quoted, for example, with the following (typical of much else) taken from a later case:

> No one would impugn the proposition that when a landlord, after a forfeiture has come to his knowledge, does anything whereby he recognizes the relation of landlord and tenant as still existing, he is precluded from saying he did not do the act with the intention of waiving the forfeiture.[2]

Here we have a forfeiture which never existed; "waiver" of that forfeiture; and estoppel from denying the "waiver." Could anything be more unreal?

AN ONTARIO DECISION. In an Ontario case, in which the lease was to be "void" upon breach of a certain stipulation it was said:

> If, therefore, any one of the quarterly instalments remain unpaid, the forfeiture is absolute, unless there is something in the contract itself to dispense with it.[3]

And the same learned judge, three months previously, said:

> I regret, therefore, that I am unable to find anything which operated as a waiver of the forfeiture.[4]

judgment which was really written by Blackburn, J. See Scarf *v.* Jardine, 1882, 7 App. Cas., 360; 51 L. J., Q. B. 612; 47 L. T. 258.

[1] Judges might have been brought back to the method of Parke, B., in Jones *v.* Carter, 1846, 15 M & W. 718.

[2] Toleman *v.* Portbury, 1871, L. R., 6 Q. B. 248; 40 L. J., Q. B. 125. To same effect is Taylor on *Landlord & Tenant*, 9th ed., vol. 1, § 287; quoted in Titus *v.* Glens Falls, etc., 1880, 81 N. Y. 419.

[3] Frank *v.* Sun, etc., 1893, 20 Ont. A. R. 567, per Burton, J. A.

[4] Manufacturer's *v.* Gordon, 1893, 20 Ont. A. R. 329.

Unless troubled with misleading words, so good a judge could not have written that which is equivalent to the assertion that, by default, "the forfeiture is absolute," and that, by "waiver," a lessor, unaided, can restore to operation a lease, which, according to its terms, had ceased to exist.

A Privy Council Decision. The Privy Council after holding that the word *void* meant *voidable*, proceeded to say:

> If then the Crown could treat the lease as voidable, the further question to be considered is, has it elected so to treat it, and waived the forfeiture.[1]

The question would be bettered by omission of its last four words. If the Crown elected to continue the lease there would be no forfeiture. And if it elected to terminate, subsequent "waiver" would be ineffective.

A House of Lords' Decision. In the House of Lords, it was said that

> The right of re-entry . . . was entirely waived by the Plaintiff; or perhaps, speaking more accurately, that the Plaintiff estopped himself from insisting on it.[2]

Confusion, in its quality, can go no further than that. But it may ascend to a still higher forum, namely to parliament, as we shall see.

A New York Decision. A passage somewhat parallel to that above quoted from Bramwell, B., is to be found in the language of Tracy, J.[3]

> We think the phrase "a continuing cause of forfeiture," found in some of the reported cases, is not strictly accurate, and is misleading. . . . When (a breach is) committed by the lessee, if the lease gives the landlord the right to re-enter for such breach, he has a right of election. He may elect to terminate the lease because of the breach, or he may elect to affirm it, notwithstanding

[1] Davenport *v.* The Queen, 1877, 3 App. Cas. 130; 47 L. J., P. C. 8; 37 L. T. 727.

[2] Croft *v.* Lumley, 1858, 6 H. L. C. 733; 27 L. J., Q. B. 321.

[3] Conger *v.* Duryee, 1882, 90 N. Y. 600.

> the breach. If he elects to terminate it, the relation of landlord and tenant ceases.

But that, too, is spoiled by the sentence which follows:

> If he elects to affirm, the affirmance is equivalent to a new lease with the same continuing covenants and conditions.

That is wrong, for nothing has happened to the old lease. The opinion is marred, too, in other parts of it, by employment of the popular phraseology:

> Receiving rent after forfeiture waives the forfeiture and affirms the lease freed from the condition.

In some of the cases estoppel is preferred to "waiver." For example, a New York court said, that after distress

> the landlord cannot say that he has terminated the tenancy. He is estopped to hold such language.[1]

MR. ADDISON. The text-writers have adopted the slip-shod language of forfeiture and "waiver." In Addison on Contracts,[2] for example, may be found the following:

> If, therefore, a lease has been forfeited, and there is an election on the part of the landlord to enter and defeat the lease or not, as he pleases, and he, by word or act manifests his intention that the lease shall continue, he waives the forfeiture, and cannot afterwards annul the lease.

When the author said "if a lease has been forfeited," he meant "if there has been a breach of covenant;" and if he had used those words, he could not have proceeded to say that "he waives the forfeiture" — meaning that he "waives the breach" — because, of course, the breach remains unaffected and may be sued upon.[3]

[1] Jackson *v.* Sheldon, 1826, 5 Cowen, 451.

[2] 11th ed., p. 713.

[3] Hartshorne *v.* Watson, 1838, 4 Bing. N. C. 178; 7 L. J. C., P. 138; Morecraft *v.* Meux, 1825, 4 B. & C. 606; 4 L. J., K. B. (O. S.) 4; Pellatt *v.* Boosey, 1862, 31 L. J. C. P. 283.

MR. LEAKE. In Leake on Contracts is the following:

> The forfeiture may be waived by a subsequent acceptance of rent or other unequivocal recognition of the tenancy by the lessor, after having notice of the cause of forfeiture.[1]

Here distinction is made between "the forfeiture" and "the cause of the forfeiture." But one thing only has happened, namely, a breach of a covenant. And if that be "the cause," what is "the forfeiture?" There is none. The breach creates, not a forfeiture, but a right of election, which may, or may not, result in a termination of the lease.

MR. BISHOP. In Bishop on Contracts is the following:

> Where a lease of lands subjects the lessee's estate to forfeiture if he assigns it, or permits an auction on the premises, or neglects to pay rent or the like, and thereupon the lessee does or suffers the prohibited thing, the lessor will waive the forfeiture, so as never afterward to be permitted to insist upon it, should he take pay for subsequent rent, or do anything else by which in legal effect he recognizes the continued existence of the lease.[2]

The sentence commences as though it might end, properly, in election ("Where a lease *subjects* the lessee's estate to forfeiture"), but the latter part excludes that idea, for it declares that "the lessor will waive the forfeiture" — a "forfeiture" which, without an election, has never come into existence.

MR. WOODFALL. In Woodfall on Landlord and Tenant it is said that:

> an acceptance of rent, or other act of waiver may make a voidable lease good.[3]

It is not made good. It was never affected. The rubric of the section is "Waiver of Forfeiture," and in it there is no word of election. How far it was from the author's mind is indicated by the statement that

[1] 6th ed., p. 483. [2] 1907, ed., pp. 330, 1. [3] 19th ed., p. 378.

> A lessee cannot avail himself of his own act or default to vacate a lease, on the principle that no man shall be permitted to take advantage of his own wrong.[1]

The principle has no relation to the case; and the fact that the author can point to judicial employment of similar language in 1817, is not sufficient justification for its insertion in a textbook of 1912.

In the same work is the following:

> A forfeiture may be expressly waived, and if the waiver be without consideration, or the right of re-entry arise on a lease by deed, it would seem that the waiver should be by deed.[2]

The learned author was confused by use of the word "forfeiture." Had he observed that he was dealing with cases in which there had, in reality, been no forfeiture, and in which, therefore, there was no "waiver;" and had he observed that it was election and not "waiver" that was applicable to the subject with which he was dealing, he would have omitted the sentence. That election of any kind has to be made by deed (save when so expressly stipulated) would not occur to anybody. The author evidently had in mind that breach of a condition *ipso facto* forfeited the lease, in the sense of terminating it; and that "waiver" would re-establish it; and so he imagined that if the lease were under seal, the "waiver" must be by deed; forgetting that, if the lease had been ended, no unilateral act of any kind could set it up again.

MR. SMITH. In Smith's Leading Cases, many pages are devoted to discussion of "the doctrine of waiver of forfeiture," phraseology that makes possible such sentences as the following:

> It is conceived that the mere receipt of subsequent rent does not, of its own proper force, operate as a waiver of a forfeiture. It is

[1] 19th ed., p. 369.
[2] *Ibid.*, p. 381.

> only evidence of the election of the lessor to retain the reversion and its incidents, instead of taking possession of the land.[1]

The second sentence is, as the present writer thinks, correct; but the first, for reasons above referred to, appears to have no meaning.

Re-Entry and Void

We have been dealing with forfeiture and "waiver" as sources of confusion in the law of landlord and tenant. Another source is failure to appreciate the difference between two kinds[2] of voidance clauses.

Various Voidance Clauses. If a tenant commit a breach of some covenant in the lease, and if the landlord, in pursuance of power reserved to him, desire to terminate the lease, what must he do? Must he do anything? Well, he must look at the terms of his particular lease, and act accordingly. Reading the document, he will probably ascertain that the relevant clause belongs to one of three classes:[3]

1. The clause may be in the nature of a conditional limitation, in which case the estate is determined by the happening of the specified event. No action by the landlord is necessary, and none that he could take would prevent the result stipulated in the lease.[4] In such cases, no difficulty arises and they are, for present purposes, omitted from consideration.

2. The clause may provide that upon breach

> it shall be lawful for the lessor at any time thereafter, into and upon the said demised premises, or any part thereof in the name

[1] 11th ed., vol. 1, p. 38.

[2] The second and third of those afterwards mentioned.

[3] There are, of course, many other forms, *e. g.*, as in Arden *v.* Boyce, 1894, 1 Q. B. 796; 63 L. J., Q. B. 338. Those most frequently employed are sufficient for the purpose of the present exposition.

[4] Fenn dem. Matthews *v.* Smart, 1810, 12 East, 448. And see Co. Litt., 215 a.

of the whole, to re-enter, and the same to have again, repossess, and enjoy, as of his former estate.[1]

3. The clause may provide that upon breach, the lease shall "cease and determine and be utterly null and void and of no effect to all intents and purposes."[2]

In the second of these cases, the lessor has a right to elect either to continue or to terminate the lease; and if he elect to terminate, he must pursue the course provided by the lease and re-enter.[3] In some jurisdictions, as in England, a statute declares that commencement of proceedings to recover possession of the land

shall stand in the place and stead of a demand and re-entry.[4]

In other jurisdictions, the courts appear to have assumed the right to declare that commencement of an action for possession is equivalent to re-entry.

In the third class of cases — where the provision is that upon default, the lease shall be "void" — the meaning of the clause is that the lease shall be "voidable at the election of the landlord";[5] and all that is necessary to terminate the lease is that the landlord should so elect.

Distinctions Neglected. Lack of observation of the distinction between the second and third kinds of voidance

[1] The statutory form in Ontario: Rev. St., 1914, c. 116, sched. B, § 12. See also Baylis v. Le Gros, 1858, 4 C. B. (N. S.) 540; 26 L. J. C. P. 176.

[2] As in Roberts v. Davey, 1833, 4 B. & Ad. 666; 2 L. J., K. B. 141.

[3] Fenn dem. Matthews v. Smart, 1810, 12 East, 443. Approved in Moore v. Ullcoats, 1908, 1 ch. 587; 77 L. J. Ch. 282; 97 L. T. 845. Arnsby v. Woodward, 1827, 6 B. & C. 519; 5 L. J. (O. S.) K. B. 199; Bowser v. Colby, 1841, 1 Hare 129; 11 L. J. ch. 132.

[4] 4 Geo. II, c. 28, § 2; 15, 16 Vic. c. 76, § 210.

[5] Bryan v. Bancks, 1821, 4 B. & Ald. 405; Malins v. Freeman, 1838, 4 Bing. N. C. 399; Bowser v. Colby, 1841, 1 Ha. 130; 11 L. J. Ch. 132; Jones v. Carter, 1846, 15 M. & W. 724; Davenport v. The Queen, 1877, 3 App. Cas. 128; 47 L. J., P. C. 8; 37 L. T. 727; Springer v. Chicago, etc., 1902, 202 Ill. 17; 66 N. E. 850, The word *void* when used in a statute may mean voidable; Davenport v. The Queen, 1877, 3 App. Cas. 129; 47 L. J., P. C. 8; 37 L. T. 727.

clauses — indeed, confusion of them under the influence of forfeiture and " waiver," induced the following:

> Though a distinction was formerly taken . . . between leases for life, which, creating a freehold, requires a re-entry to take advantage of a breach of condition, and leases for years — it being then held, in respect to the latter class, that the lease became void by the mere happening of the breach and could not be set up again by a waiver thereof — the modern decisions have exploded the distinction, holding that in either case, the lease becomes void only on the lessor's electing so to treat it, and that the only difference between a lease for life and one for years is that, in case of the former, election must be manifested by a formal entry which is unnecessary in case of a lease for years.[1]

The old distinction between leases for life (passing an estate in freehold) and leases for years was that, inasmuch as an estate in freehold was created by livery of seizen, its determination had to be by re-entry; and for this reason it was held that even if the lease provided that, upon the happening of some event, it should be *ipso facto* void, yet the re-entry was necessary in order to end it.[2] That distinction was exploded, not by the decisions, but by the abolition of the necessity for livery of seizen. And it is, now, not true to say that the modern cases require that, in the case of a lease for life, the election must be manifested by a formal entry, while in the case of a lease for years simple election suffices. The courts are governed by the agreement of the parties, and the lease is void, or not, according to the terms of that agreement. The difference now is not between the two kinds of estate, but between the two kinds of voidance clauses.

English Legislation

Forfeiture and " waiver " are responsible for some curious legislation. A few examples will now be noticed. Others may be found in chapters III and VI.

[1] Note to Viele *v.* Germania, etc., 1868, 26 Iowa, 70.

[2] Co. Litt. 215 a.

DUMPOR'S CASE. The court in Dumpor's case [1] in dealing with a clause in a lease prohibiting alienation by the lessee without assent of the lessor, held that an assent given to one alienation "determined the condition" — even if the condition forbade alienation not only by the lessee but by his assigns — so that a second alienation without assent was no breach of the condition. In a subsequent case,[2] the lessee made an underlease, without the lessor's assent; afterwards the lessor received rent (thus "waiving the forfeiture"); afterwards the lessee made a second underlease, and contended, upon the authority of Dumpor's case, that the waiver "had determined the condition," and, therefore, that no assent was necessary. The court held against him, saying that the argument

> that this tolerance is tantamount to a license . . . is too strong a proposition.[3]

In other words, a previous license to do the act would "determine the condition," but a subsequent tolerance of it — a subsequent "waiver" of it — would not. No statute was rendered necessary by that decision, but (probably) to remove any doubt as to its correctness, the following act was passed:

> Where any actual waiver of the benefit of any covenant or condition in any lease on the part of any lessor or his heirs, executors, administrators or assigns, shall be proved to have taken place, after the passing of this act, in any one particular instance, such actual waiver shall not be assumed or deemed to extend to any instance or any breach of covenant, or condition other than that to which such waiver shall specially relate, nor to be a general

[1] 1603, 4 Coke, 119 b. See Smith's L. C., 12 ed., vol. 1, p. 35.

[2] Boscawen *v.* Bliss, 1813, 4 Taunt. 735. In this case, Mansfield, C. J., said that "the profession have always wondered at Dumpor's case." Lord Eldon spoke to the same effect in Brummell *v.* Macpherson, 1807, 14 Ves. 173. The decision was reversed in England by statute 22, 3 Vic. c. 35, § 1.

[3] Boscawen *v.* Bliss, 1813, 4 Taunt. 735.

waiver of the benefit of any such covenant or condition, unless an intention to that effect shall appear.[1]

If this language be given an application that nobody intended it should have, it has some meaning — although a useless one; otherwise it has none. Take it as meaning that when there has been some

> actual waiver of the benefit of any covenant . . . in any one particular instance (meaning a waiver of the right to sue upon the particular breach) "such actual waiver shall not . . . be a general waiver of the benefit of any such covenant" (meaning that it shall not take away the right to sue upon any other breaches) —

that is intelligible, but useless and undesigned. The draughtsman had in mind the erroneous idea that a breach of covenant (being a forfeiture) determines a lease, and that it may be re-established by "actual waiver." (What *actual* waiver may be, the statute does not indicate.) If the draughtsman had observed that he was dealing not with "waiver" but with election, he would have dropped his pen for he could not have proposed that parliament should enact that

> when a lessor, upon the happening of any occurrence enabling him to elect whether to continue or to determine the lease, elects to continue it, that election shall not be deemed to be an expression of his election upon the happening of some subsequent occurrence; nor shall it deprive him of any right to make any subsequent election given to him by the lease.

THE ENGLISH COMMON LAW PROCEDURE ACTS. Explanation of the complications by the statutes of 15, 16 Vic. c. 76, §§ 210–2, and 23, 4 Vic. c. 126, § 1, due to wrong employment of the phraseology of forfeiture, would require too much space, and is omitted.

THE CONVEYANCING ACT, 1881. The English statute, 44, 5 Vic. c. 41, § 14, provided as follows:

[1] 23 & 24 Vic. c. 38, § 6. See Rev. St. Ont., 1914, c. 155, § 26.

> A right of re-entry or forfeiture under any proviso or stipulation in a lease, for a breach of any covenant or condition in the lease, shall not be enforceable by action or otherwise, unless and until the lessor serves on the lessee a notice specifying the particular breach complained of, and, if the breach is capable of remedy, requiring the lessee to remedy the breach, and, in any case, requiring the lessee to make compensation in money for the breach, and the lessee fails, within a reasonable time thereafter, to remedy the breach, if it is capable of remedy, and to make reasonable compensation in money, to the satisfaction of the lessor for the breach.[1]

The effect of this clause upon leases containing powers of re-entry is clear. The re-entry, except under the prescribed conditions cannot be made; and the lease therefore remains unaffected. But has the clause any application to a lease voidable by election only — without necessity for re-entry? In such a case, the lessor can take no proceedings " by action or otherwise " to recover possession until he has elected to terminate the lease; and there would be no " forfeiture " capable of enforcement until after election. If it be said that the clause may mean that the lessor shall not elect, the reply appears to be that the prohibition is directed against the enforcement, and not against the creation, of a right. And if the lessor be left free to make his election, and the statute apply to the case, the position would be that the lessor could terminate the lease without giving the notice referred to in the statute, but that he could not, afterwards, sue for possession without giving a notice which would be inappropriate to a terminated lease. The draughtsmen had not in mind the termination of leases by mere election.

The difficulty produced by the use of the word *forfeiture* was illustrated in an action brought under the statute.[2] Covenants in a lease (1) to erect certain buildings on the

[1] For similar statute, see Rev. St. Ont., 1914, c. 155, § 20 (2).

[2] Stephens *v.* Junior Army, etc., 1914, 2 Ch. 516.

demised premises by a certain date, and (2) to keep in repair present buildings, and all others which should be erected on the demised premises; proviso for re-entry for breach of covenants; no building erected, as required by the first covenant; rent received after the day on which the buildings ought to have been completed; action in ejectment by lessor claiming breach of the covenant to repair the *non-erected* building. The court said that

> the admitted waiver of forfeiture for not building extends to and carries with it a waiver of any forfeiture for non-repair, as it is impossible to repair or keep in repair what has never been built.

As there was no forfeiture, but only a right of election, would it not have been better to say that the acceptance of rent was evidence of an election to continue the tenancy, notwithstanding the non-erection of the building, and that, with reference to non-repair, no right of election had arisen?

THE CONVEYANCING ACT, 1892. The false phraseology of forfeiture and "waiver" appears also in the clause of the English Conveyancing Act of 1892 which provides that a lessor shall be entitled to sue a lessee for costs paid to solicitors and surveyors

> in reference to any breach giving rise to a right of re-entry or forfeiture, which, at the request of the lessee, is waived by the lessor by writing under his hand.

The section assumes that when, after some breach of covenant by the tenant, the lessor elects to continue to lease, he has "waived" a forfeiture, and it enacts that, when the forfeiture is waived at the request of the tenant, he must pay certain costs. But prior to election to terminate the lease nothing happens to it — there has been no forfeiture and there is nothing to waive. And after election to terminate has been made, nothing which may be called "waiver" can have any effect. The statute should have provided that the costs should be paid when, in reference to any breach giving to the lessor a right to elect to terminate the lease, the lessor, at the request of the lessee by writing under his hand, elects to continue the lease.[1]

Division of the Subject

Election. Having to some extent exhibited the existing confusion, an attempt will now be made to introduce order and consistency.

A breach of some stipulation in a lease, giving to the landlord a right to terminate the lease, having happened, the question for discussion, in the language of most of the cases, is "How may the breach, or the forfeiture incurred by the breach, be waived?" and, in more careful phraseology, "What acts of the landlord indicate an election to continue or determine the tenancy?" The cases group themselves under the following headings:

1. Election by action to recover possession.
2. Election by demand of rent.
3. Election by acceptance of rent.
4. Election by distress for rent.
5. Election by other acts.

1. Election by Action to Recover Possession

Of all possible acts indicative of an election to terminate a lease, perhaps the clearest and least equivocal is the institution of an action for recovery of possession of the land based upon the breach complained of.

> By bringing an ejectment, the plaintiff elects to consider the defendant as a trespasser, and not as tenant from the day on which the right of possession is claimed in the writ; and he cannot distrain or sue for any subsequent rent.[2]

[1] The clause was considered in Nind v. Nineteenth, etc., 1894, 2 Q. B. 226; 63 L. J., Q. B. 636; 70 L. T. 831.

[2] Cole on Eject. 82. And see Birch v. Wright, 1786, 1 T. R. 387; Bridges v. Smyth, 1829, 5 Bing. 410; 7 L. J. (O. S.) C. P. 143; Franklin v. Carter, 1845, 1 C. B. 750; 14 L. J., C. P. 241.

2. Election by Demand of Rent

Demand as Evidence of Election. A demand for the payment of rent which fell due after a breach of a stipulation is evidence of an election to continue the tenancy notwithstanding the breach; for the demand necessarily implies the continued existence of the lease (without that there could be no *rent*), and is inconsistent with election to terminate. *A fortiori*, the institution of an action for the recovery of such rent furnishes similarly satisfactory evidence.[1]

Confusion by "Waiver." These propositions would appear to be indisputable, but if the language of forfeiture and "waiver" be employed, a contrary opinion appears to be quite possible. For example, in one case, Parke, B., said:

> You may say that a demand of rent is not a waiver of a forfeiture, because the landlord in effect says, if you will pay me the rent I will accept you as a tenant, and the tenant does not do so; therefore it is incomplete. Some distinct act ought to be done to constitute a waiver.[2]

But the landlord does not say, "If you will pay me the rent, I will accept you." He is not in a position to use that language. The tenancy has been in no way affected. Were it true that default worked a forfeiture of the lease, and that by default, the lease had been terminated, then, no doubt, the landlord might make proposals for renewal of relations, and might proffer as supposed. But default having no effect upon the lease, all offers of renewal, prior to election to terminate, are premature.

Cole on Ejectment, too, has the following:

> A mere demand of subsequent rent which is not complied with, or even a distress for subsequent rent which is not submitted to,

[1] Dendy *v.* Nicholl, 1858, 4 C. B. (N. S.) 376; 47 L. J., C. P. 220.

[2] Doe dem. Nash *v.* Birch, 1838, 1 M. & W. 405; 5 L. J., (N. S.) Ex. 185.

> but replevied by the tenant, will not be sufficient to waive the forfeiture.[1]

But it would be quite impossible to say that a distress for rent was not an acknowledgment of the existence of a tenancy during the period in which the rent accrued.

Lord Coke used the word "wayveth," but it was in unnecessary addition to the statement that an action for rent "affirmeth the rent to have a continuance":

> Here it appeareth that if the condition be broken for non-payment of rent, yet if the feoffer bringeth an assise for the rent due at that time, he shall never enter for the condition broken, because he affirmeth the rent to have a continuance, and thereby wayveth the condition.[2]

RENT DUE BEFORE BREACH. Demand of rent which fell due prior to the breach, even if the demand were made after the breach, would not indicate an election to continue the tenancy after the breach, for, in that event, the landlord is entitled both to the rent, and to terminate the lease. Being entitled to both, he is not put to choice between them, and there is no case for election.

> If the feoffer had distrained for the rent for non-payment whereof the condition was broken, he should never enter for the condition broken, but he may receive that rent and acquite the same and yet enter for the condition broken. But if he accept the rent due at a day after, he shall not enter for the condition broken, because he thereby affirmeth the lease to have a continuance.[3]

By demanding payment of rent, he affirms the existence of the tenancy during the time in which the rent accrued, and

[1] p. 409. Blyth *v.* Dennett, 1853, 13 C. B. 178; 22 L. J., C. P. 79, appears to be authority for the proposition that a demand, without payment, will not waive a notice to quit. But as to that see *post* pp. 180, 181. Somewhat the same idea has been applied to a demand of payment of an insurance premium after breach of some condition. *Infra*, p. 231.

[2] Co. Litt., 211 b.

[3] Co. Litt., 211 b. See *post*, p. 176.

down to the date of accrual only. He makes no indication of his wish as to any later period. Demand of rent is an acknowledgment (in the inappropriate language of forfeiture)

> that no forfeiture was then complete. He does not thereby admit that a forfeiture may not have been inchoate, but merely that it was not completed so as to entitle him to bring an ejectment.[1]

3. Election by Acceptance of Rent

Acceptance as Evidence of Election. A demand for payment of rent which fell due after the breach, being evidence of election to continue the tenancy, so also, and *a fortiori*, is acceptance of the rent. And in this case, as in the other, the evidence is supplied only when the rent accrued after the breach. For, if a lessor have a right to terminate for non-payment of rent, he may, after the breach, both accept the money and elect to terminate because of the default — in accepting the rent, he has not acknowledged the existence of the tenancy after the date of the default.

> In order to render the receipt of rent a waiver, it is necessary that the rent should have accrued, as well as have been received subsequent to the forfeiture. It proceeds upon the principle that the lessor, by receiving the rent, affirms the lease to have continuance.[2]

Confusion by "Waiver." It has been said that receipt of rent from an under-tenant must be distinguished from a distress upon him for the rent, because the mere receipt of the money

> amounts to no more than going and asking for the rent, and finding persons willing to pay the money and taking it;

[1] Bryan *v.* Bancks, 1821, 4 B. & Ald. 407.

[2] Jackson *v.* Allen, 1824, 3 Cowen (N. Y.) 230. See also Griffith *v.* Pritchard, 1833, 5 B. & Ad. 780; 3 L. J., K. B. 11; Price *v.* Worwood, 1859, 4 H. & N. 516; 28 L. J. Ex. 329; Silva *v.* Campbell, 1890, 84 Cal. 422; 24 Pac. 316; Morrison *v.* Smith, 1899, 90 Md. 83; 44 Atl. 1031; Denison *v.* Maitland, 1891, 22 Ont. R. 171. And see the quotation from Co. on Litt., ante, p. 169.

whereas distress for the same amount

> does away with all previous forfeiture.[1]

The mistake is due to the use of the phraseology of forfeiture and "waiver." For no one would think of suggesting that demand and acceptance of rent from anybody did not indicate election to continue the lease by which alone it became payable. It is said also, that

> A landlord who receives rent from a subtenant, thereby *prima facie* waives the stipulation in the lease against subletting without his written consent.[2]

But that, too, is not quite correct, for he may sue upon the stipulation for any damages he has sustained. Receipt of the rent indicates election. That is all.

Rent or Compensation. Sometimes when a landlord has received money from his tenant, the question arises as to whether it is to be regarded as rent, or as damages for use and occupation, or as *mesne* profits. The inference as to election will be affected by the answer.

Double Value. If a tenant continue in possession after the termination of his tenancy, he is no longer a tenant, and although he does not pay rent, he must make compensation. The statute 4 Geo. 2, c. 28, for example, provided, that where a tenant holds over after the determination of his term, and after demand made and notice given in writing requiring delivery of possession, he shall

> pay . . . at the rate of double the yearly value of the lands.

This statutory provision applies only to tenants overholding after determination of their terms by expiry of them, or by notice to quit, and not to cases where the term is ended by exercise of the landlord's right of re-entry for condition broken. In these latter cases the law awards compensation

[1] Price *v.* Worwood, 1859, 4 H. & N. 516; 28 L. J. Ex. 329.

[2] Lorefice *v.* Sardella, 1915, 150 N. Y. Supp. 980; 85 Misc. R. 522.

estimated upon the single, not the double, yearly value of the lands.

It will therefore be apparent that, if, after breach of a stipulation, the landlord receive money from the tenant, the important question at once arise, "Did he receive it as rent?" If so, he has acknowledged the existence of a tenancy. But if he received it

> as a satisfaction for the injury done by the defendant in continuing on the plaintiff's land as a trespasser.[1]

he is asserting that the tenancy has ended.[2] This would seem to be a mere question of fact, but observe the following:

A tenancy was ended by notice to quit; the tenant held over; "the landlord received rent, *eo nomine*, for a quarter of a year which became due after the expiry of the term"; and Lord Mansfield's Court said

> that is only a waiver of his right to double rent under the statute 4 Geo. 2, and does not necessarily imply a consent that the tenancy should continue. . . . What then is the case when a landlord accepts the single rent only. The taking half, when he is entitled to an action for the whole, is an act of lenity; but it does not import a consent that the tenant shall continue in possession, or a waiver by the landlord of his remedy to ejectment.[3]

With deference, that is not correct. Taking *rent* does "import a consent that the tenant shall continue in possession." Nevertheless it was not a "waiver" of anything. For the tenancy had been ended by exercise of the lessor's election to terminate it — by the notice to quit; the lessor could not withdraw or "waive" his election; nor could he "waive" his remedy by ejectment. On the other hand, the

[1] Charter *v.* Cordwent, 1795, 6 T. R. 220. See also Cheny *v.* Batten, 1775, 1 Cowp. 243; Griffith *v.* Pritchard, 1833, 5 B. & Ad. 780; 3 L. J., K. B. 11; Croft *v.* Lumley, 1858, 6 H. L. C. 706, 714; 27 L. J., K. B. 321.

[2] Soper *v.* Littlejohn, 1901, 31 Can. S. C. 580.

[3] Cheny *v.* Batten, 1775, Cowp. 246. This case was, in effect, distinguished by Lord Mansfield in Walter *v.* Davids, 1778, 2 Cowp. 803. It was disapproved in Charter *v.* Cordwent, 1795, 6 T. R. 219: McKildoe *v.* Darracott, 1856, 13 Grat. (Va.) 278.

parties were at liberty to agree to re-establish the old lease, or to constitute a new one. And the payment and acceptance of *rent* would be evidence of such an agreement. If the money had not been paid and received as rent, *eo nomine*, ascertainment of the intention of the parties might be difficult. The defendant ought to have succeeded.

PAYMENT AS RENT AND ACCEPTANCE AS COMPENSATION. A further question has arisen: What happens if the money be paid as rent, and received by the landlord, not as rent but as compensation? The answer is that the debtor has the right of appropriation, and the legal consequences of the receipt of rent cannot be avoided by protesting against it.[1]

USE AND OCCUPATION. If, after a breach, the lessor accept or sue for compensation for the subsequent use and occupation of the premises by the tenant, does he thereby elect to continue the lease? or is his action some evidence of an agreement to restore the old lease? or is it evidence merely of the creation of a new relationship? The answer depends upon the view taken of the basis upon which the action for use and occupation rests. If it be consistent only with the existence of the relationship of landlord and tenant, then it may be election to continue, or of restoration, or of new creation, according to circumstances. If it do not necessarily import the existence of the relationship, it has no such significance. Settlement of that question is outside of the scope of the present work; and the authorities are by no means satisfactory. It is said by one author that

> the action for use and occupation is founded on contract;

and in the same sentence it is said

> that the lessor in ejectment may, if he please, waive the trespass and recover the *mesne* profits in an action for use and occupation.[2]

[1] Croft *v.* Lumley, 1858, 6 H. L. C. 694, 697, 706, 722, 725, 730, 734; 5 E. & B. 680; 27 L. J., Q. B. 321. See *ante*, p. 86.

[2] 1 Chitty's Pleadings, p. 193; quoted in Cavanagh *v.* Cook 1915, 94 Atl. 663.

On the other hand, sharp distinction is sometimes made between *mesne* profits and use and occupation; and it is said that the lessor

> would be entitled to maintain, not an action for use and occupation, but one for *mesne* profits for the time intervening between the accruing of his title and his obtaining possession.[1]

On the one hand, it is said that an action for use and occupation would be a " waiver of the forfeiture " caused by default in payment of rent, because the action is based upon the existence of the relationship of landlord and tenant,[2] while on the other hand it is said that

> The action for use and occupation does not necessarily suppose any demise; it is enough that the defendant used and occupied the premises by the permission of the plaintiff.[3]

Settlement of these differences is not within the scope of the present work.

4. Election by Distress for Rent

Distress as Evidence of Election. As demand of rent, and acceptance of rent, which fell due after a breach of some stipulation, is evidence of an election to continue the tenancy, so, *a fortiori*, is distress for such rent:

> I take it to be clear that the lessor could not do an act affirming the tenancy and yet say that he did not elect not to treat the breach as a forfeiture; for instance he could not distrain for rent . . . and at the same time effectually say that he did not elect not to treat an antecedent breach of covenant as a forfeiture; his act would be taken to be rightful and bind him, rather than his words make his act wrong.[4]

[1] Per Martin B in Croft *v.* Lumley, 1858, 6 H. L. C. 706; 27 L. J., Q. B. 321. And see Woodfall, L. & T., 1912, p. 638.

[2] Cavanagh *v.* Cook, 1915, 94 Atl. 663.

[3] Rochester *v.* Pierce, 1808, 1 Camp. 466. And see Woodfall L. & T., 1912, 630.

[4] Croft *v.* Lumley, 6 H. L. C. 706; 27 L. J., Q. B. 321.

RENT PRIOR TO THE BREACH. But what is to be said of a case in which the rent distrained for fell due prior to the breach? Demand for, or acceptance of such rent (without distress for it) would of course have no significance, for the rent being for a period prior to the breach, the landlord, by receiving it, does not recognize a tenancy subsequent to the breach.[1] Is there any difference in cases of distress? In Green's case

> It was clearly resolved that the bare receipt of the rent after the day was no bar, for it was a duty due to him (the landlord), but a distress for the rent, or a receipt of the rent due at another day, was a bar; for these acts do affirm the lessee to have lawful possession.[2]

> There is no inconsistency in a man who has given notice to determine a tenancy receiving rent due before the supposed determination of it, and consequently there is no waiver by receiving the rent. . . . Waiver by distress depends upon a different principle, viz., that at common law a distress for rent can only be made during the existence of the tenancy . . . and if the lessor chooses to distrain for rent after the tenancy has determined, that shows that he considers the tenancy as subsisting. . . . According to the doctrine of election, he treats the reversion as existing and the rent as still accruing from time to time, instead of electing to take the land from the tenant. The doctrine of waiver rests on the inconsistency of a man saying, by his distress, that a tenancy is subsisting, when by claiming a forfeiture, he asserts that it has been determined.[3]

In other words, by receiving past-due rent, you affirm nothing as to the present condition of the tenancy; but by distraining for it, you necessarily acknowledge that the tenancy still exists,

> for after the lease determined, he cannot distrain.[4]

[1] *Ante*, p. 169.

[2] 1 Cro. Eliz. 3; 2 Tiffany on Landlord and Tenant, vol. II, p. 1387; 2 Taylor on Landlord and Tenant, vol. II, p. 94; Johnson *v.* Electric, etc., 1911, 150 Iowa 720; 130 N. W. 808.

[3] Ward *v.* Day, 1863, 4 B. & S. 352.

[4] Lord Coke; Pennant's Case, 1596; 3 Rep. 64 b.

Indeed distress is said to be so clearly an election that no question as to the intention with which it was made should be left to the jury:

> There could be no question of intention left to the jury, as the taking a distress was an act not to be qualified, and an express confirmation of the tenancy.[1]

Such is the argument. Is there sufficient reply to it in the fact that, in England, since the statute of 8 Anne, c. 14, distress may be made within six months *after* the termination of the tenancy, and during possession of the tenant? No; for the statute has been held to apply only

> to the case of the determination of the tenancy in the ordinary course, and not by a forfeiture.[2]

Notwithstanding the statute, therefore, it still remains true that distress for rent (whether it accrued before, or after the breach) is an affirmation that the landlord has elected to continue the tenancy, and not to determine it.

Rent Subsequent to the Breach. With reference to rent which accrued subsequent to the breach, another distinction must be made between accepting money and distraining for it. Bear in mind that if a tenant continue in possession after a breach, he is not free from liability to pay for his occupation, and that (either by way of payment for use and occupation, or as *mesne* profits) the amount he will have to pay, will sometimes be the same sum as the rent.[3] After a breach has taken place, therefore, a landlord may, with perfect consistency, terminate the tenancy, and demand and accept money, not as rent, but as compensation for the tenant's possession. If he distrain, however, he is enforcing

[1] Zouch Dem. Ward. *v.* Willingale, 1790, 1 H. Bl. 312.

[2] Grimwood *v.* Moss, 1872, L. R. 7 C. P. 365; 41 L. J., C. P. 239; 27 L. T. 268; Doe dem. David *v.* Williams 1835, 7 C. & P. 322; Baker *v.* Atkinson, 1886, 11 Ont. R. 750; Linton *v.* Imperial etc., 1889, 16 Ont. A. R. 343.

[3] See *ante*, pp. 171, 172.

payment, not of compensation, but of rent (and so electing to continue the lease), for there is no remedy by distress for compensation. By distress, therefore, a landlord indicates his election to continue the tenancy; whereas if he receive the money without distress, he may contend that it was paid to him, not as rent but as compensation for occupation by a non-tenant.[1]

LEASE VOID AND FUTURE RENT PAYABLE. A further point arises in connection with leases in which there is the provision that, upon bankruptcy of the lessor (or upon other event), the lease shall be void, and the rent for the current and the next ensuing quarter shall be at once payable, and may be distrained for. Clear views of election were not in the possession of the first draughtsman of that clause (for if election to terminate the tenancy be exercised no future *rent* can become due) and he has caused the courts not a little difficulty.

Baker *v.* Atkinson[2] puts the matter with sufficient clearness: Upon the happening of the event, the landlord had a right of election between continuing and determining the lease; by distress he evidenced a previous election to terminate (for in the absence of such election he could not distrain); and tenancy having been ended, the lessor's right of distress was also ended, for, at common law, there can be no distress after expiry of the relationship of landlord and tenant, and the statute of Anne permits it only when the expiry has been by effluxion of time. Moreover the statute sanctions distress, after expiry of the term, only for rent due before the expiry, and, in the case in hand, it became due after the expiry and

> as a consequence upon that event having taken place; it did not accrue, therefore, during the term.[3]

[1] See *ante*, pp. 171, 172. [2] 1886, 11 Ont. 751.
[3] Griffiths *v.* Brown, 1870, 21 U. C., C. P. 17.

Another view is that the right to the future rent depends,

> not upon the lessor's election to forfeit the term, but upon the fact of the lessee having made an assignment. . . . I think the clause is divisible, and the lessor may distrain for the rent so long as he has not elected to forfeit the term. If he elects to do that, he loses his remedy by distress, and is perforce driven to recover the rent in some other manner.[1]

In other words, upon the bankruptcy of the tenant —

(1) The landlord may elect to continue the tenancy; and, in that case, he may both sue, and distrain for, the future rent. All that has happened is that the dates for payment of the future rent, as fixed by the lease, have been moved forward.

(2) Or the landlord may elect to terminate the tenancy; and, in that case, he may sue, but not distrain for, the future rent. The tenancy having ceased, he may sue, but not distrain.

If that be the true view of the clause, its operation is unobjectionable. The interpretation, however, appears to be arrived at, not by consideration of what the parties probably meant, but in order to evade the supposed incompatibility of terminating the lease and distraining for the agreed amount. There is no such incompatibility. No doubt a distress at common law is consistent only with the existence of a tenancy; but distress by agreement may be made under any relationship — by a mortgagee against his mortgagor, and by a grocer against his customer.

5. Election by other Conduct

Remembering that demand of rent, acceptance of it, and distress for it are more properly evidence of election than election itself, we are prepared for the statement that other acts may also furnish some indication of election.

[1] Linton *v.* Imperial, etc., 1889, 16 Ont. 344.

For example, if a lessor transfer his reversion subject to the lease, he has indicated election to continue it.[1]

So also, a notice to repair is evidence of an election to continue; for it assumes the continuation of the relation of landlord and tenant.[2]

So also, if an action for non-repair has been brought, the lessor, when subsequently bringing ejectment (based upon default), may be told that he has, by his former suit, indicated his election to continue the tenancy.[3]

So also, if, in a receipt given after the breach for rent which accrued prior to the breach (rent which the landlord might therefore accept without, by so doing, indicating election) the tenant be spoken of as a tenant, evidence of election to continue the tenancy is supplied.[4]

So also, negotiation for a new lease "after the termination of the present lease," is evidence of election, for the lease is referred to as in existence.[5]

Cases of contradictory elections have already been dealt with.[6]

Changing Election

Withdrawal of Notice to Quit. If a landlord, after breach by his tenant of some obligation, elect to terminate the lease, can he afterwards change his election? Suppose, for example, that the tenant makes restitution and pleads for withdrawal of a notice to quit, can the landlord restore the lease by what is spoken of as "waiving" the notice?

We have already seen that an election is irrevocable and irreversible.[7] By the contract, the parties have agreed that

[1] Hunt *v.* Bishop, 1853, 8 Ex. 680; 22 L. J. Ex. 337.

[2] Griffin *v.* Tompkins, 1880, 42 L. T. 362.

[3] Pellatt *v.* Boosey, 1862, 31 L. J., C. P. 284.

[4] Green's Case, Cro. Eliz. 3; Nash *v.* Birch, 1836, 1 M. & W. 406; 5 L. J. Ex. 185.

[5] Ward *v.* Day, 1863, 4 B. & S. 335.

[6] *Ante*, p. 98.

[7] *Ante*, pp. 100–104.

the lease is to be void if the lessor shall so elect; he has elected; the lease is at an end; the legal relationship of landlord and tenant has terminated. That it can be re-established otherwise than by contract; that the estate, which has returned to the lessor, can be revested in the tenant, without some new agreement to that effect, is comparable to the notion that a fee simple reverts to a grantor of it by the destruction of his deed. And it is wrong to say, as in Woodfall on Landlord and Tenant,[1] that

> a notice to quit can be waived, and a new or continual tenancy created, only by the express or implied consent of both parties,

for the notice is not "waived;" and a new agreement is necessary because its effect remains. All that need be said is that the election

> put an end to the tenancy. The right of possession reverted to the landlord . . . and the tenancy, being at an end, there could be no new contract except by mutual agreement.[2]

But suppose that, after election to terminate and notice to quit, the landlord should distrain for subsequent rent, would not that be a "waiver" of the notice, would it not be a recognition of the continuation of the tenancy? Put it the other way; Would the distress have any effect upon the election? Can an election once made be changed? The authorities answer in the negative.[3] Then what is the effect of the distress? Merely this; that the former landlord has committed a trespass.

In one case,[4] Maule, J., agreed that termination of the lease was the effect of a notice to quit; and that such notice

[1] 19th ed., p. 423.

[2] Nisbet *v.* Hall, 1895, 28 Nova Scotia, 801. And see Jones *v.* Carter, 1846, 15 M. & W. 725; Blyth *v.* Dennett, 1853, 13 C. B. 180; 22 L. J., C. P. 79; Thompson *v.* Baskerville, 1877, 40 U. C., Q. B. 616.

[3] Blyth *v.* Dennett, 1853; 13 C. B. 180; 22 L. J., C. P. 79.

[4] Serjeant *v.* Nash, etc., 1903, 2 K. B. 311; 72 L. J., K. B. 630; 89 L. T. 112.

could not be " waived," for it had already put an end to the term " by the agreement of the parties "; but he said:

> There is this difference between a determination of a tenancy by a notice to quit and a forfeiture: in the former case, the tenancy is put an end to by the agreement of the parties, which determination of the tenancy cannot be waived without the assent of both; but, in the case of a forfeiture, the lease is voidable only at the election of the lessor; in the one case, the estate continues though voidable, in the other the tenancy is at an end.

The learned judge did not sufficiently observe that his cases were alike, for in both of them the lease was voidable at the election of the lessor, and in both it was determined " by the agreement of the parties " — the agreement which settled beforehand the effect of the lessor's action.

In the same case, it was said that although a demand of rent, after the expiration of a notice to quit, would not be a " waiver " of the notice, yet that payment and acceptance of the rent would have that effect. But " waiver " cannot re-establish a terminated lease. That can be done by contract only. And the fact of payment and acceptance of *rent* is evidence of the existence of some agreement, as well after a notice to quit as at other times.

In a much earlier case [1] Lord Kenyon said:

> I cannot assent to the doctrine laid down in the cases cited, that the receipt of rent accruing after the expiration of the notice to quit is not a waiver of it; for, according to that doctrine, the same person might stand in the relation of tenant and trespasser to his landlord at the same time.

In other words, if the effect of the notice remain, the occupant of the premises is a trespasser, and yet he is paying rent as a tenant. But the reply is that although the notice has terminated the tenancy, and turned the tenant into a trespasser, yet that subsequent agreement (of which the payment is evidence) has reconstituted the previous relationship.

[1] Goodright dem. Charter *v.* Cordwent, 1795, 6 T. J. R. 220.

CONTINUING BREACHES

Inasmuch as a right of election usually arises upon the happening of every recurring breach by the tenant of his covenants, it becomes important to consider the case of continuing breaches.

VARIOUS CONDITIONS. Note, for example, the difference between a covenant to insure by a certain time, and a covenant to keep insured during the tenancy. In the former case the breach is complete when the specified time has elapsed; and consequently the right of election must be exercised within a reasonable time after the default, or not at all. Where, however, the agreement is to keep the premises insured, a new breach arises every successive moment of default, and gives an ever-recurring new right of election.[1] In such a case, where rent was received on the 23d of December, and ejectment (because of no insurance) was brought the next day it was held that the "waiver" was of breaches only to the 23d — a new right of election (we would say) arose because of the subsequent breach.[2] It is clear corollary from this, that an agreement to insure may be "waived" by acceptance of rent (as the case puts it), and yet an agreement to keep insured may remain unaffected.[3]

It is not always quite easy to distinguish between a completed and a continuing breach. For example, as has been noted, a covenant to insure by a certain time is not a continuing covenant; but it is said that a covenant to repair within a reasonable time is of that character,[4] and it has been

[1] Muston *v.* Gladwin, 1845, 6 Q. B. 963; 14 L. J., Q. B. 189; Jackson *v.* Allen, 1824, 3 Cowen (N. Y.) 231; Bleecker *v.* Smith, 1835, 13 Wend. (N. Y.) 533; McKildoe *v.* Darracott, 1856, 13 Grat. (Va.) 285.

[2] Price *v.* Worwood, 1859, 4 H. & N. 512; 28 L. J. Ex. 329; Flower *v.* Peck, 1830, 1 B. & Ad. 438; 9 L. J. (O. S.) K. B. 60; Muston *v.* Gladwin, 1845, 6 Q. B. 963; 14 L. J., Q. B. 189.

[3] Hyde *v.* Watts, 1843, 12 M. & W. 269; 13 L. J. Ex. 41.

[4] Baker *v.* Jones, 1850, 5 Ex. 498; 19 L. J. Ex. 405; Coward *v.* Gregory, 1866,

held, that where the reasonable time had elapsed and rent had subsequently been received, the landlord might act upon the subsequent continuation of the breach and terminate the tenancy, for otherwise,

> if a landlord once knew that his premises were out of repair, and did not sue instantly, he could never after re-enter for a breach of covenant committed for their not being repaired.[1]

In the same way it is held that a covenant to build within twelve months is " completely broken " at the end of the twelve months; but that a covenant to keep the buildings " so to be erected " in repair is a continuing covenant for it means that

> at all proper times the messuage referred to shall be in proper repair.[2]

A covenant to repair forthwith, is said to be capable of but one breach, and,

> when damages were once recovered in respect of the breach no more could be recovered;

but a covenant not to interrupt the lessor's reserved right of way is of perennial sort;[3] as is also a covenant not to use the land for certain purposes.[4] Breaking a door through a brick wall is said not to be a continuing breach of a covenant to repair and keep in repair.[5]

Where there is a covenant not to assign, and not to permit any other person to occupy the premises; and the landlord, with notice of an assignment and other occupancy by the

L. R. 2 C. P. 153; 36 L. J., C. P. 1; 15 L. T. 279; Ainsley *v.* Balsden, 1857, 14 U. C., Q. B. 535.

[1] Doe dem. Boscawen *v.* Bliss, 1813, 4 Taunt 735.

[2] Jacob *v.* Down, 1900, 2 Ch. 161; 69 L. J. Ch. 493; 83 L. T. 191. And see Stephens *v.* Junior Army, etc., 1914, 2 Ch. 516.

[3] Jackson *v.* Allen, 1824, 3 Cowen (N. Y.) 220.

[4] Doe dem. Ambler *v.* Woodbridge, 1829, 9 B. & C. 376; 7 L. J. (O. S.) K. B. 263; Mulligan *v.* Hollingsworth, 1900, 99 Fed. 20; Farwell *v.* Easton, 1876, 63 Mo. 446.

[5] Holderness *v.* Lang, 1886, 11 Ont. R. 1.

assignee, accepts subsequent rent, the effect, it is said, is that his right to terminate the tenancy because of the assignment is gone.[1] But is that quite right? While the covenant not to assign is of single character, is not the covenant not to permit others to occupy of a continuing quality? Do not breaches of it occur *de die in diem;* and may not the lessor, therefore, re-enter at any time? [2]

In one case the question was answered by construing the language of the agreement as meaning

> not to assign or (without assigning) permit others to occupy.[3]

But where this solution is not possible what are we to say? Possibly one of two things: (1) The permission given by the tenant to his assignee to occupy was not a repeated permission. It was given once for all, namely, by the assignment of the lease. After that the lessee did not *permit* occupation, for after that he had nothing to do with occupation.[3] Or (2) it may be urged, that the landlord by electing to continue the lease notwithstanding its assignment, has assented to the transfer, and, if so, he cannot object to possession under it.

STANDING-BY. Much the same point has arisen in another form: Suppose that the lessee covenant that he will not permit the premises to be used for the purposes of trade; that nevertheless, the buildings are, by the lessee, converted into shops, and one of them rented to a plumber; and that, with knowledge of these facts, the landlord receives subsequent rent; is continuation of the trade a continuing breach for which the landlord may re-enter?

To such questions Cockburn, C. J. has replied as follows:

> But I cannot help thinking that where a lessor, with full knowledge that a breach of this particular description has been com-

[1] Goodright dem. Walter *v.* Davids, 1778, Cowp. 803.

[2] Ambler *v.* Woodbridge, 1829, 9 B. & C. 376; 7 L. J. (O. S.) K. B. 263.

[3] Walrond *v.* Hawkins, 1875, L. R. 10 C. P. 348; 44 L. J., K. B. 116; 32 L. T. 119; Griffin *v.* Tomkins, 1880, 42 L. T. 359.

mitted, waives the forfeiture . . . that amounts not merely to a waiver of the past breach but to *a license to continue the breach in future*. There is to my mind an obvious distinction between the case of something which is to be done, and which remains undone, and the doing of which may be postponed; and the doing of something which is forbidden, but which having once been done may be acquiesced in for the future. I think it would be monstrous if it were otherwise. It would amount to this: that the lessor with a full knowledge that the thing had been done which was prohibited by the lease, and upon which a forfeiture was to accrue if it was done, might continue as long as it suited his purposes to receive his rent and so waive the forfeiture up to the time that rent was received, and then, when it suited his purpose upon a change of circumstances, turn round on the tenant and say " Although I have allowed you, thus by implication to suppose that I was licensing what you were doing, I now take advantage of it and turn you out of what is to you a beneficial lease." It seems to me that is a very different thing from saying " Though I take my rent to-day you have not done the repairs which you are bound to do, and, unless you do those repairs, there is a continuing obligation to do something " which is not the case in the other breach suggested.[1]

In some cases, the lessor might be estopped on the ground that he stood by while the conversion of the building was in progress; that he was aware of the tenant's purpose; and that he remained silent.

If an owner of land, who stands by and sees another building upon his, the owner's land, under the honest belief that he, the one who is building, is building upon his own land, and does not stop him and inform him of his mistake, is afterwards precluded from recovering the land so built upon by such other person, I think the like rule may well be applied to a landlord who stands by and sees his tenant doing an act which is a forfeiture of his term, and who, by the landlord's conduct, is led to believe that the landlord is an

[1] Griffin *v.* Tompkins, 1880, 42 L. T. 359. And see Laurie *v.* Lees, 1880, L. R. 14 Ch. D. 262 for a *quaere*, as to the construction when the covenant is not against a sub-lease but merely against user in a particular way. See also Doe dem. Ambler *v.* Woodbridge, 1829, 9 B. & C. 376. 7 L. J. (O. S.) K. B. 263.

assenting party to such act; and that he should equally be estopped from setting up such act afterwards as a ground of forfeiture.[2]

If the tenant, however, knew that his contemplated action was a breach of his agreement, could he plead estoppel? To sustain that defence, three things must be proved: (1) that the lessor was aware of his own right; (2) that the lessee was unaware of his right; and (3) that the lessor had reasonable ground for assuming the lessee's ignorance.[2]

INAPPLICABILITY OF FORFEITURE AND "WAIVER." The inapplicability of the phraseology of forfeiture and "waiver" to breaches of covenant becomes conspicuous in connection with continuing covenants. Breaches of a covenant may happen at the rate of sixty to a minute, but it appears to be foolish to say that in every minute sixty forfeitures occurred, and that every one of them terminated the lease unless afterwards "waived." If none of them was ever "waived," did the lease end with the first of the series? And if so, how could there have been any subsequent forfeitures? Perhaps it is wrong to say that there were sixty forfeitures, and we ought to say that there is "*a description* of forfeiture *de die in diem?*"[3] But what does that mean? Why should we not say that there may be a continuing breach, or, if you will, rapidly recurring breaches, and that, on the occurrence of any breach (no matter how many had already happened), the lessor may elect to terminate the lease?

[1] Holderness *v.* Lang, 1886, 11 Ont. R. 16.
[2] Ewart on Estoppel, p. 90.
[3] Hernings *v.* Durnford, 1832, 2 C. & J. 669; 1 L. J. Ex. 251.

CHAPTER VIII

VENDOR AND PURCHASER OF REAL PROPERTY

The subject of vendor and purchaser of real property is a part of the larger department of contract, but presents some points which deserve separate treatment.

" WAIVER " OF A GOOD TITLE. English law furnishes scores of cases in which the word " waive " and its derivatives are used in connection with the purchaser's right to receive a good title, and the general rule is laid down as follows:

> I am of opinion that the obligation to which a vendor is subject to make out a good title is intended for the benefit of the purchaser only, and that, if he thinks fit to waive it, he has a right to do so.[1]

But the word is inaccurate and misleading. Substitute for the phrase " thinks fit to waive it " the words " thinks fit to accept a title which is not good," and you have in simple and unambiguous language that which, when so expressed, is so clearly obvious that there is no necessity for saying it.

Test the word " waiver " by comparing contracts for the sale of land with contracts for the sale of goods: Wheat is sold by sample; a lower grade is tendered; the purchaser considers and accepts; and he must pay. Land is sold; the title is to be good; a defective title is tendered; the purchaser considers and accepts; and he must pay. In the

[1] Bennett *v.* Fowler, 1840, 2 Beav. 304.

former case, no one would found liability upon "waiver." In the latter, liability is almost universally so founded. Both are simple cases of election.

The evil of treating the land case as one of "waiver" is that attention and inquiry are wrongly directed. You are inquiring whether the purchaser "waived" an objection, instead of whether he accepted the title — whether he relinquished one thing, instead of whether he accepted another. And you may eventually be heard saying, that

> Where such waiver distinctly appears . . . the party will be estopped.[1]

ACCEPTANCE OF TITLE. Usually it is agreed that an act is a "waiver" of a good title if it indicate an intention to accept the title. But argument is clear and direct only when addressed to the establishment of relationship between the act and the intention. Reasoning from the act to "waiver," and from "waiver" to acceptance, leaves ample room for all the fallacies associated with the undistributed middle of the logicians. Keeping in mind that the alleged act must indicate something quite definite, namely, intention to accept, you will have a standard by which to test its importance. Arguing that the act was a "waiver," while leaving undetermined what "waiver" is, may be a tactful method of presenting a bad case. In a good case, assertion that the act was a "waiver," and that "waiver" amounts to acceptance of title, is only paying a befogging deference to misleading terminology and risking success.

There is ample authority for the proposition that effective acts of "waiver" must be such as indicate an acceptance of title. Indeed, in many places, the two things are treated as identical. And this much, at all events, is certain, that no attempt has been made to distinguish between them — no-

[1] Queen *v.* Young, 1888, 86 Ala. 430; 5 So. 116.

body has asserted that there are acts which amount to a "waiver" of all objections to title, and yet which do not amount to an acceptance of the title.[1] Many such expressions as the following could be supplied:

> Acts of ownership on the part of the purchaser may . . . work an acceptance of title and a waiver of all objections.[2]
>
> Apologizing for not paying the purchase money which was, of course, only payable if the title was accepted, have been considered strong acts of waiver.[3]
>
> It . . . amounts to a waiver of his objections to title, and that he must be considered as having accepted the title.[4]
>
> The question then . . . will be whether the purchaser waived all proof of the abstract which would amount to an acceptance of the title.[5]
>
> *Prima facie*, however, taking possession after an abstract has been delivered, and not in pursuance of any provisions in the conditions of sale, is a waiver of the objections appearing on the abstract, and it lies on the purchaser to rebut this presumption. This is not to be done by merely saying at a subsequent time "I did not so intend it;" it must be shown that the presumption is rebutted by the fair inference to be derived from the acts of the person himself. The rule it is to be observed is founded on reason, because after the purchaser has taken possession of the property it may become altered, delapidated, or employed for injurious purposes. To all which the vendor can say nothing, if the property really belongs to the purchaser, which it does when he accepts the title.[6]
>
> The mere fact of taking possession and exercising acts of ownership over the land will not preclude the purchaser from his right to investigate the title, unless it clearly appears that he intended to

[1] The statement in Warren *v.* Richardson, 1830, 1 Young 1, that "a waiver of the defendant's right to make the plaintiff produce his title does not seem necessarily to import that he will accept the title though it should manifestly appear to be bad," is not a contradiction of the above. The case was one of specific performance in which discretion, arising out of hardship, was the determining factor.

[2] Fry on Sp. Perf., 5th ed., p. 657.

[3] *Ibid.*, p. 658.

[4] Hull *v.* Laver, 1838, 3 Y & C. Ex. 196.

[5] Southly *v.* Hull, 1837, 2 My. & Cr. 217.

[6] Brown *v.* Stenson, 1857, 24 Beav. 637.

> waive and has actually waived such right. . . . It is better, however, that the purchaser should not take possession until every objection to the title has been removed, lest the act should be deemed an acceptance of the title.[1]
>
> The mere taking possession by a purchaser is not necessarily a waiver of the right to an inquiry as to title. The court will not hold it to be so unless satisfied that it was the intention of the purchaser to take the land without such inquiry.[2]

Mr. Armour treats "waivers" of objections as the equivalent of acceptance of title.[3]

"WAIVER" INAPPROPRIATE. The considerations above offered will, it is hoped, sufficiently indicate the impropriety of such language as the following:

> But a purchaser may, after the contract, expressly or impliedly waive, wholly or in part, his right (whether absolute or qualified) to a marketable title, or to the usual evidences thereof.[4]
>
> The fact of an intended lessee having advertised the property for sale, though not considered conclusive, has been relied on as one among other evidences of his having waived the production of the lessor's title.[5]

For when that has been said, we still need to be told what "waiver" is. Why not simply say (if that be necessary) that a purchaser may accept a defective title if he wants to. He does not "waive" defective wheat.

But may there not be a "waiver" of one of several objections, in which case there would be no acceptance of title? No. A mere statement by the purchaser that a point is "waived" is inconclusive. Under certain circumstances it may help to prove a new contract, or an estoppel.[6] And it

[1] Warville on Vendors, 2d ed., p. 392.

[2] Mitcheltree *v.* Irwin, 1867, 13 Gr. 542. And see Simpson *v.* Sadd, 1854, 4 De G. M. & G. 685.

[3] On Titles, 3d ed., p. 24, *et seq.*

[4] Dart's *Vendors and Purchasers*, 7th ed., vol. 1, p. 508.

[5] *Ibid.*, p. 511.

[6] Fry on Sp. Perf., 5th ed., p. 656; Lesturgeon *v.* Martin, 1834, 3 My. & K.

may be called " waiver " if you wish, but it will remain contract or estoppel. A stipulation in a contract for a good title cannot be eliminated by the unilateral act of the purchaser.[1] Test that statement by trying to think of some act of a purchaser which, although not amounting to contract or estoppel or acceptance of the title, would deprive a purchaser of his right to a good title on the ground of " waiver."

255; Alexander *v.* Crosby, 1844, 1 J. & LaT. 666; 7 Ir. Eq. 445; Goss *v.* Lord Nugent, 1833, 5 B. & Ad. 64; 2 L. J., K. B. 127.

[1] See *ante* pp. 131–142.

CHAPTER IX

INSURANCE

To the laborious inquirer, the immense number of insurance cases in the American courts affords an unequalled opportunity for the study of the subject of this work. And there is no department of the law from which the elimination of " waiver " is more necessary.

Courts *vs.* Companies. The history of the cases is, very largely, the history of a struggle between the insurance companies and the courts. Too frequently the companies have repudiated liability upon trumpery grounds — that a written notice of the loss was not given in proper form to the proper officer; that assent to other insurance was not indicated by indorsement upon the policy; that the contract was never obligatory, because of the breach, well known to the company, of some condition contemporaneously with the delivery of the policy; and so on. And the courts, endeavoring to compel fair play, but trammelled and often thwarted by the stringent terms of the contracts, have devised doctrines and asserted principles which are sometimes more creditable to the ingenuity and sublety of the judges than easily harmonized with decisions rendered, under less violent bias, in other departments of the law. "The doctrine of waiver," it is said,

> has been an efficient means by which to prevent insurers from treating the contract as valid when it is to their interest, and repudiating it when called upon to respond to its burdens, thus playing fast and loose with the insured.[1]

It is the purpose of the following chapters to point out that the courts have unduly handicapped themselves by the adoption of ideas associated with forfeiture and "waiver"; that the principles which they ought to have applied are, principally, those of election and estoppel; and that the substitution of these will not only relieve the courts of some of their difficulties but will clarify and elucidate the law.

VOID AND VOIDABLE. The mistake of the courts is traceable to the fact that policies usually provide that upon breach of conditions they are to be "void;" that the word is sometimes thought to mean that, by the breach, the policy becomes *ipso facto* void, instead of merely "voidable at the election of the company;" that even when the true meaning is accepted in theory, it is not sufficiently carried into thought; and that forfeiture and "waiver" are usually believed to contain principles properly applicable to the subject. Read for example the following typical passage:

> Conditions prescribed by insurance companies for their benefit or protection can of course be waived by them at any time; and since forfeitures are deemed odious, courts are prompt to lay hold of circumstances that indicate an election to waive the conditions imposed.[2]

There is no "waiver" of the conditions. They remain unaffected. The election is to continue the policy.

If the language of the policies had not been (as is usual) that "the policy shall be void," but (as that language must be construed) "the policy shall be voidable at the election of the company," it is inconceivable that the cases should

[1] Parsons *v.* Lane, 1906, 97 Minn. 98.

have proceeded upon grounds of forfeiture [1] and "waiver." If a contract of sale, for example, provided for monthly delivery of goods and for monthly payments, and stipulated that, if one party made default, the other might if he so chose rescind the contract, we would not say that the defaulter had "forfeited" the contract and that, afterwards, the forfeiture had been "waived" by the other party.[2] We should simply say that the one party had made default, and that, nevertheless, the other party had elected to continue the contract.

FORFEITURE AND "WAIVER." And so a person insured does not "forfeit" his policy. He gives to the company a right to terminate it, a right which may never be exercised, and very probably never will be — unless a loss happens. There is therefore no "forfeiture" of the policy, and consequently no "waiver" of forfeiture. The contract is not void, but voidable only. It continues until the company elects to terminate it. Election once made is irreversible. And lapse of time, without election to terminate, is evidence of election to continue.

PLEADING AND PROOF. That is what is now suggested; and, as a corollary of it, that when an insurance company pleads that, by some default, the policy has been forfeited, and asks you to prove, if you can, any "waiver" of the forfeiture, you should refuse to accept the issue; and that, on the contrary, you should turn upon the company, and ask whether it ever elected to terminate the policy — if so, how, when, and by whom? The company's plea ought not to be forfeiture; and the insured's reply ought not to be "waiver." On the contrary, the company, if it would succeed, must plead default, and election, consequent upon the default, to terminate the policy. Upon that plea, issue will be joined.

[1] Frasier *v.* New Zealand, etc., 1901, 64 Pac. 814; 39 Or. 342.

[2] For discussion of the word "Forfeiture" see pp. 59–65.

Confusion by "Waiver." Repetition of what has already been said as to the mischief worked by adherence to the phraseology of forfeiture and "waiver" is unnecessary.[1] One reference only will here be added. A Canadian court, holding that certain correspondence indicated an election to continue liability, said:

> Upon default being made in the payment of the note, the insurers might have elected to forfeit the policy, or they might have elected not to forfeit it but to continue it; and upon the evidence before us, I think it clear that they elected not to forfeit but to continue it.[2]

Two appellate courts overruled this decision,[3] the judges being misled by ideas of "waiver" and of forfeiture followed by revivor:

> It became incumbent on the plaintiff to establish with reasonable clearness, some act of the company to revive the lost liability. There was no waiver of the forfeiture, etc.

The case is an excellent example of the benefit to be derived from the substitution of election for forfeiture and "waiver." One appeal judge appears to have been looking for something which would "revive the lost liability," whereas nothing had happened to the liability. And another declared that there had been no "waiver of the forfeiture" — overlooking the fact that there had been no forfeiture, for until the company elected to make the policy "void," it remained absolutely unaffected.

Customary Phraseology. The following may be regarded as fair samples of the language usually applied to the subject of insurer's liability after breach of condition:

> If the insurer, with knowledge of the facts by reason whereof it is entitled to insist upon forfeiture, continues to recognize the policy

[1] *Ante*, caps 1–4.

[2] McGeachie *v.* North Am., etc., Co., 1892, 22 Ont. R. 164.

[3] 20 Ont. R. 187; 23 Can. S. C. 148.

as in force, or does any act inconsistent with insistence upon the forfeiture, the forfeiture is waived and may not be relied upon thereafter.[1]

If with knowledge of the circumstances, it continued to treat the contract as of binding force, and induced plaintiff to act in that belief, the rule holding that it thereby waived the forfeiture is a very just one.[2]

Such statements may be found by the score or hundred. Upon the other hand the use of the word "election" is not only exceptional, but its employment still more rarely indicates conscious reference to the department of the law which it is sometimes employed to denote. Very frequently it is confused with forfeiture, "waiver," and estoppel. For example:

Conditions prescribed by insurance companies for their benefit or protection can of course be waived by them at any time; and since forfeitures are deemed odious, courts are prompt to lay hold of circumstances that indicate an election to waive the conditions imposed.[3]

. . . it was only voidable at their election, and that it was therefore competent for them to waive a strict compliance with it after the time stipulated for the payment of such premium, and that in case of such waiver the policy would be revived . . . .[4]

Such language is very misleading, and causes much misapprehension, with occasional resulting injustice. For it turns inquiry into an improper channel. It posits the question, "Did the company waive the forfeiture and revive the

[1] Hunt *v.* State, etc., 1902, 66 Neb. 127; 92 N. W. 921. And see to same effect Johnston *v.* Phelps, 1901, 63 Neb. 21; 88 N. W. 142; Prudential, etc. *v.* Sullivan, 1901, 59 N. E. 873; 27 Ind. App. 30.

[2] Hollis *v.* State, etc., 1884, 65 Iowa, 454; 21 N. W. 774; approved in Corson *v.* Anchor, etc., 1901, 85 N. W. 806; 113 Ia. 641. It will be observed that this formula introduces an element of estoppel that is not found in the one preceding it.

[3] Frasier *v.* New Zealand, 1901, 64 Pac. 814; 39 Or. 347. And see Phœnix, etc. *v.* Spiers, 1888 87 Ky. 293; 8 S. W. 453; Home, etc. *v.* Myer, 1879, 93 Ill. 275; Insurance Co. *v.* Norton, 1877, 96 U. S. 234; Insurance Co. *v.* Eggleston, 1877, 96 U. S. 572.

[4] Bouton *v.* American, etc., 1857, 25 Conn. 550.

policy ? " instead of, " Did the company elect to terminate (to forfeit, if you insist upon it) the policy ? " It removes the onus from the company to prove election; and places it upon the assured to prove " waiver." It requires proof of the " waiver " by some person who had authority from the company for the purpose, instead of requiring the company to prove that the official who is said to have elected had been duly authorized.

ESTOPPEL. The idea of " waiver " resulting in estoppel, or of estoppel resulting in " waiver " — of building " waiver " upon estoppel, or estoppel upon " waiver," is frequently encountered. We have seen that one text-writer insists that

> parol waiver . . . must always be based upon estoppel or new consideration,[1]

and also says, that a waiver having taken place, " the company is said to be estopped," if the other party has been misled.[2] The courts, too, use language such as this:

> We are of opinion that the natural and reasonable presumption is that the company retained the proofs because it elected to waive a technical defence and thereby concluded itself from insisting upon the forfeiture.[3]

And the effect of the misconception is that there appears in a useful book on insurance the following:

> Again where the policy, during its life, whether before or after loss, becomes voidable at the option and to the knowledge of the insurers, words or acts of the insurers confirmatory of the continued validity of the contract ought to be taken as good evidence of the exercise of this option to condone the default, if otherwise their effect would be to mislead the insured to his prejudice. To this last proposition substantially all the authorities agree, provided the representative of the insurer, acting on its behalf, has sufficient power to waive.[4]

[1] *Ante*, p. 35.

[2] *Ante*, pp. 36, 37.

[3] Insurance Co. *v.* Norton, 1877, 96 U. S. 234.

[4] Richards on Insurance, p. 163.

Here both the essentials of the "words or acts," and their relevancy are mistaken. For (1) it is not at all necessary to effective election that it should, or should not, have any tendency to mislead the insured, and (2) the "words or acts" are relevant not as condonation of any default (for that may still be sued on), but as indication of the election of the insurer, notwithstanding the default, to continue the policy.

Ample confirmation and illustration of what has been said will appear in the succeeding chapters.

EXCEPTIONAL DOCTRINES. Writers upon the law of insurance find themselves confronted with, and confounded by, the fact, that although a contract of insurance is indubitably a contract, yet that there are

> certain exceptional doctrines of law by which it is governed;

and a recent author[1] has offered the following as an explanation of the phenomenon:

> We must keep in mind that the contract of insurance inherently differs from the lease of a house or the ordinary sale of merchandise. The storekeeper sells a hundred dollars worth of potatoes for one hundred dollars. The underwriter sells one thousand dollars worth of insurance for two dollars, but only upon conditions. The disparity between the premium and the amount of insurance demonstrates that the conditions are a vital part of the contract, indeed, much more than that, that substantially the whole contract, as regards the underwriters' interest must be in some way bound up in the conditions.
>
> Surely we cannot escape the conclusion that insurance is, in its nature and its relation to public interests, somewhat peculiar. To the exceptional character of the contract, we may attribute the adoption of certain exceptional doctrines of law by which it it governed.

But the companies do not sell "one thousand dollars worth of insurance for two dollars." Pay them two dollars,

[1] Mr. Richards: Columbia Law Rev., vol. 13, p. 55. To a prior article by Mr. Richards in vol. 12, p. 135, the present writer replied at p. 619.

and they promise to pay one thousand dollars upon the happening of an event the likelihood of which is (say) in the ratio of one dollar to one thousand. They sell their liability not at an absurd loss, but at a reasonable profit.

There can be no reason for the existence of "certain exceptional doctrines" in the law of insurance. There are none. If election and estoppel were substituted for "waiver," there would not appear to be any.

APPLICATION OF ELECTION SUBSEQUENT TO LOSS. Objection to the views here maintained has been made, on the ground that election can have no application after the loss has occurred. For example, in reply to an article by the present writer in the Columbia Law Review advocating the application of the doctrines of election to insurance cases,[1] Mr. Richards said:

> In weighing the advantages and disadvantages involved in giving to the standard fire policy the new meaning, let us at the outset observe that, in the vast majority of instances of breach of condition committed before loss, the insurance company has no knowledge of the facts constituting breach until after loss, and therefore, is in no position to cancel. In this larger class of cases, then, if the legal effect of the policy is to be modified as proposed, the insured would be able to violate the provisions of the policy to any extent and with perfect impunity.
>
> So far as I am aware no court has ever advocated such a view, no one of the cases cited in the article gives countenance to it, nor can I persuade myself that Mr. Ewart desires to press his theory to such an extreme. Though he does not so state or intimate, I must believe that he intended to limit the application of his rule to instances in which the insurer, prior to loss, has obtained knowledge of the facts constituting breach. If so, then upon his own showing, it becomes no longer a matter of interpreting the phraseology of the standard fire policy, adopted by statute, but of constructing, in place of it, a new contract for the parties. If this be the proposal, then our policy must be extended to read somewhat as follows: "void if the party for whose benefit the

[1] Vol. 12, p. 619.

> provision was made — the company — so elects, in those instances in which the company, prior to loss, acquires knowledge of the facts constituting breach, and cancels the contract: and in other cases void without such cancellation."
>
> But does not such a provision again plunge us into the midst of confusion and difficulty? What do we mean by "knowledge of the facts?"[1]

To these criticisms, the following replies are submitted:

(1) The policy permits election to be made within a reasonable time after knowledge of the event has reached the insurer — whether before or after loss, or before or after Christmas, is immaterial.

(2) The suggestion that the voidance clause should be read one way prior to loss, and another way subsequent to loss, does not come from those who point out that the clause has but one meaning, an indisputable meaning; that it does not mean that, upon breach, the policy is forfeited — that is, *ipso facto* terminated; that it does mean that, upon breach, the company may elect between continuation and termination; and that the right of election exists so long as the contract endures, and at every stage of its existence.

(3) If it be true that election has no application after the loss, neither has forfeiture or "waiver." For either the clause providing that the policy shall be void is, or is not, in force after the loss. If it is, it provides for election, and the right to elect therefore exists. And if it is not in force, then the only ground upon which forfeiture can be suggested has vanished.

(4) The difficulty is supposed to lie in the fact that election after a loss cannot cancel a completed liability — the loss occurred while the policy was in full force, and how can a subsequent election have any effect upon it? Gunpowder, for example, had been stored upon the premises prior to the

[1] Columbia Law Rev., vol. 13, p. 51. And see *ante*, Chap. 1, p. 15.

loss; of that the insurer had no notice until after the loss; how can election relieve him from liability? The reply is that termination of the contract does not date from the time of election, but from the time of the breach. Look at the contract. It says (if in usual form) that a certain act shall make void the policy — if the company so says. The company does so say. Says what? That the act voids the policy. When did the act void the policy? At the only time it could do so, namely when it occurred. What the company elects is, that a certain act shall or shall not have a certain effect. The company does not change the contract. It says: We elect that the voidance clause shall operate.

(5) If a prerequisite of election be knowledge of the facts, and if, therefore, it be necessary to make answer to the question, "What do you mean by knowledge of the facts?" [1] the reply is that that inquiry "will plunge us into the midst of confusion and difficulty" no deeper than if we have recourse to forfeiture and "waiver," for (1) forfeiture does not exist; (2) nobody knows what "waiver" is; and (3) the usual definition of "waiver" being "an intentional relinquishment of a known right," [2] the difficulties by which we shall be confused are: (A) What do we mean by *intentional?* (B) What do we mean by *relinquishment?* and (C) What do we mean by a *known right?* The second of these may be found to be specially troublesome.

(6) It is not quite correct to say that "no court has ever advocated such a view," for Mr. Richards himself includes an instance in his *Cases on Insurance.*[3] The defence was a breach (by vacancy of the premises) unknown to the company until after the loss, and the court said:

[1] The answer may be found *ante*, pp. 72–83. [2] *Ante*, p. 6.

[3] Moore *v.* Phœnix, etc., 1882, 62 N. H. 240. Another instance is Glens Falls, etc. *v.* Michael, 1906, 167 Ind. 659; 79 N. E. 905. See the extract from it, *ante*, cap. 1, p. 17. And another is Milkman *v.* United, etc., 1897, 20 R. I., 10; 36 Atl. 1121; quoting Phœnix, etc. *v.* Lansing, 1884, 15 Neb. 494.

> The defendants might have waived the condition altogether, or might have waived its breach; but having had no opportunity before the loss to make their election to waive the breach, their refusal to pay, when notified of the loss and unoccupancy, was an effectual election that they insisted upon the condition of the policy.[1]

In another, a life-insurance case, the company, although aware, after the death of the insured, of a misrepresentation made at the inception of the risk, requested that letters of guardianship of the children should be obtained, and negotiated for a compromise; held that the facts justified the view that the company had

> elected to waive the right to repudiate and rescind the contract.[2]

In better language, the company had elected to continue its liability; for it did not "waive the right to repudiate," it exercised its right to elect between continuation and termination.

In a Canadian case, the court said:

> The question is, whether, whenever the loss happened, the policy was, or was not, an existing risk. If the defendants accepted the payments as alleged, whether before or after the fire, I do not see how they can be allowed to fall back on an alleged prior forfeiture. . . . They treat the plaintiff as insured with them, when they called on him to pay for a period long after his alleged default.[3]

That there are not many other such decisions is due to the fact that the courts, even when recognizing the element of election, confuse themselves with forfeiture and "waiver."

Take, for example, the following from a frequently cited case in the Supreme Court of the United States.[4] An agent for an insurance company, after the due date of a premium note, extended the time for its payment, and afterwards

[1] Upon other points, the case is not satisfactory.
[2] Baker *v.* N. Y., etc., 1896, 77 Fed. 550.
[3] Lyons *v.* The Globe, etc., 1877, 27 U. C., C. P. 567.
[4] Knickerbocker, etc. *v.* Norton, 1877, 96 U. S. 234.

declined to receive the money. If the time had been extended *before* the due date, the company would have admitted liability. But the extension having been made *after* the due date, it declined to pay a loss. The case is one of simple election. When the note fell due and was dishonored, the company had a right of election between continuing and terminating its liability; and by agreeing to extend the time for payment, it supplied evidence of election to continue. There was no "forfeiture" and no "waiver of the forfeiture." Now read the following extract from the judgment of the Court:

> The material question is, whether the forfeiture was waived; and we see no reason why this may not be done as well by an agreement made for extending the note after its maturity, as by one made before. In either case, the legal effect of the indulgence is this: The company say to the insured, Pay your note by such a time and your policy will not be forfeited. If the insured agreed to do this and does it, or tenders himself ready to do it, the forfeiture ought not to be executed. In both cases, the parties mutually act upon the hypothesis of the continued existence of the policy. It is true if the agreement be made before the note matures and before the forfeiture is incurred, it would be a fraud upon the assured to attempt to enforce the forfeiture when, relying on the agreement, he permits the original day of adjustment to pass. On the other hand, if the agreement be made after the note matures, such agreement is itself a recognition, on the company's part, of the continued existence of the policy, and consequently of its election to waive the forfeiture. It is conceded that the acceptance of payment has this effect; and we do not see why an agreement to accept, and a tender of payment according to the agreement, should not have the same effect. Both are acts equally demonstrative of election of the company to waive the forfeiture of the policy. Grant that the promise to extend the note is without consideration and not binding upon the company — which is perhaps true as well when the promise is made before maturity as when it is made afterwards — still it does not take from the company's act the legitimate effects of such act upon the forfeiture of the policy. Perhaps the note might be sued on

> regardless of the extension; but if it could be, that would not annihilate the fact that the company elected to waive the forfeiture by entering into the transaction. If it should repudiate its agreement, it could not repudiate the waiver of the forfeiture, without at least giving to the assured reasonable notice to pay the money.

The Court has election in mind, but always "an election to waive the forfeiture" instead of election to continue or terminate the obligation. And it is thus led into consideration of the company's repudiation "of the waiver of the forfeiture," whereas there was no forfeiture, and no "waiver," and nothing to repudiate.

CHAPTER X

INSURANCE

BREACHES CONTEMPORANEOUS WITH DELIVERY OF POLICY

Scope of Chapter. Perusal of previous chapters will probably have convinced readers that breach by a policy-holder of a stipulation of the contract does not work a forfeiture of the policy; that usually it gives to the company a right to elect either to continue or to terminate the policy; that, if the company desire to terminate the contract, it must so elect promptly; and that failure in that regard will either (1) put an end to the right to elect, or (2) supply evidence of election to continue. We are now to see that all this is quite as true of breaches contemporaneous with the issue of the policy as of subsequent breaches.

CLASSIFICATION. The cases may be divided into three classes:

1. Cases in which the company had knowledge of the breach at the time of issuing the policy.

2. Cases in which the company had no knowledge of the breach at the time of issuing the policy.

3. Cases in which the company had no such knowledge when the preliminary insurance slip or premium receipt was issued, but acquired it prior to the issuing of the policy.

1. KNOWLEDGE WHEN POLICY ISSUED

SYMPATHETIC COURTS. The courts have always sympathized with the policy-holder who, having answered all his application questions, paid his premium, obtained his policy, and suffered a loss, is confronted with refusal to pay upon the ground that the company was never for a moment liable upon the policy, because of the existence, at the time of its delivery, of some breach of condition well known to the company.

> The general rule that an insurance company cannot take advantage of conditions in a policy whereby such policy is to be void, by reason of circumstances existing at the time the policy issued, in case the facts were known to its agent at the time, has been recognized universally.[1]

But the courts have not seen very clearly upon what ground the insured can be relieved.

FRAUD. Sometimes they have founded their decision upon fraud:

> To deliver a policy with full knowledge of facts upon which its validity may be disputed, and then to insist upon these facts as

[1] German, etc. v. Shaden, 1903, 68 Neb. 1; 93 N. W. 972. The judgment asserts that 27 States have so declared the law and many authorities are cited in support of the statement. And see Gray v. Germania, etc., 155 N. Y. 180; 49 N. E. 675; Frasier v. New Zealand, 1901, 64 Pac. 814; 39 Or. 342; Cassimus v. Scottish, 1902,

ground of avoidance, is to attempt a fraud. . . . Such an issue is tantamount to an assertion that the policy is valid at the time of delivery.[1]

ESTOPPEL. Sometimes it is estoppel:

An insurance company that knowingly takes a premium for a policy under conditions that would render it invalid, will not be permitted to say it is not a binding contract for that reason.[2]

It is well settled . . . that the insurer is estopped to plead . . . the breach of conditions against other insurance or incumbrances, without the consent of the company in writing on the face of the policy, if it appears that when the agent of the company, with authority to deliver or withhold policies, delivered the policy in question, when he knew of the existence of the other insurance or incumbrance.[3]

"WAIVER." Sometimes it is waiver:

Conditions which enter into the validity of a contract of insurance at its inception may be waived by agents, and are waived if so intended, although they remain in the policy when delivered.[4]

135 Ala. 256; 33 So. 163; Allen *v.* Home, etc., 1901, 133 Cal. 29; 65 Pac. 138; Prudential, etc. *v.* Sullivan, 1901, 59 N. E. 876; 127 Ind. App. 30.

[1] Gray *v.* Germania, 1898, 155 N. Y. 180; 49 N. E. 675. And see Home, etc. *v.* Garfield, 1871, 60 Ill. 124; Union, etc. *v.* Chipp, 1879, 93 Ill. 96; Green *v.* National, etc., 1913, 90 Kan. 523; 135 Pac. 586; Elliott on Insurance, § 188.

[2] Germania, etc. *v.* Hick, 1888, 125 Ill. 361; 17 N. E. 792. And see Farley *v.* Spring Garden, etc., 1912, 134 N. W. 1054; 148 Wis. 622; Norfolk, etc. *v.* Wood, 1912, 74 S. E. 186; 113 Va. 310; Coats *v.* Camden, etc., 1912, 135 N. W. 524; 149 Wis. 129.

[3] London, etc. *v.* Fischer, 1899, 92 Fed. 500. And see Wood *v.* American, etc., 1896, 149 N. Y. 382; 44 N. E. 80; Osborne *v.* Phœnix, etc., 1901, 64 Pac. 1103; Hartford, etc. *v.* Post, 1901, 62 S. W. 140; Benjamin *v.* Palatine, etc., 1903, 80 N. Y. App. 260; 80 N. Y. Supp. 256; Phœnix & Co. *v.* Randle, 1903, 33 So. 500; New Amsterdam, etc. *v.* New Palestine, etc., 1915, 107 N. E. 554; Fink *v.* Anchor etc., 1915, 153 N. W. 1048.

[4] Berry *v.* Ins. Co., 1892, 132 N. Y. 49; 30 N. E. 254. Approved in Grabbs *v.* Farmers, etc., 1899, 125 N. C. 389; 34 S. E. 503. And see McFarland *v.* Kittaning, etc., 1890, 134 Pa. 590; 19 Atl. 796; Sproul *v.* Western, etc., 1898, 54 Pac. 180; 33 Or. 98; Merchants, etc. *v.* Harris, 1911, 51 Col. 95; 116 Pac. 143; Bear *v.* Atlanta, etc., 1901, 34 N. Y. Misc. 613; 70 N. Y. Supp. 581; Germania, etc. *v.* Klewer, 1889, 129 Ill. 609; 22 N. E. 489; Fireman's, etc. *v.* Horton, 1897, 170 Ill. 258; 48 N. E. 955; First Nat. Bank *v.* Am., etc., 1894, 58 Minn. 492; 60 N. W. 345; Home, etc. *v.* Wilson, 1913, 159 S. W. 1113; 109 Ark. S. C. 324; Murphy *v.* Lafayette, etc., 1914, 83 S. E. 461; 167 N. C. 334; Elliott on Ins. § 188.

MISTAKE. Sometimes it is held that the circumstances are evidence of mistake in preparation of the contract, and that it ought to be reformed:[1]

VARIOUS. Sometimes different conceptions are confused as in the following:

> It is well settled in this state that when an insurance company issues a policy with full knowledge of facts which would render it void in its inception, if its provisions were insisted upon, it will be presumed that it, by mistake, omitted to express the fact in the policy, waived the provisions, or held itself estopped from setting it up, as a contrary inference would impute to it a fraudulent intent to deliver and receive pay for an invalid instrument.[2]
>
> If at the time of closing the contract the insurers have knowledge of the existence of a cause of forfeiture which would invalidate the policy from the time of its inception, they are held by accepting the premium or delivering the policy, to waive the forfeiture or to be estopped from insisting upon it.[3]
>
> Under these circumstances it is to be presumed that if anything else was omitted which was necessary to make the policy valid it was by mistake, or that the condition was waived, or the defendant held itself estopped from setting it up.[4]

JUSTICE. Sometimes general notions of justice, with an estoppel flavor, are deemed to be sufficient for the case:

> It cannot be contended that the company with knowledge of the execution of the mortgage, could retain the premium, treat the policy as in force, knowing that the assured was relying upon its validity, and then insist upon the . . . breach of the condition.[5]

[1] United States *v.* Budd, 1891, 144 U. S. 154. See Northern, etc. *v.* Grand View, etc., 1901, 183 U. S. 308; 101 Fed. 77.

[2] Gray *v.* Germania, etc., 1898, 155 N. J. 183; 49 N. E. 675.

[3] Richards on Ins., 3rd ed., p. 175. And see Forward *v.* Continental, etc., 1894, 142 N. Y. 387; 37 N. E. 615.

[4] Robbins *v.* Springfield, etc., 1896, 149 N. Y. 477; 44 N. E. 159. See also McNally *v.* Phœnix, etc., 1893, 137 N. Y. 389; 33 N. E. 475; Tilton *v.* Farmers etc., 1913, 143 N. Y. Supp. 112, 3; Gray *v.* Germania, etc., 1898, 49 N. E. 675; 155 N. Y. 180.

[5] Phœnix, etc. *v.* Hart, 1894, 144 Ill. 513; 36 N. E. 990; New Jersey, etc. *v.* Commercial, etc., 1900, 46 Atl. 777; 49 Atl. 157; 64 N. J. Law, 51; 580.

ALTERATION OF POLICY BY PAROL EVIDENCE. Sometimes the courts find themselves compelled to decide in favor of the companies. They may regard the plaintiff's claim as meritorious, and may be anxious to discover legal ground upon which to maintain the action, but they succumb to the rule that parol evidence cannot alter a written contract. For example, Mr. Justice Shiras, in the United States Supreme Court, said:

> The only way to avoid the defence and escape from the operation of the condition, is to hold that it is not competent for fire insurance companies to protect themselves by conditions of the kind contained in this policy. . . . This case is an illustration of the confusion and uncertainty which would be occasioned by permitting the introduction of parol evidence to modify written contracts.[1]

And in a New Jersey action, the court said that consideration of the case had

> excluded the faintest idea that upon legal principles this case can be successfully carried through.
>
> Nor do I think, if this court should sustain the present action, that it would be practicable to preserve, in any useful form, the great primary rule that written instruments are not to be varied or contradicted by parol evidence.[2]

CRITICISM. This last case is specially noteworthy because of its recognition of the justice of the classes of claims under consideration and its frank avowal of inability to find legal ground upon which to make the companies pay. Indeed, apart from cases of mutual mistake in the wording of the policy (that it misrepresented the real agreement between the parties — very seldom capable of proof), the courts supply us with no such ground. It is clear that the rule as to parol evidence is good and ought to be adhered to. Fraud,

[1] Northern, etc. *v.* Grand View, etc., 1901, 183 U. S. 308; 101 Fed. 27.
[2] Dewees *v.* Manhattan, etc., 1872, 6 Vroom (N. J.), 366.

if proved, might enable the policy-holder to rescind the contract and recover the premium, but would entitle him to no greater relief. Estoppel as against a term of a contract, because of something known at the time of its execution to both parties, cannot be supported. " Waiver of the forfeiture " is out of the question, for there has been no forfeiture. What then?

ELECTION. There is not the least reason for amending, or " waiving," or disregarding the terms of the policy. All that is necessary is that it should be properly construed. Giving the word " void " its accepted meaning — voidable at the election of the company — the situation is this: The company delivered a policy knowing of a contemporaneous breach of it; the company was therefore entitled to rescind it the next moment; instead of rescinding and asking its immediate redelivery, the company permitted the assured to carry it away, and put the premium in its cash box intending to keep it there. That conduct was evidence of election to continue the obligation.

Current law declares that under such circumstances the voidance clause in the policy must, in some way, be got rid of: Enforcement of it would be " to attempt a fraud." " The insurer is estopped to plead it." The insurer must be held to have " waived " it. Its insertion in the policy was due to mistake. A proper sense of justice forbids its assertion. Parol evidence will be admitted (so sometimes, in effect, held) to contradict it. Better advised and construing the clause correctly, the policy-holder depends upon none of these suggestions; he is content that the clause shall remain unaffected and unqualified; and, confidently, he asks the court to decide whether the company elected to continue the policy or to terminate it.

The onus of proof, moreover, is on the company. If he allege election to terminate, he must prove the fact. And to discharge the onus, the company must ask the court to believe that it prepared the policy, and sealed it, and delivered it, in order to end it. One would assume that it was delivered with the intention of its becoming a real obligation. The company must prove the contrary. The question is not one of fraud, or estoppel, or waiver, or mistake, but this merely: Do the company's actions prior to, at the time of, and subsequent to, the delivery of the policy, indicate an intention to elect to continue or to rescind the contract?

ANALOGY TO CASES ALREADY CONSIDERED. If, as is anticipated, readers accept the view that, when a breach occurs at a time subsequent to the issue of the policy, the company must, within a reasonable time, elect to terminate the policy (if that is what it desires), there can be little difficulty in applying the same rule to cases in which the breach is contemporaneous with the issue of the policy, and the knowledge subsequent. And to cases, also, in which the breach and the knowledge both date from the issue of the policy, or prior thereto.

THE VOIDANCE CLAUSE. Observe, too, that if the voidance clause of the policy do not apply to the case, or if there be no voidance clause, the insurer is in still worse case, for his only plea would be that he had been deceived, whereas, in the case we have in hand, he is assumed to have had knowledge of the facts. If he had knowledge, he must depend upon the voidance clause of the policy; that clause provides for election in case of breach; in order to escape, he must establish election to cancel; and election he cannot prove, for he did not elect.

NORTHERN, ETC. V. GRAND VIEW, ETC. What has been said is not in conflict with the ground of the decision of the United States Supreme Court in the very elaborately considered case of Northern, etc. *v.* Grand View, etc.[1] The

[1] 1901, 183 U. S. 308; 101 Fed. 27.

policy provided that it should be void if other insurance existed at its date; other insurance did exist; the agent of the company was aware of the fact; but the company was not. The court declared

> that parol contemporaneous evidence is inadmissible to contradict or vary the terms of a valid written instrument unless in cases where the contracts are vitiated by fraud or mutual mistake.

That is indisputable. But some of the *dicta* in the opinion cannot, for the reasons above mentioned, be agreed to:

> Accordingly it is a necessary conclusion that, by reason of the breach of the condition, the policy became void and of no effect, and no recovery could be had thereon by the insured unless the company waived the condition.

But it did not become void, for there had been no election to cancel it. And if it did become void (terminated) how could it be restored to contract status by the unilateral act of the company?

2. No Knowledge When Policy Issued

Distinction. Cases in which a breach existing at the date of the policy was unknown to the company differ, in one respect, from those in which the company was aware of the breach. In both cases the company, if it desire to terminate the policy, must so elect within a reasonable time after becoming aware of the existence of the fact enabling it to elect. But in the one case, the company may base its right to elect upon two grounds, while in the other it has only one. If the company have no knowledge of the breach until after issue of the policy, it may (usually) assert a right to cancel (1) because of the clause in the contract, and (2) because of the common law right to rescind a contract induced by misrepresentation. If, on the other hand, the company, when it issues the policy, have knowledge of the breach, the common law power is not available, and the company, for its right to rescind, must rely solely upon the terms of the contract.

3. Knowledge When Policy Issued, But None at Date of Preliminary Receipt

Morrison v. Universal, etc.[1] In the application for insurance, a material fact was concealed; the company issued an insurance "slip" (sometimes called an interim receipt), assuming liability; the company, almost immediately afterwards, became aware of the concealment; but, nevertheless, it subsequently issued a policy. The question appears to be a simple one of election — issue of the policy, after knowledge of the facts, was strong evidence of election to continue the obligation. But evidence of a custom to hand out policies, irrespective of intermediate happenings, was thought by the jury to outweigh the prima-facie view, and they declared against election to continue. The judges in the Court of Exchequer decided, but upon different grounds, that the company was liable. Martin, B., held that the company was estopped because, by handing out the policy, it had led the insured to suppose that it was delivered to him as a binding contract. Bramwell, B., thought that the company was liable upon the ground that, when knowledge of the concealment came to the company,

> It then became not only their right but, I think, also their duty to say, within a reasonable time, either "We find that there has been a material concealment, and we elect to avoid the policy and to return the premium;" or "We will retain the premium, and elect to go on with an insurance which is not at present enforceable against us."

[1] 1872, L. R. 8 Ex. 40; 197.

And Cleasby, B., dissented, saying:

> I agree that a man may, by words or conduct, elect to waive an objection which entitles him to avoid a contract;

but held that there was no evidence of election. In the Exchequer Chamber, the judgment was reversed on the ground that the proved custom deprived the delivery of the policy of any significance. But to this the reply is that the time at which the policy was delivered was the time at which the election should have been made, and that lapse of the time within which to make election either (1) is evidence of an election to continue, or (2) puts an end to the right to elect.[1]

[1] *Ante*, p. 105.

CHAPTER XI

INSURANCE

NON-PAYMENT OF PREMIUMS

FORFEITURE AND " WAIVER." Provisions in policies declare that they shall be " void " if recurring premiums are not promptly paid; the courts declare that parties to such contracts may agree as they please; that such provisions are perfectly valid; that non-payment works a forfeiture of the policy; and that forfeiture may be " waived."

> More liberal views have obtained on this subject in recent years, and an insurance policy now often provides express modes of avoiding the odious result of forfeiture. The law, however, has not been changed, and if a forfeiture is provided for in case of non-payment at the day, the courts cannot grant relief against it. The insurer may waive it, or may by his conduct lose his right to enforce it; but that is all.[1]

Here, as elsewhere, the courts proceed upon the assumption that non-observance of some requirement of the policy has

[1] Thompson *v.* Ins. Co., 1881, 104, U. S. 258. To same effect, New York, etc. *v.* Statham, 1876, 93 U. S. 24; Schmertz *v.* U. S., etc., 1902, 55 C. C. A. 104; 118 Fed. 255; Northern, etc. *v.* Stout, 1911, 117 Pac. 621.

the effect of forfeiting it — has terminated it, and that it can be revived by some act of "waiver."

FORFEITURE, "WAIVER," ELECTION, AND CONTRACT. Sometimes forfeiture and "waiver" are commingled with election, and even with new contract, in most confused manner:

> The consequence of a default in the payment of the premium is defined in the policy itself. It declares that, if not paid on the days named and in the lifetime of the insured, the policy shall "cease and determine." By this I understand that it is suspended; it ceases to bind the company and to protect the assured, and this without any act or declaration on the part of the former. It does not require a formal forfeiture. This term is often used, and, I think inaccurately in such cases. Nor is the policy void in the general sense of that term. It is voidable at the election of the company, and that election can be exercised without notice to the assured, for the reason that the policy itself is notice that his rights ceased with the non-payment of the premium. As to him it is a dead policy. It is true it may be restored to life, by the subsequent payment of the premium and its acceptance by the company. This, however, is a new contract by which the company agrees in consideration of the premium to continue in force a policy which had previously expired; in other words, it it a new assurance, though under a former policy: Want *v.* Blunt, 12 East, 183. I do not understand it to be contended that, had the assured died between the nineteenth of February and the second of March, there could not have been a recovery of this policy. It seems almost a work of supererogation to cite authorities for so plain a proposition, and I will refer to but few, out of an abundance.[1]

In other words, the effect of election is to suspend the policy although the only power was to elect between continuation and termination; although only suspended, it is, as to one of the parties a dead policy; it became such not by the election of the company but by the non-payment;

[1] Lantz *v.* Vermont, etc., 1891, 139 Pa. 546.

and subsequent payment and acceptance of the premium are the formation of a new contract.

ELECTION. Probably at this stage of the present work, all that need be said is that non-payment of the premium has no effect whatever upon the policy; that it merely gives, to the company, a right to elect whether or not it will continue or terminate the contract; that forfeiture and "waiver" phraseology is inappropriate; that if the company desire to terminate the policy it must so elect within a reasonable time; that if it do not, its inaction is evidence of election to continue; and that if it elect to terminate, the obligation ceases as of the date of the default.

A COURSE OF DEALING

THE DECISIONS. In very many cases, evidence has been given of a course of dealing by which companies have been said to have "waived" prompt payment, or to be estopped from pleading forfeiture, because of failure in strict compliance; and, under certain circumstances, it is held that the company

> will be deemed to have waived the right to claim the forfeiture, or will be estopped from enforcing the same, although the policy expressly provides for forfeiture for non-payment of premiums as stipulated, and even though it is also conditioned that agents cannot waive forfeitures.[1]

The classic quotation is from the Supreme Court of the United States:

> Any agreement, declaration, or course of action, on the part of an insurance company, which leads a party insured honestly to believe that, by conforming thereto, a forfeiture of his policy will not be incurred, followed by due conformity on his part, will and ought to estop the company, though it may be claimed under the

[1] Joyce on Ins., vol. 2, § 1356; quoted in Loftis v. Pacific, etc., 1911, 38 Utah, 532; 114 Pac. 138.

> express letter of the contract. The company is thereby estopped from enforcing the forfeiture.[1]

The same principle has been enunciated in a case in which a lessee had, by the terms of the lease, an option to purchase the demised premises:

> Where a person is entitled to an option, and leads the grantor to believe that he does not intend to exercise it; if the grantor acts on that belief, and is thereby induced to alter his position, the person who formerly held the option will be precluded from subsequently exercising it, and will be held to have waived it: Nova Scotia Steel Co. Limited *v.* Sutherland Steam Shipping Co. Limited (1899), 5 Com. Cas. 106; Re Tyrer & Co. and Hessler & Co. (1901), 84 L. T. 653. In the latter case, Phillimore, J., says: "I think here the charterer did alter his position, and he altered his position upon the faith that the forfeiture would not be enforced, and he was allowed to do so by reason of the delay in giving notice of the forfeiture."[2]

Confusion. Introduction of the idea of forfeiture; confusion of "waiver" with estoppel and contract; and absence of reference to election, preclude true appreciation of the points involved. As there has been no forfeiture, there can be no "waiver"; but, under varying circumstances,

[1] Ins. Co. *v.* Eggleston, 1877, 96 U. S. 572. And see Wing *v.* Harvey, 1854, 5 DeG. M. & G. 265; Buckbee *v.* United States, etc., 1854, 18 Barb. 541; Chicago, etc. *v.* Warner, 1875, 80 Ill. 410; Ins. Co. *v.* Wolff, 1877, 95 U. S. 326; Thompson *v.* Ins. Co., 1881, 104 U. S. 252; Tattersall *v.* People's, etc., 1904, 9 Ont. L. R. 611; Redmond *v.* Canadian, etc., 1891, 18 Ont. App. 335; Phœnix *v.* Boster, 1882, 106 U. S. 35; Tripp *v.* Vermont, etc., 1882, 55 Vt. 100; James *v.* Mutual, etc., 1898, 148 Mo. 1; 49 S. W. 978; Supreme, etc., *v.* Hall 1900, 24 Ind. App. 316; 56 N. E. 781; Schmertz *v.* U. S., etc., 1902, 55 C. C. A. 104; 118 Fed. 250; Illinois, etc. *v.* Wells, 1902, 200 Ill. 445; 65 N. E. 1072; Farmer's, etc. *v.* Kinney, 1903, 101 Va. 236; 43 S. E. 339; Neal *v.* Gray, 1905, 124 Ga. 510; 52 S. E. 622; Lord *v.* Des Moines, etc., 1911, 99 Ark. 476; 138 S. W. 1008; Workingmen's, etc. *v.* Leverton, 1912, 178 Ind. 151; 98 N. E. 871; Fenn *v.* Northwestern, etc., 1913, 90 Kan. 34; 133 Pac. 159; Edmiston *v.* The Homesteaders, etc., 1914, 93 Kan. 485; 144 Pac. 826; Head Camp, etc. *v.* Bohanna, 1915, 151 Pac. 428.

[2] Matthewson *v.* Burns, 1913, 30 Ont. L. R., p. 198. The court, probably, did not observe that the judgment of Phillimore, J., had been reversed (86 L. T. 697). His view of the law, however, was not affected.

the insurer may be liable, notwithstanding failure in prompt payment, upon the ground of contract, estoppel, or election.

CLASSIFICATION. There are two classes of cases: (1) those in which a general course of dealing with reference to all policy-holders is alleged; and (2) those in which a course of dealing with reference to the particular policy-holder is asserted.

GENERAL CUSTOM. In the first class of cases, the defaulter's difficulty is that the contract has to be modified by parol evidence. The policy fixes a specific date, and the evidence is said to supply a different date. That, indeed, might not be insuperable, for contracts sometimes are modified in that way. The due-date of promisory notes, for example, was originally postponed by evidence of custom, and is now deferred by the undisputed existence of the custom. That is, however, a general custom; and the cases do not sanction the application of the idea to the methods of any particular individual or company. Efforts to prove the existence of a general custom have so far failed — because there is none.

PARTICULAR CUSTOM. The assertion that a course of dealing between insurer and insured — between two particular persons — may sufficiently establish a modification of the contract by new agreement rests upon better foundation; and sometimes that ground, rather than estoppel, ought to be the *ratio decidendi*. "An agreement, declaration, or course of action" by the company, "followed by due conformity" by the insured [1] looks like contract rather than estoppel. The subject is fully discussed in the chapter on Contract.[2]

ESTOPPEL. Estoppel may arise in cases in which, the evidence being insufficient to prove a new contract, the con-

[1] *Ante*, p. 217. And see Royal Guardians, etc. *v.* Clark, 1914, Que. R. 21 K. B. 541; 49 S. C. Can., p. 241.

[2] *Ante*, pp. 124–150.

duct of the insurer has been such as was "calculated to inspire confidence and throw him off his guard." And there appears to be no difference in principle between cases in which such conduct has led the assured to delay delivery of his proofs of loss, and those in which he has been lulled into security with reference to payment of his premiums. The former point is discussed in a subsequent chapter,[1] and reference may be made to the present writer's book on Estoppel.[2]

ELECTION. The company's right of election to continue or to terminate the policy arises upon the happening of every default; and the fact that the company has, on many occasions, elected to continue its liability can have no effect upon its right to make contrary election upon a subsequent default. A landlord may accept rent a score of times after the due-dates, and thus repeatedly elect to continue the lease, but upon the next occasion he may elect to terminate. Indeed, what has to be shown by the policy-holder, or by the tenant, is that, for some reason, the right of election cannot be exercised. He is not in a position to demand that there should be election to continue. The best he can hope for is that there shall be no election to terminate.

The insurer may elect to terminate the policy, but he must do so within a reasonable time. If he do not, then (1) either his right ceases, or (2) he has supplied evidence of election to continue his liability.[3] And in considering the question of reasonable time, a previous course of dealing may have a very important effect. For it may be thought to indicate the existence of a general system of continuing policies, notwithstanding defaults, and thus throw more heavily upon the company the onus of proving that it intended to make an exception in the case in hand. Even a short lapse of time might be held sufficient to evidence the company's intention to deal with the default according to its usual method.

[1] *Post*, p. 220. [2] Pp. 40; 105, 106; 133–136. [3] *Ante*, p. 115.

CUSTOM TO GIVE NOTICE. Sometimes it is said that a custom to give notice of the approach of the date for payment may afford foundation for " waiver," and sometimes for estoppel. In an Indiana case, both are asserted:

> But as forfeitures are not favored, appellants' custom of giving notice of the time regular assessments are due was a waiver of the right of forfeiture for non-payment without the giving of such notice . . . .
>
> Nor should a forfeiture be permitted, where, during a long term of years — here the full term of membership — it has been the uniform policy of the society to give notice. Its own acts should estop it.[1]

Estoppel, upon the ground that the conduct of the insurer was such as is " calculated to inspire confidence and throw him (the insured) off his guard," is an available ground of decision.

CUSTOM TO COLLECT PREMIUMS. A custom to send for premiums has been held to prevent forfeiture when the custom was omitted, upon the ground that the

> beneficiary was justified in believing that the insurer would not insist on a forfeiture when its agents failed to appear to receive the money at the proper time, on the first day of the month.[2]

In a recent case in the Canadian Supreme Court, the following dictum of a French author was approved:

> " La résiliation ou la suppression de l'assurance n'ont lieu qu'au cas ou la prime arrièrée était portable, c'est à dire qu'elle devait être payée par l'assuré au domicile de l'assureur ou de ses agents. D'ordinaire les compagnies stipulent que les primes seront portable, mais comme elles ont l'habitude de faire encaisser les primes à domicile par les agents, pour être plus sûres de leur rentrées, la jurisprudence décide que cette circonstance change la nature de la prime qui, de portable qu'elle était d'apres la

[1] Supreme, etc. *v.* Grove, 1911, 176 Ind. 356; 96 N. E. 159. A number of supporting authorities are quoted.

[2] Boutin *v.* National, etc., 1915, 86 Wash. 372; 150 Pac. 449.

police, devient quérable (tres nombreux arrêts depuis cinquante ans: Cass. 21 août, 1854; D. 54.1.366; S. V. 54.1.359; Cass. 31 janvier, 1872; D. 73.1.86.; S. V. 75. 1. 113).

Cette jurisprudence à été pendant longtemps très énergiquement conbattue par les compagnies; elle n'est plus discutée aujourd'hui. Vide Laurent, vol. 16, No. 182, page 245; Fuzier-Herman, vo. Assurance, Nos. 697, *et seq.*"[1]

[1] Royal Guardians, etc. *v.* Clark, 1914, 49 S. C. Can. 229. The quotation may be translated as follows:

" The rescission or termination of the insurance takes place only when the overdue premium is *portable*, that is to say that it is to be paid by the insured at the domicile of the insurer or of his agents. Ordinarily, the companies stipulate that the premiums are to be *portable*, but as they customarily collect the premiums through their agents at the domicile of the insured, to be more sure of receiving them, jurisprudence decides that that circumstance changes the nature of the premium, which, from being *portable* according to the policy, becomes *quérable* (many decisions during the last fifty years . . .). That jurisprudence was for a long time very energetically combatted by the companies. To-day it is no more discussed."

The word *quérable* means that the premiums are sent for by the companies, instead of being brought to them by the persons insured.

CHAPTER XII

INSURANCE

Demanding, Accepting, or Retaining Premiums

DEMANDING OR ACCEPTING PREMIUMS

FORFEITURE AND "WAIVER." Almost all of the many cases on this subject proceed upon ideas of forfeiture, and "waiver" or estoppel — by default in payment of a premium, the policy has been forfeited; the company is not liable unless the insured can establish "waiver" or estoppel; and the insured endeavors to discharge that *onus* by proving that, after the default, the company demanded or accepted a premium. Premising (or rather reaffirming) that in such cases there is no forfeiture and no "waiver," but only a right of election by the company to continue or to terminate the policy as it pleases, and that we must regard demand or acceptance of premiums as evidence of election to continue the policy, let us endeavor, in some measure, to systematize the subject.

CURRENT PHRASEOLOGY. The following are fair examples of declarations as to the effect of acceptance by a company of insurance premiums:

> If, after the policy has been forfeited by non-observance of a condition annexed to it, the insurers, or their agent, continue to receive the premiums with full knowledge of the breach of the condition, they will be deemed to have waived the forfeiture, and will not afterwards be permitted to avoid the policy.[1]

> . . . they could not afterwards set up its forfeiture. It would be an estoppel, which is the true ground upon which the doctrine of waiver in such cases rests.[2]

ELECTION. Here, as elsewhere, election is seldom mentioned. Fortuitously, it may be referred to, but, even then, usually in mistaken conjunction with estoppel, forfeiture or "waiver." Venturing to correct current phraseology, the

[1] Addison on Contracts, 11th ed. pp. 1231, 2. To the same effect, Frasier *v.* New Zealand, etc., 1901, 64 Pac. 814; 39 Or. 342.

[2] Elliott *v.* Lycoming, etc., 1870, 66 Pa. St. 22, 26. And see Masonic, etc. *v.* Robinson, 1913, 156 Ky. 371; 160 S. W. 1078; Ferguson *v.* Massachusetts, etc., 1884, 32 Hun. 306; 102 N. Y. 647; Carroll *v.* Charter, etc., 1862, 38 Barb. 402.

present writer suggests that we ought to say that there is, in such cases, neither forfeiture, nor estoppel. Non-payment of the premium gives the company a right to elect whether to terminate or to continue its liability — that is all. The following is approximately correct:

> . . . but, although having the right to treat it as forfeited, if the insurer does not do so, but demands payment thereafter of the assured of the premiums, it elects to treat the policy as a living valid obligation, and when he has elected to do so, he cannot thereafter change the election when it becomes to his interest to regard the policy as forfeited.[1]

CONFUSION. The word *forfeited*, in that particular sentence is harmless, but its use leads to " waiver " and estoppel as in the following:

> By recourse to the foregoing propositions, we have here a situation where appellant, with knowledge of the existence of facts and circumstances constituting a breach of warranty, as indicated, failed to elect to declare the contract of insurance void, or to forfeit all rights of the insured and beneficiary thereunder, but on the contrary, with knowledge aforesaid, collected and retained assessments for about 16 months. Under such circumstances it must be held that appellant at the decease of the insured had waived said breaches of warranty, and was estopped to assert the invalidity of the contract of insurance.[2]

> Waiver by acceptance of the premium is not based upon contract, but on estoppel of the company to insist on conditions of the policy inconsistent with the acceptance or retention of the premium.[3]

A STATED RULE. Using the word " waives " in the least objectionable way, an Oregon court stated the current rule in this way:

> The rule is well settled that if an insurer voluntarily accepts, or compulsorily collects, a premium after knowledge of a breach of a condition in its policy which annuls it upon election, or retains

[1] National Council, etc. *v.* Thomas, 1915, 173 S. W., 813; 163 Ky., 364.

[2] Sovereign Camp, etc. *v.* Latham, 59 Ind. App. 290; 1915, 107 N. E., 749.

[3] Simmons *v.* Modern Woodmen, etc., 1915, 172 S. W., 492; 185 Mo. App., 483.

> an unearned premium after such knowledge . . . it thereby waives the right to invoke the breach as a defense to an action by the insured on the policy to recover the indemnity provided for by the contract of insurance.[1]

DISTINCTIONS. Thus stated, the rule is much too wide for 1. Premiums which fell due prior to a breach may be demanded and accepted after the breach, without prejudicing the company's right to cancel the policy.

2. The company may, under certain circumstances, be entitled both (1) to receive premiums which fall due after the breach, and (2) to deny liability because of the breach; and, in such cases, acceptance of the money would have no effect upon the company's liability. Whether the company be so entitled depends, of course, upon the terms of the policy, but the distinction is important, and the following warning is somewhat necessary:

> Confusion with resulting injustice in cases of this sort will occur from want of appreciation of the distinction between acceptance by the insurer of money from the assured to continue the policy which he might decline to pay at his pleasure and suffer only the penalty of forfeiture, and acceptance or collection of money from the assured on account of an absolute liability created and persistent until discharged, regardless of any forfeiture after such liability became fixed. In the former situation acceptance of money would be inconsistent with insisting upon the forfeiture, in the latter it would not.[2]

[1] Frasier *v.* New Zealand, etc., 1901, 39 Or. 350; 64 Pac. 816. And see Wing *v.* Harvey, 1854, 5 DeG. M. & G. 265; Hemings *v.* Sceptre, etc., 1905, 1 Ch. 365; Lyons *v.* The Globe, etc., 1877, 27 U. C., C. P. 567; Erdmann *v.* Mutual, etc., 1878, 44 Wis. 376; Shafer *v.* Phœnix, etc., 1881, 53 Wis. 665; 10 N. W. 381; Schimp *v.* Cedar Rapids, etc., 1888, 124 Ill. 354; 16 N. E. 229; Continental, etc. *v.* Chew, 1894, 11 Ind. App. 330; 38 N. E. 417; Milkman *v.* United, etc., 1897, 20 R. I. 10; 36 Atl. 1121; Moreland *v.* Union, etc., 1898, 46 S. W. 516; Morrow *v.* Lancashire, etc., 1898, 29 Ont. 377; Sun, etc. *v.* Phillips, 1902, 70 S. W. 603; Manning *v.* Connecticut, etc., 1913, 176 Mo. App. 678; 159 S. W. 750; Fidelity, etc. *v.* Goza, 1913, 13 Ga. App. 20; 78 S. E. 735; Melick *v.* Metropolitan, 1913, 84 N. J. Law 437; 87 Atl. 75. There are some contrary statements, e. g. McGeachie *v.* North Am., etc., 1892, 22 Ont. 150; 20 Ont. App. 187; 23 Can. S. C. 148.

[2] Bennett *v.* Beavins, etc., 1914, 150 N. W. 181; 159 Wis. 145.

PREMIUMS DUE PRIOR TO BREACH. The first of these assertions is sufficiently supported by analogous cases in the law of landlord and tenant. Rent which fell due prior to a breach of covenant may be demanded and received, and the landlord may also terminate the lease. For his acceptance of the rent is an affirmance of the existence of the tenancy only down to the day upon which it fell due; and the breach occurred subsequently.[1]

PREMIUMS DUE AFTER BREACH. Secondly, it is not true that demand or acceptance of a premium which fell due after the breach, always " waives " the forfeiture; for there are many cases in which, by the terms of the policy, the company is entitled both to receive the premium and to deny liability.[2] Cases occur in which the premium has been accepted on condition that the insured is in good health, and that there is to be no " waiver " unless that be the fact;[3] or on condition that the insurer will furnish proof of the truth of certain representations;[4] or for the purpose of reinstatement of the insured;[5] or for the " revival " of the policy from the date of receipt of the money;[6] or for the purpose of keeping the policy alive while the insured is engaged in a prohibited occupation;[7] or the policy may have provided that although it is to be void, yet that the whole premium shall be payable.[8]

SUSPENSORY CLAUSES IN POLICIES. One class of cases, in which the insurer may be entitled to a premium without being under corresponding liability, and in which, therefore,

[1] The subject is treated in the chapter on Landlord and Tenant; *ante*, pp. 152–186.

[2] United States, etc. *v.* Smith, 1899, 34 C. C. A. 506.

[3] New York, etc. *v.* Scott, 1900, 23 Tex. C. A. 541; 57 S. W. 677; Mutual, etc. *v.* Lovenberg, 24 Tex. C. A. 355; 59 S. W. 314.

[4] McQuillan *v.* Mutual, etc., 1902, 112 Wis. 665; 87 N. W. 1069.

[5] Continental *v.* Peden, 1913, 145 Ky. 775; 141 S. W. 43; Société, etc. *v.* Moisan, 1898, Que. Rep. 7 Q. B. 128; Royal, etc. *v.* Clark, 1914, 49 S. C. 229, per Duff, J.

[6] Dale *v.* Continental, etc., 1895, 95 Tenn. 38; 31 S. W. 266.

[7] Northwestern, etc. *v.* American, 1887, 119 Ill. 329; 10 N. E. 255.

[8] As in Anchor, etc. *v.* Corbett, 1882, 9 Can. S. C. 73.

he may accept a premium without prejudicing his position, deserves special treatment. Policies sometimes provide, not for their termination upon default in payment of a premium, but for suspension of the obligation of the company during default, and reservation of the right of the company, nevertheless, to the whole premium. In such cases questions arise as to whether by accepting the whole premium, the insurer has "waived" the suspensory clause and become liable for a loss happening during the suspensory period.

If the policies had provided for a reduction in the amount of the premium, corresponding to the duration of the suspended liability, the courts would probably have been favorably influenced by their reasonableness. Without such reduction, the courts appear to be inclined, with the help of "waiver" and estoppel, to make the liability coterminous with the premium — to say that the premium does not run during suspension of liability, and that if the insurer receive the whole premium, he receives it in respect of a corresponding obligation; in other words, that receipt of the whole premium means liability during the whole period.

JOLIFFE *v.* MADISON, ETC.[1] A policy provided that

> when a note is taken for the cash premium, if it is not paid within sixty days after due, all obligations of the company to the insured, until such note is paid, are suspended.

A note was taken; during default a loss happened; after the loss, the company accepted full payment of the note; and it was held liable for the loss. The reasoning is this: The policy did not contain any provision declaring (as sometimes) that upon default, the whole premium shall be considered to have been earned;[2] during suspension of liability, no premium is being earned; the company, therefore, would be entitled to the whole premium only upon the basis of liability

[1] 1875, 39 Wis. 111.

[2] Such a clause would have altered the result: Williams *v.* Albany, etc., 1870, 19 Mich. 451.

for the whole period; the insured paid, and the company received, the whole premium; and, therefore, liability for the loss. The court said:

> But the defendant received the whole cash premium for which the note was given. By so doing, it received compensation for the note covering the time when the loss occurred; and we think that it cannot now be heard to allege that, at the time of the loss, it had no risk on the property insured.

PHŒNIX, ETC. *v.* TOMLINSON.[1] A policy provided that

> this policy shall cease to be in force, and remain null and void, during the time said note remains unpaid after its maturity, and no legal action on the part of this company to enforce payment shall be construed as reviving the policy. The payment of the premium, however, revives the policy and makes it good for the balance of the term.

A note was taken for a premium covering a period of five years; before loss, judgment upon the note was recovered; and after loss, the company received payment in full — only seventeen months of the period having expired. There was no specific declaration in the policy that, upon default, the company should be entitled to the whole premium. But the clause appears sufficiently to provide that liability shall be suspended during default, and that only by payment in full should liability be restored. Nevertheless, judgment was given against the company. The court fixed upon the words " reviving " and " revives." It said that the payment might have been accepted, either (1) as a waiver of the clause, or (2) for the purpose of reviving the policy; that it

> cannot be justly affirmed that the parties meant to revive a policy in a case where, as here, the act which revived it was performed after the loss occurred;[2]

and that there was, therefore,

[1] 1890, 125 Ind. 84. And see New Zealand, etc. *v.* Maaz, 1899, 13 Col. App. 493; 59 Pac. 213.

[2] As the loss was only partial, the revival might have applied to the undestroyed goods.

> a waiver of the right to declare a forfeiture of the policy. . . . In such a case there is no interregnum in which there was a lifeless policy.

The company lost that case because of the stupidity of the phraseology of its policy. Provision for a contract becoming "null and void," and afterwards undergoing revivification, misled the court. The company had meant to say (1) that its liability (not *that the contract*) should be suspended during default; (2) that payment in full should not affect that suspension; and (3) that upon payment in full, liability should recommence.

JOHNSTON *v.* PHELPS.[1] In another case, the policy was as follows:

> If the member who holds this policy fails to pay any assessment . . . this policy shall become null and void; but if he, afterward, pay the amount due from him, this policy shall be holding from the date of the receipt of said amount then due. The company, however, will not be held liable during the time that this policy was made void by such delinquency.

That appears to be fairly clear; and yet, as the company had received payment of some subsequent assessments, it was held liable for a loss which happened during default. The court agreed that if the loss had not been total — if there had remained some property to which liability might have re-attached — acceptance of the money could have been referred to a revival of the policy, but held that, that being impossible, the only other interpretation which could be placed upon the act was that it was a "waiver" of the forfeiture. With deference, that cannot be right. Receipt of the money may have been evidence of an agreement to modify the policy. If it fell short of that, the clause remained, and was (it is submitted) conclusive.

WALLS *v.* THE HOME, ETC.[2] A policy provided that:

[1] 1901, 63 Neb. 21; 88 N. W. 142.

[2] 1903, 114 Ky. 611; 71 S. W. 650. See Dale *v.* Continental, etc., 1895, 95 Tenn. 38; 31 S. W. 266; Home, etc. *v.* Karn, 1897, 19 Ky. 273; 39 S. W. 501.

The company shall not be liable for loss during such default, and the said policy shall lapse until payment is made. . . . The company may collect . . . any past due notes . . . and a receipt from the Chicago office . . . must be received by the assured before there can be any revival of the policy; such revival to begin from the time of such payment.

The intention is clear enough, but the phraseology is a bungle; and the company was held to be liable for a loss because, during default in payment of a premium-note, it had demanded payment of the installments which would have covered the date of the subsequent loss. The court said that if the policy had really "lapsed," the whole amount of the premium could not have been due, and that, by demanding the whole amount, the company had waived the condition for suspension of liability. The question was really one of the construction of the contract, and for its ambiguity the company deserved to lose.

WILLIAMS *v.* ALBANY, ETC. Consideration of the subject will be aided by perusal of some good analysis (notwithstanding "waiver" blemishes) in Williams *v.* Albany, etc.[1]

DEMAND AND NO PAYMENT. While there is general agreement that acceptance of a premium is, under certain circumstances, a "waiver of the forfeiture" (really an election to continue the policy), it is sometimes said that a demand, not followed by payment, has no such effect.

> We have found no case which goes to the extent of holding that merely a demand of the overdue premium, without its payment, is sufficient to reinstate a policy which is forfeited.[2]

But the court was misled by its idea that the policy had been forfeited — had come to an end — and that its reinstatment was a necessary prerequisite of liability. If the

[1] 1870, 19 Mich. 451.

[2] Cohen *v.* Continental, etc., 1887, 67 Tex. 325; 3 S. W. 296. A like opinion has been expressed with reference to a mere demand by a landlord, after breach of some covenant, for payment of rent: Cole on Eject. 409. See *ante*, pp. 168, 169.

policy really had terminated, no doubt a demand would not re-establish it; and one is rather surprised that, arguing from forfeiture, the courts do not always so declare.

If it be urged that the company is not treated fairly by holding that demand without payment is an election to continue liability — for, in that case, liability remains without corresponding compensation — the answer is that the company may do as it likes; it may continue or terminate its liability — it cannot do both; and a demand for payment can be made only upon the basis of continuation. The company, moreover, is not without remedy if default continue longer than it wishes; for, although the company cannot change its election, it is entitled to treat refusal to pay as a repudiation of the contract, and, upon that ground, to terminate it.[1] In other words, election under the provisions of the policy has been exercised; the election is irreversible; and the policy is to continue; but upon the same terms as other contracts, namely, that if one party refuse to perform his part of it, the other may cancel.

Retention of Premium

If, when a breach of condition occurs, the company has, in its possession, money paid as a premium for an unexpired period, what effect has retention of the money upon an allegation of election by the company to terminate the contract? The terms of the policy may answer the question; express language may provide one way or the other; but, that apart, what shall we say?

Three Points Involved. The answer to the question involves three points:

1. Upon the premature termination of the policy, who is entitled to that part of the premium applicable to the unexpired period — the insurer or the insured?

[1] Edge *v.* Duke, 1849, 18 L. J. (N. S.) Ch. 183. The language of the judgment is unscientific, but, probably, the above is its proper translation.

2. Is there, indeed, any part of the premium so applicable? In other words, is the premium divisible?

3. If the premium be divisible, and if the insured be entitled to that part of it applicable to the unexpired period, can the insurer terminate the policy without returning or offering to return that part?

1. WHO ENTITLED? Were we to say (as is customary) that, by his breach of the condition, the assured had "forfeited" his policy — that he had brought to premature conclusion, a policy which, but for his act, would have further continued — we should be of opinion that the assured could have no right to a return of any part of the premium which he had paid; and that if he had given a note for that premium, he would have to pay it. We should say that although he had wrongfully cancelled his policy, he could not cancel his note. We should say that

> As a result of the forfeiture, the entire premium is treated as earned, and the collection does not constitute a waiver.[1]
>
> If the risk attached, and the policy became void subsequently, through the conduct of the assured, no part of the premium can be recovered.[2]
>
> If the company had taken advantage of the forfeiture, there was no unearned premium which the plaintiff was entitled to.[3]
>
> But Penner's violation of his insurance contract did not invest him with a right of action against the Home Company to recover the premium which he had paid the company therefor, or any part of that premium.[4]

FORFEITURE AND "WAIVER." Argument from forfeiture and "waiver" seems inevitably to lead to the conclusion that the company is entitled to retain the full premium, and to collect any part of it that remains unpaid: The insured has, by his wrongful act, terminated the policy; he has lost

[1] German, etc. v. Emporia, etc., 1900, 9 Kan. App. 803; 59 Pac. 1092.
[2] U. S. Ins. Co. v. Smith, 1899, 34 C. C. A. 506; 92 Fed. 503.
[3] Home, etc. v. Kuhlman, 1899, 58 Neb. 493; 78 N. W. 936.
[4] Farmer's, etc. v. Home, etc., 1898, 54 Neb. 742; 74 N. W. 1101.

all rights in respect of it; his wrongful act cannot give him a claim to the return of money which he voluntarily paid to the company, and which the company rightfully received; nor can it form any defence to an action for payment of his obligations. This also appears to be clear: that if the insured is not entitled to the money, the company does not "waive" anything by keeping it.

Election. Dropping forfeiture (for there was none); observing that the assured did not (for he could not) cancel the policy; and turning to election, we say that the assured was at liberty to commit the breach, if he wanted to; if he did, the company could (although he could not) shorten the insurance period, if it wanted to; it did shorten the period; and having prematurely terminated its liability, the question is, Upon what ground can it claim to retain the amount paid for the full period? The cases supply no answer to that apparently simple question — indeed, none of them so state it. Some judges, nevertheless, while using the language of forfeiture and "waiver," reach the conclusion which reasoning from election supplies, namely, that if the insurer exercise the power given to him by the policy to terminate, prematurely, his liability, he cannot retain the part of the premium applicable to the unexpired part of the agreed period of his liability — in the absence, of course, of agreement to that effect.

Rescission and Termination. We must distinguish between rescission *ab initio* and termination of a contract. Take an example of each and then apply them to an insurance policy: A contract for sale of land provides for payment by installments; and that, upon default, the vendor may cancel the contract; default is made; the election to cancel is exercised; the vendor cannot sue for any of the future installments; and he must return those already paid. The law is succinctly stated as follows:

> As any party rescinding the contract for another's breach is entitled to be restored to his former position, so, it is conceived, he is in general bound to return to the other any property or profit which he himself received under the partial execution of the agreement. It is thought that in every case in which a party to a contract lawfully rescinds it, whether for the other party's breach of some stipulation which goes to the root of the whole consideration; for the other's renunciation of the contract; for non-fulfillment of some condition subsequent under an express power to rescind it; or for misrepresentation, duress, or undue influence, the rule is that he shall not enjoy the advantage of rescission without yielding every benefit he has taken by the previous part performance of the contract.[1]

That is a case of rescission. For an example of termination, take the case of a lease: If a lessor, upon breach by the lessee of some covenant, elect to terminate the lease, he cannot sue for any future rent; but he may retain money already received as rent; and he may sue for installments overdue at the date of his election to terminate. The reason is obvious: He retains rent received (although the vendor could not retain installments received) because the tenant has received value for it; and he may sue for overdue rent for the same reason. If some of the money which he had received had been a payment in advance for a period not yet expired, he ought to return a ratable portion of the rent.[2]

Applying the distinction to insurance cases, we say:

1. If the election of the insurer be a rescission of the contract, *ab initio*, he must return the premiums already paid.[3]

2. If the election merely terminate the contract, the insurer may retain the premiums already paid, so far as he has given value for them; he must return moneys for which

[1] Williams on V. & P., 1911, vol. 2, p. 1054.

[2] A question might arise as to the divisibility of rent. In some jurisdictions, statutes provide that rent shall be deemed to arise *de die in diem*.

[3] The effect of the introduction of a fraud-factor is not here considered.

he has given no value; and he is not entitled to any further payments.

2. ARE PREMIUMS DIVISIBLE

> When a contract has been in part performed, no part of the money paid under such contract can be recovered back, unless the consideration is clearly severable.[1]

Apprenticeship, and some other premiums have been held not to be intended to be divided, or to be capable of division.[2] What are we to say of insurance premiums?

FIRE INSURANCE. No difficulty can arise, in fire-insurance cases, as to the divisibility of a premium. Nothing is more usual than its apportionment. Policies which provide for premature termination, at the will of the company, usually. refer to the well-known practice.[3]

LIFE INSURANCE. There is much reasonableness in the French view as to the divisibility of life insurance premiums.[4]

> La prime étant le prix de l'assurance, son taux devrait varier chaque année: il tombe sous le sens qu'au fur et à mesure qu'une parsonne vieillit, ses chances de mortalité vont en augmentant. Néanmoins et à juste titre, car dans les dernières années le chiffre aurai pu être excessif, il a paru plus pratique et plus rationnel dene pas tenir compte des différence qui se produisent d'année en année et de rendre la prime uniforme. On reporte sur les premières années une partie de ce qui serait à payer pour les dernières, en prenant la moyenne des chiffres donnés par toutes les primes prévues pour l'assurance vie entière et indiquées par les tables de mortalité. Ce chiffre de la prime uniformisée comprend deux parties: l'une correspond à la prime simple d'assurance pour l'année, l'autre est destinée à parfaire l'insufisance des primes futures, c'est ce qui constitue la *réserve*.[5]

[1] Addison on Contracts, 1911, p. 137.

[2] Whincup *v.* Hughes, 1871, L. R. 6 C. P. 78; Ferns *v.* Carr, 1885, 28 Ch. Div. 409. Addison on Contracts, 1911, p. 137.

[3] Pollock *v.* German, etc., 1901, 127 Mich. 460; 86 N. W. 1017.

[4] The extract, and its accompanying notes are taken from Lefort: *Contrat d'assurance sur la vie*, vol. III, pp. 18, 19.

[5] Couteau: op. cit., T. 11, p. 294.

Quand pour une raison ou pour une autre, l'assuré arrête le contrat, l'assureur a le droit incontestable de conserver la somme représéntant la prime pour chacune des années écoulées, mais il ne peut retenir d'une façon absolue la réserve, puisque cette réserve se rapporte à des années durant lesquelles lui, assureur, ne sera nullement engagé. Quand une personne traite pour une assurance sur la vie avec une compagnie, cette dernière lui ouvre un compte qui comprend deux éléments: la prime simple due chaque année; la somme destinée à parfaire l'insufisance des primes futures. Si l'assuré se retire, il faut liquider cette situation; la compagnie doit rembourser le solde créditeur,[1] mais nullement, quoiqu'il ait pu être soutenu,[2] dans son intégralité: pendant tout le temps qu'a duré le contrat elle à eu a supporter des frais généraux, frais que motivait la participation de l'assuré, et dont il ne saurait s'exonérer en excipant de son départ, la compagnie n'étant pas un mandataire chargé de faire gratuitement les affaires de leur clientéle.[3]

The extract may be translated as follows:

The premium being the price of the insurance, its amount must vary each year: for the reason that in the measure that a person grows old his chances of death are increased. Nevertheless, and rightly so, for in the last years the figure would have to be excessive, it appears to be more practical and more rational not to take into account the differences which are produced from year

[1] C'est là une différence essentielle avec l'assurance contre l'incendie: quand une police de ce genre a été résilliée, l'assuré n'a rien à réclamer pour les primes par lui versées, parceque les primes encaissées sont l'exacte contre-partie du risque couru: V. Dormoy: *Thèorie mathèm. des assur. sur la vie*, T. 11, p. 79. ("There is here an essential difference in fire insurance cases: when a policy of this kind has been rescinded, the assured has nothing to claim, for the premiums are the exact counterpart of the risk run.")

[2] V. Laurent: *Les Compagnies d'assurance sur la vie humaine.* (*La réforme économique*, 1875); de Serbonnes: *Des contrats discontinués.* (Monit. des assur., 1875, p. 429); *La valeur de rachat* (*ibid.*, 1877, p. 87). Cf. Dormoy: *op. cit.*, p. 79; Karup: *Theoretisches Handbuch des Lebens Versicherung.* T. 111, p. 135.

[3] De Courcy: *Précis de l'assurance sur la vie*, p. 289. Ce prélèvement est destiné à couvrir les dépenses générales de l'entreprise et à procurer un bénéfice suffisamment rémunérateur aux capitaux qui y sont engagés. Conf.: *Des entreprises d'assurances sur la vie* (L'Opinion, avril, 1870, p. 55). (This assessment is destined to cover the general expenses of the enterprise, and to procure a sufficiently remunerative return upon the capital engaged in it).

to year and to render the premium uniform. We carry back the part of that which is to be paid in the last years to the first year, and take the mean of the figures given by all the premiums for the entire life insured and indicated by the tables of mortality. The amount of the premium thus made uniform comprises two parts: the one corresponds to the simple premium of insurance for the year; the other is destined to equalize the insufficiency of the future premiums. It is this which constitutes the reserve. When for one reason or another the assured puts an end to the contract, the insurer has the incontestable right to keep the sum representing the premium for each of the years already past, but he cannot retain in absolute fashion the reserve, since this reserve has relation to the years during which the assurer will not be under obligation. When a person agrees for a life insurance with a company, the company opens with him an account which comprises two elements: the simple premium due each year; the sum destined to equalize the insufficiency of the future premiums. If the assured withdraws, it is necessary to liquidate this situation: the company ought to reimburse the amount at the credit of the account; but not in its entirety—although that has been argued. During all the time that the contract was in force the company had to pay its general charges—charges which warranted the participation of the assured and from which he cannot exonerate himself by his withdrawal, the company not being a mandatory charged with transacting gratuitously the affairs of their customers.

Marine Insurance. As to divisibility of marine insurance premiums, Lord Mansfield said

> that if the risk of the contract of indemnity has once commenced, there shall be no apportionment or return of the premium afterwards. For though the premium is estimated, and the risk depends upon the nature and length of the voyage, yet if it has commenced, though if it be only for twenty-four hours or less, the risk is run, the contract is for the whole entire risk, and no part of the consideration shall be returned; and yet it is as easy to apportion for the length of the voyage as it is for the time.[1]

Lord Mansfield, however, admitted an exception to this rule: A marine policy from London to Halifax, with a war-

[1] Tyrie *v.* Fletcher, 1777, Cowp. 668.

ranty by the insured of convoy from Portsmouth to Halifax; one premium for the whole distance; breach of warranty by insured as to convoy; action by insured for return of part of premium, because no insurance between Portsmouth and Halifax; and Lord Mansfield said:

> This is not a contract so entire that there can be no apportionment. For there are two parts in this contract; and the premium may be divided into two distinct parts relative as it were to two voyages. . . . Equity implies a condition that the insurer shall not receive the price of running the risk if he runs none.[1]

EFFECT OF NON-DIVISIBILITY. If we are to hold that a premium which has been received by the insurer is not divisible, and, that, therefore, upon premature termination of the policy, he may retain the whole of it, what are we to say as to the insurer's right to sue for a premium overdue at the time of the premature termination, but covering an unexpired period? Can he sue for the whole amount, while admitting that, for part of it, he has given no consideration?

3. TERMINATION WITHOUT RETURN OF PREMIUM. If we are right in the opinion that upon premature termination of a policy by the election of the insurer, the insured is usually entitled to that part of any premium which has been paid in respect of a future period; and that, for that purpose, the premium is divisible; the next question is what effect has retention of the money upon an allegation of election by the company to terminate the policy?

TWO POINTS. Two points are involved and they must be kept separate:

1. Retention of the money may be evidence upon the question whether or not the company has, as a matter of fact, elected to terminate the policy.

2. Is election to terminate effective, in the absence of a return, or offer to return, the money?

[1] Stevenson v. Snow, 1761, Burr. 1238. The English rule in cases of marine insurance is now prescribed by statute, 6 Ed. VII, c. 41, § 84.

Retention as Evidence of Election. In the first of these cases, we assume that there has been no expressly declared election, and the question to be decided is whether or not retention of the money has any evidentiary value?

Forfeiture and "Waiver." Before replying, let us observe how argument along the lines of forfeiture and "waiver" induces decision in favor of the insurer: By the breach, the insured has forfeited his policy; his wrongful act can give him no claim to the money; the company has done nothing to "waive the forfeiture;" silence and inactivity do not amount to "waiver" for the policy is at an end and the company is merely keeping its own money; therefore retention can have no prejudicial significance.

Election. Application of principles of election leads to contrary conclusion: The breach gave to the insurer a right to elect either to continue or to terminate the policy; if it elected to continue, it would be entitled to retain the money; if it elected to terminate, it ought to return the money;

> The retention of the money was — in morals certainly — inconsistent with an intention to avoid the policy.[1]

and, therefore, retention of the money is some evidence of election to continue. But observe some distinctions: If a company not only retained the unearned premium, but upon request refused to give it up, there would be strong ground for inference of election to keep the money, and, therefore, of election to continue the risk. On the other hand, if the company sent notice of cancellation, intimating that the money had been placed to the credit of the assured, there would be very little appearance of election to continue. In other words, retention of the money may not, of itself, be sufficient proof of election. The surrounding circumstances must be considered.

[1] Schreiber *v.* German-American, etc., 1890, 43 Minn. 367; 45 N. W. 708; Baker *v.* New York, etc., 1896, 77 Fed. 550; 27 C. C. A. 658.

ELECTION EFFECTIVE WITHOUT RETURN. Upon the second question — whether election to terminate is effective unless accompanied by a return, or an offer to return, the money, the decisions are inconclusive; for, not usually employing the phraseology of election, they do not sufficiently deal with the point. Some of the courts hold that the money need not be returned.[1] Others hold that it must, upon the ground that, having failed

> to return the premium, it waived the provision for a forfeiture and became liable for the amount of the policy.[2]

The Indiana courts have repeatedly held not only that the company must return, or offer to return, the money, but, in pleading election to terminate the policy, it must allege one or other of those facts.[3]

With deference, it is submitted that although retention of the money may be some evidence of election to continue the policy, return of it is not an essential element in an election to terminate. On the contrary, election to terminate and obligation to return the money, so far from being parts of one whole, are related to one another as cause and effect. Why is the company under obligation to return the money? Because, by its election, the policy has been terminated. The obligation exists because the election has been made. If the company had not elected to terminate, it would have been entitled to keep the money.

Retention of the money is not an element, therefore, in the essence or requisites of an election to terminate; it is a factor in the proof or disproof of the fact of an election having

[1] Phœnix, etc. *v.* Stevenson, 1879, 78 Ky. 161. Georgia, etc. *v.* Rosenfield, 1899, 37 C. C. A. 102; 95 Fed. 358.

[2] Scott *v.* Liverpool, etc., 1915, 86 S. E. 484. And see Fisbeck *v.* Phœnix, etc., 1880, 54 Cal. 427; Schmurr *v.* States, etc., 1896, 30 Or. 29; 46 Pac. 363; Patterson *v.* American, etc., 1912, 164 Mo. App. 157; 148 S. W. 448.

[3] Metropolitan, etc. *v.* Johnson, 1911, 49 Ind. App. 233; 94 N. E. 785; and cases there cited. And see *ante*, pp. 16–21.

been made. Were the company, while continuing to hold the money, to make express declaration of its election to terminate, a court might, indeed, point to the retention of the money as evidence of election to continue, and hold that the company had not proved its election to terminate. But that would not warrant the assertion that return, or offer to return, is an essential element in election.

As to the necessity for alleging a return or an offer to return as part of a plea of election to terminate, observe that if one of these be an essential element of election, then, obviously, a plea of election is complete without the additional allegation of return or offer. Indeed, such additional allegation would be mere redundancy, and ought, for that reason, to be omitted. On the other hand, if failure to return the premium, be merely some evidence upon the fact of the existence of an election, then, also, no reference to it should appear in the pleading.

Return or Offer Sometimes Impracticable. Under certain circumstances return or offer to return the money may be impracticable. Election to terminate must be exercised promptly. Delay gives occasion for inference of election to continue. But the assured may be in the wilds of Africa, or may be dead and there may be no known legal representatives. It is not a sufficient reply to this, that, under such circumstances, return and offer will be excused; for if one of them be a necessary part of election, there can be no election in their absence. The alternative to this would be to say that the presence of the difficulty postponed the time for election — that the company might, indeed would be compelled, to keep its option open until the difficulty was removed. That is not acceptable.

Must the exact amount, too, be returned or offered? Yes. If return or offer be necessary to election, return or tender of too little would be useless. A deduction for postage on the letter might give rise to debate.

OFFER USELESS. Less can be said for the necessity of a mere offer to return than for tender of the money; for, being only an offer to do that which the law requires shall be done, it can be of no use to anybody. By electing to terminate the policy, the company incurred a liability to repay certain money. An offer to repay adds nothing to that liability, nor does it in any way change it. If the election of the company did not itself terminate the policy — if it were merely a proposal to end it, then, very properly, as part of that proposal, there might be necessity for an offer to return the money. But there is no proposal. There is a severance of legal relationship, and a consequent legal liability. An offer is inappropriate.

ANALOGY. Whether when a release of damages has been executed, it can be sufficiently repudiated upon the ground of fraud, without returning, or offering to return, the money paid as consideration for the release, is a somewhat similar question, and has been answered diversely.[1] It is submitted that retention of the money is merely some evidence of election to affirm the settlement.

CANCELLATION WITHOUT BREACH. Sometimes policies provide that, apart from any question of default, the company may cancel the policy at any time, and, if it be cancelled, the company

> shall retain a *pro rata* premium for the time the policy has been in force.[2]

[1] The Indiana courts have held in the affirmative: Supreme, etc. *v.* Lennert, 1911, 93 N. E. 869; 98 N. E. 115; 178 Ind. 124; Brashears *v.* Perry, 1912, 51 Ind. App. 8; 98 N. E. 891. In the negative are: Chicago, etc. *v.* Doyle, 1877, 18 Kan. 58; Mullen *v.* Old Colony, etc., 1879, 127 Mass. 86; Lumley *v.* Wabash, 1896, 43 U. S. App. 476; 22 C. C. A. 60; British Columbia, etc. *v.* Turner, 1914, 18 B. C. 132; 49 S. C. Can. 470; Lee *v.* Lancashire, etc., 1871, L. R. 6 Ch., at pp. 532, 533.

[2] See the New York Standard policy.

In such cases, the courts disagree as to the power of the company to cancel the policy without refunding the money.[1] But there is no difference between them and those with which we have been dealing. Both are cases of election; and a return of the money is not a necessary ingredient in election.

[1] See Tisdell *v.* New Hampshire, 1898, 155 N. Y. 163; Schwarzchild *v.* Phœnix etc., 1903, 124 Fed. 52; Hansell-Elcock, etc. *v.* Frankfort, 1913, 177 Ill. App., p. 500, and cases referred to at p. 506.

CHAPTER XIII

INSURANCE

" Waivers " of Breaches Prior to Loss, by Subsequent Activities

Election. A breach of a condition in a policy has occurred prior to loss; the company has become aware of the breach, either prior or subsequent to the loss; nevertheless, after the loss, and with knowledge of the fact, it proceeds as though the policy were in force: upon what ground ought its liability to be alleged? The answer is that the case is a simple one of election. By the terms of the policy, the policy was, upon the happening of the breach, voidable at the election of the company, and the allegation ought to be that the company has indicated its election to continue its liability.

" Waiver " and Estoppel. Indubitable as that appears to be, the application of election has been almost universally overlooked. " Waiver " and estoppel are everywhere invoked. And the most recent author on the law of insurance, in the course of a Review interchange with the present writer, said as follows:

"Keep clear of forfeiture," says Mr. Ewart, "substitute election to terminate." So far as I am aware no court has ever advocated such a view, no one of the cases cited in the article gives countenance to it, nor can I persuade myself that Mr. Ewart desires to press his theory to such an extreme. Though he does not so state or intimate, I must believe that he intended to limit the application of his rule to instances in which the insurer, prior to loss, has obtained knowledge of the facts constituting breach.[1]

THE NEW YORK CASES. The most frequently quoted dictum is to be found in a case in which, after loss, and after knowledge of a breach by the happening of foreclosure proceedings, the company required the assured to submit to examination — a proceeding to which the company had a right (as the court said) "only by virtue of the policy." The company was held liable upon the following ground:

> But it may be asserted broadly that if in any negotiations or transactions with the insured, after knowledge of the forfeiture, it recognizes the continued validity of the policy, or does acts based thereon, or requires the insured by virtue thereof to do some act or incur some trouble or expense, the forfeiture is as a matter of law waived; and it is now settled in this court, after some divergence of opinion, that such waiver need not be based upon any new agreement or estoppel.[2]

A few years afterwards, the rule was stated in somewhat modified form:

> When an insurance company, with knowledge of all the facts constituting a breach of a condition with a warranty, requires the assured, by virtue of the contract to do some act or incur some trouble or expense, the forfeiture is deemed to have been waived, as such requirement is inconsistent with the position that the contract has ceased to exist, and consistent only with the theory that the obligations of the contract are still binding upon both parties.[3]

[1] Columbia Law Rev., vol. 13, p. 52. For a reply, see *ante*, pp. 199–204.

[2] Titus *v.* Glens Falls, 1880, 81 N. Y., 419.

[3] McNally *v.* Phœnix, etc., 1893, 137 N. Y., p. 397; 33 N. E. p. 477.

CONFUSION. It will be observed that the element indicative of election to continue liability is identical with that to which the court points as ground for the assertion that

> the forfeiture is as a matter of law waived [or] that the forfeiture is deemed to have been waived.

But the evil of positing a forfeiture which never happened (a right of election only was created), and then extinguishing it with " waiver " (which could have no effect upon a real forfeiture[1]), is not only indicated by the dispute (referred to in the first of the quotations) as to the basis of " waiver," but clearly misleads authors [2] as well as judges. For example, the writer above referred to has said that:

> Demanding the usual verified proofs of loss, in itself, effects no waiver or estoppel;

the company is (he said) merely requesting performance of a " reasonable requirement " of the contract:

> the request may benefit the insured by calling his attention to a condition precedent which might otherwise be overlooked;

from that no intention to waive can be gathered;

> and as to estoppel, the essential element of injury or prejudice to the insured is lacking, since the insured is bound by his contract to do the very same thing, though the company make no affirmative request at all. . . . It must be observed also that one great difficulty with all parol waivers is that written terms of the contract are sought to be set aside by testimony which at best is uncertain and unreliable.[3]

CLARITY BY SUBSTITUTION OF ELECTION. Substitution of election for forfeiture and " waiver," it will be observed, obviates what the author describes as the " one great difficulty with all parol waivers "; for, by election, " the written

[1] *Ante*, p. 62.

[2] Mr. Richards in his work on Insurance declared that the New York rule is " very dubious in principle," and works very badly in practice.

[3] Richards on Ins., 1909, pp. 180–182.

terms of the contract are " *not* " sought to be set aside " by parol testimony. The contract gives a right to elect; and the evidence is directed to the fact of election.

The substitution also provides the answer to the assertion (in relief of the company) that the proofs

> were not furnished upon the request of the defendant after the loss, but in pursuance of the obligation of the plaintiff as expressed in the policy.[1]

Applied to the rule, that, for " waiver," the company must require the insured " to do some act, or incur some trouble or expense," [2] the observation is pertinent. But it has no application to election, for, there, the material question is, not what actuated the insured in furnishing the proof, but what sort of election was indicated by the fact of the company's request.

CONTRADICTORY AUTHORITIES. The cases upon the subject in hand are very numerous, and, proceeding as they do (in the opinion of the present writer) upon erroneous principles, the conclusions arrived at are naturally contradictory. The author above quoted refers to some of those which support his view.[3] Some of the others are cited at the foot of this page.[4]

The phraseology in those of the latter class, even where election obtains partial recognition, is almost always to the effect that

[1] Fitzpatrick *v.* Hawkeye, etc., 1880, 53 Ia. 335; 5 N. W. 151. And see Phœnix Ins. Co. *v.* Stevenson, 1879, 8 Ins. L. J. 922; 78 Ky. 150. Ronald *v.* Mutual, etc., 1898, 23 Abbott, N. C. 271; 10 N. Y. Supp. p. 632.

[2] *Ante*, p. 246.

[3] Richards on Ins., 1909, pp. 180–183.

[4] Webster *v.* Phœnix, etc., 1874, 36 Wis. 71; Northwestern, etc., *v.* Germania etc, 1876, 40 Wis. 446; Silverberg *v.* Phœnix, etc., 1885, 67 Cal. 36; 7 Pac. 38; Carpenter *v.* Continental, etc., 1886, 61 Mich. 635; 28 N. W. 749; Marthinson *v.* North British, etc., 1887, 64 Mich. 372; 31 N. W. 291; Rockford, etc. *v.* Travelstead, 1888, 29 Ill. App. 654; German, etc. *v.* Gibson, 1890, 53 Ark. 494; 14 S. W. 672; Replogle *v.* American, etc., 1892, 132 Ind. 360; 31 N. E. 947; Western, etc. *v.* Ashby, 1913, 53 Ind. App. 518; 102 N. E. 44; Corson *v.* Anchor, etc., 1901, 113 Iowa 641, 85 N. W. 806.

> the requiring of further proofs of loss after the company was chargeable with notice . . . is a waiver of the breach, and estops the company to claim a forfeiture of the policy.[1]

One of them may be referred to for the purpose of illustration. An insurance company, having knowledge of a breach of the stipulation against further insurance, wrote to the insured as follows:

> If Mr. C. has a fair and legal claim for loss . . . he should make out such proofs as the policy requires and send same here; and, on receipt of same, the claim shall be investigated at once, and you shall be promptly advised of our views of same.

The court said that, as the insured was put to trouble and expense, the company was estopped from denying its liability.[2] Regarded from the standpoint of election, we should say that the letter was some evidence of the election of the company to continue its liability; that suggestion of trouble and expense to the assured makes denial of such election difficult; and that consequential action by the assured was immaterial.

Adjustment Proceedings, etc. As request for delivery of proofs is evidence of election to continue a policy notwithstanding prior breaches of conditions known to the insurer, so also is conduct of other sorts, for example, joining in adjustment proceedings. The general rule (expressed in " waiver " phraseology) has been stated as follows:

> If the company, after knowledge of the breach, enters into negotiations or transactions with the assured, which recognize and treat the policy as still in force, or induce the assured to incur trouble or expense, it will be regarded as having waived the right to claim the forfeiture.[3]

[1] Gans v. St. Paul, etc., 1877, 43 Wis. 112.

[2] Cannon v. Home, etc., 1881, 53 Wis. 585; 11 N. W. 11. See also Webster v. Phœnix, etc., 1874, 36 Wis. 71; Rockford, etc. v. Travelstead, 1888, 29 Ill. App. 659; Rundell v. Anchor, etc., 1905, 128 Iowa, 575; 101 N. W. 517.

[3] Queen Ins. Co. v. Young, 1888, 86 Ala. 424; 5 So. 116. Approved in United States v. Lesser, 1900, 126 Ala. 568; 28 So. 646.

From the point of view of election, we should say, that recognition of " the policy as still in force " is evidence of election by the company to continue its obligations; and that the estoppel element — " induce the insured to incur some trouble or expense " (the basis of many of the decisions) — is of no consequence save as helpful evidence of that election.

OFFERS OF COMPROMISE — REBUILDING. Offers of compromise are sometimes said to be "waivers."[1] But substitution of election for " waiver " indicates that the result thus arrived at cannot be correct. The company cannot be recognizing its liability, and, at the same time, denying it and offering to agree to a compromise of the dispute. The company should note, however, that while it is dallying, the reasonable time within which it may elect to terminate its liability may expire. Propositions for rebuilding may indicate election to continue.[2]

COUNTERVAILING CONSIDERATIONS. Activity by the company after the loss may be accompanied by circumstances which contradict the assumption of election to continue. Each case must be judged according to its own circumstances. For example, while adjustment proceedings are usually held to be " waivers," [3] investigations " to enable the company to show the breach " would not,[4] especially if conducted without the aid of the insured.[5] So appraisal

[1] Lycoming, etc. *v.* Schreffler, 1862, 42 Pa. 188; Larkin *v.* Glens Falls, etc., 1900, 83 N. W. 409; 80 Minn. 527; Phœnix, etc. *v.* Center, 1895, 31 S. W. 446; 10 Tex. Civ. App. 535; Ætna, etc. *v.* Simmons, 1896, 69 N. W. 125; 49 Neb. 811; Providence, etc. *v.* Wolf, 1907, 168 Ind. 690; 72 N. E. 606. But see Logan *v.* Commercial, etc., 1886, 13 S. C. Can. 270.

[2] Thieroff *v.* Universal, etc., 1885, 110 Pa. St. 37; 20 Atl. 412.

[3] Lewis *v.* Monmouth, etc., 1846, 52 Me. 492; Corson *v.* Anchor, etc., 1901, 85 N. W. 806; 113 Iowa 641; German-Am., etc. *v.* Evants, 1901, 61 S. W. 536; 62 S. W. 417; 94 Tex. 490; Mutchmoor *v.* Waterloo, etc., 1902, 4 Ont. L. R. 608; Georgia, etc. *v.* Allen, 1898, 119 Ala. 436; 24 So. 399; 128 Ala. 451; 30 So. 537.

[4] Niagara, etc. *v.* Miller, 120 Pa. 517; 14 Atl. 385.

[5] Blossom *v.* Lycoming, etc., 1876, 64 N. Y. 162; People's, etc. *v.* Ætna, etc., 1896, 74 Fed. 507; 20 C. C. A. 630.

may have in view the ascertainment of the amount of that part of the loss in respect of which there is no defence.[1] And where the breach complained of is the existence of other insurance, request for the particulars of that insurance may not prove election,[2] for the alleged conduct must indicate election to continue the liability.[3] Action for the purpose of enabling the company to elect,[4] or without prejudice to its right to elect, may fall short of election.

ESTOPPEL. As above indicated, the courts sometimes hold insurers liable, notwithstanding breaches of condition, upon the ground of estoppel. It is said that if, by the conduct of the company (in demanding proofs, in entering into adjustment proceedings, etc.), the insured is induced to incur expense, the insurer is estopped from setting up prior breaches of condition.[5] But the courts overlook the fact that by such conduct the insurers do not in any way mislead the insured, and that there is therefore no possibility of estoppel. The conduct indicates election by the insurers to continue the policy. The insured so understands it. The insurer makes no misrepresentation. And the insured makes no mistake.

[1] Kiernan *v.* Dutchess, etc., 1896, 150 N. Y. 190; 44 N. E. 698.

[2] Sheldon *v.* Michigan, etc., 1900, 82 N. W. 1068; 124 Mich. 303.

[3] Niagara, etc. *v.* Miller, 1888, 120 Pa. 517; Carpenter *v.* German, etc., 1892, 135 N. Y. 298; 31 N. E. 1015.

[4] Queen *v.* Young, 1888, 86 Ala. 424; 5 So. 116.

[5] Marthinson *v.* North Br., etc., 1877, 64 Mich. 372; 31 N. W. 291; Oshkosh, etc. *v.* Germania, etc., 1888, 71 Wis. 454; 37 N. W. 819; McGonigle *v.* Agricultural, etc., 1895, 167 Pa. St. 364; 31 Atl. 626; German-Am. *v.* Evants, 1901, 94 Tex. 490; 61 S. W. 536; 62 S. W. 417; Mutchmoor *v.* Waterloo, etc., 1902, 4 Ont. L. R. 606.

CHAPTER XIV

INSURANCE

"WAIVER" OF PROOFS OF LOSS

CONDITIONS OF LIABILITY AND CONDITIONS OF ENFORCEMENT. Breaches prior to loss (e. g. as to vacancy, increase of risk, and so on) are naturally felt to be more serious than disregard of prescribed methods of proof of loss. Some conditions, it is said,

> are essential to its obligatory character. Others relate only to the steps to be taken by the insured for the recovery of the loss, and a neglect to comply with the requirements of the former might render the contract itself void; whilst a failure to follow the latter would only defeat the right of the insured to maintain his action upon it.[1]
>
> Proofs of loss are but conditions precedent to the bringing of an action, and not of the insurance.[2] They belong to the class of stipulations termed a "formal" requirement, as distinguished from a "substantive" requirement; and as to formal requirements, the courts lean strongly against depriving the insured of the insurer's liability, and sometimes seemingly resort to quite slender and far-fetched inferences of waiver or estoppel for that purpose.[3]

And so it is said that

> conditions affecting the risk itself are more strictly enforced than those relating to the mode of establishing the loss.[4]

VARIOUS FORMS OF POLICIES. Provisions in policies with reference to proofs of loss are of great variety, but substantially, they fall into two classes, and they may be so dealt with in this chapter:

1. Policies which provide that they are to be "void;" are to "cease and determine;" and so on, upon failure to produce proofs.

2. Policies which provide merely that no action shall be commenced unless proofs are delivered within a certain specified time.

[1] Bowes *v.* National, etc, 1880, 20 N. B. 437. And see Carpenter *v.* German, etc., 1892, 135 N. Y. 303; 31 N. E. 1015; Washburn, etc. *v.* Merchants, etc., 1900, 110 Iowa 423; 81 N. W. 707.

[2] Jones *v.* Mechanics, etc., 1872, 36 N. J. Law, 29. And see Phœnix, etc. *v.* Spiers, 1888, 87 Ky. 285; 8 S. W. 453; Lebanon, etc. *v.* Erb, 1886, 112 Pa. St. 160; 4 Atl. 8; Priest *v.* Citizens, etc., 1862, 3 Allen (Mass.) 604.

[3] Peninsular, etc. *v.* Franklin, 1891, 35 W. Va. 673; 14 S. E. 237.

[4] Phœnix, etc. *v.* Spiers, 1888, 87 Ky. 285; 8 S. W. 453. Approved in Kenton, etc. *v.* Downs, 1890, 12 Ky. L. R. 115; 13 S. W. 882.

1. Policies Void upon Failure of Proofs

Election. Here, as elsewhere, the word *void* means *voidable at the election of the insurer*. At the expiration of the period prescribed for production of the proofs, if default have occurred, the insurer may elect to continue or to terminate his liability. During the running of the period, there can be no opportunity for election. No default having occurred, there can be no election based upon default. But after expiry of the period — after breach of the condition has occurred — a right of election arises. The breach has not caused a "forfeiture," as is so frequently alleged. The policy is still in force, and the liability of the company is, as yet, unaffected. Whether the breach is to oust the liability, is a matter for the election of the insurer, and, until he elect, liability remains.

"Waiver." In some cases of the class in hand, the courts hold the insurers liable upon the ground of "waiver."[1] For example, it has been said that

> a distinct recognition of the liability of the defendant for the loss, after the expiration of the ten days for the service of the preliminary proof . . . is sufficient to establish a waiver of such proof within the ten days.[2]

With deference, it would have been better to have said that the recognition was evidence of an election to continue the liability. And so the Indiana courts, having adopted the principles of election[3] (although, upon occasion recurring to the language of forfeiture), hold that the company may be liable, although no proofs have been delivered within the prescribed period, by

> conduct tending to evince the election of the company.[4]

[1] Carroll *v.* Girard, etc., 1887, 72 Cal. 297; 13 Pac. 863; McGonigle *v.* Susquehanna, 1895, 168 Pa. 1; 31 Atl. 868; Sagers *v.* Hawkeye, 1895, 94 Iowa 519; 63 N. W. 194; Ervay *v.* Fire Assce., etc., 1903, 119 Iowa 304; 93 N. W. 290.

[2] Owen *v.* Farmers, etc., 1869, 57 Barb. 521.

[3] *Ante*, pp. 16–21. [4] Germania, etc. *v.* Pitcher, 1902, 160 Ind. 392; 64 N. E. 922.

For example, if the company proceeded to repair some of the buildings covered by the policy,[1] or if it paid part of the claim,[2] we should say, not that it had " waived " delivery of the proofs, but that it had evinced its election to continue the policy notwithstanding their non-delivery. And so, also, if it proceeded to adjust the amount of the loss.[3] As to offers of compromise, see *ante*, p. 250.

It will be observed that appraisals and investigations, prior to the expiry of the period for furnishing proofs, cannot be " waivers " of default in sending them in; nor could such proceedings be an election, for as yet no opportunity for election has arrived.

ELECTION AND " WAIVER." The importance of substituting election for " waiver " becomes very apparent when we read dicta such as the following:

> After the thirty days had expired without any statement, nothing but the express agreement of the company could renew or revivify the contract.[4]

For the expiry of the thirty days has no effect whatever upon the policy. It merely gives to the insurer a right of election.

DEFECTIVE PROOFS. What has been said applies to cases of delivery of defective proofs equally with cases in which no proofs of any kind have been supplied. In neither case is there any default until expiry of the period, and in neither, therefore, is the insurer, until then, in a position to make an election between continuing and terminating liability. There

[1] Hibernia, etc. *v.* O'Connor, 1874, 29 Mich. 241.

[2] Westlake *v.* St. Lawrence, etc., 1852, 14 Barb. 206; Westchester, etc. *v.* McAdoo, 1899, 57 S. W. 409; *Quaere*, if the amount be paid to a mortgagee with better claim than the original insured: King *v.* Watertown, etc., 1888, 54 N. Y. 1.

[3] Lewis *v.* Monmouth, 1846, 52 Me. 492; Bowes *v.* National, etc., 1901, 20 N. B. 438.

[4] Beatty *v.* Lycoming, etc., 1870, 66 Pa. St. 9. Approved in Everett *v.* London, etc., 1891, 142 Pa. St. 343, 21 Atl. 819. And see Wood on Fire Ins., § 452; Westchester, etc. *v.* Coverdale, 1899, 9 Kan. App. 651; 58 Pac. 1029.

is, however, one point of difference between the two cases. The British Privy Council has said that silence

> cannot possibly be a waiver of the not sending the proper proofs in, and not sending them in within proper time.[1]

But while that may be true (using the language of "waiver") in the case of the absence of all proofs, it may not be true (as we shall see) where defective proofs have been delivered, for silence may indicate acceptance of the documents as sufficient. And silence may, under certain circumstances, estop the company from alleging the informality.

Denial of Liability upon other Grounds. As we shall soon see, difference of opinion has been expressed as to the effect of denial of liability (upon some ground other than non-delivery of proofs) on the obligation of the policy-holder to furnish proofs, in cases in which the policy provides that, in case of default, no action shall be brought.[2] But there can be little question that, when non-delivery merely supplies the company with a right to elect to terminate the policy, denial of liability upon some other ground has no eliminating effect upon the duty to furnish the proofs. By the denial, the company is alleging that, because of some default, it has elected to terminate the policy altogether; and if the policy-holder urge that the company ought not to be permitted to say both (1) that the policy is ended, and (2) that the assured ought to have complied with its provisions as to proofs, the company may equally say that the assured ought not to be allowed to contend (1) that the policy has not been terminated, and, at the same time (2) that, although it is in force, he may disregard its conditions.

In truth, the company's action is perfectly consistent. It says:

[1] Whyte *v.* Western, etc., 1875, 22 L. C. Jur. 215; 7 Rev. Leg. 106 (Que.).

[2] *Post*, pp. 259–268.

Because of a certain default prior to loss, we elected to cancel the policy; and, if for any reason, that election was ineffective, we now elect to cancel for failure in delivery of proofs.

2. Time Specified for Delivery

Scope of the Inquiry. We are now to deal with policies which provide that no action for a loss shall be brought unless proofs are delivered to the company within a certain specified period. And the points which we have to consider relate to the nature of some of the replies which may be made to defences which the companies may base upon (1) total non-compliance, and (2) defective compliance, with the provisions of the policies. In a former chapter, two possible replies have been considered; (1) that, by a new contract, the stipulation as to time had been eliminated from the policy and (2) that, by a new contract, the time specified had been extended.[1] Other replies, more usual in insurance cases, are those which will now engage attention. The subject may conveniently be divided as indicated in the conspectus at the head of this chapter.

No Proofs Delivered within the Prescribed Period

Estoppel. During the period within which proofs must be tendered, the company may estop itself from objecting to their non-production, if its conduct towards the assured is

> calculated to inspire confidence and throw him off his guard.[2]
>
> If assurer in any case is guilty of such conduct as to render some mere matter of detail, in the establishment of a claim for loss under a policy, useless, and to lead the assured to assume, reasonably, that compliance with provision of the policy in that regard

[1] *Ante*, pp. 131–142.

[2] Thierolf *v.* Universal, etc., 1885, 110 Pa. 37; 20 Atl. 412; Kenton, etc. *v.* Wigginton, 1889, 89 Ky. 330; 12 S.W. 668. And see Hughes *v.* Metropolitan, etc., 1877, 1 C. P. D. 135; 2 A. C. 439. Ewart on Estoppel, pp. 40; 105, 106; 133–136.

> will not be insisted upon, it does not, strictly speaking, work a waiver of such provisions, but it estops the company from insisting thereon.[1]

Silence, under certain circumstances, may mislead and so work an estoppel.

> It is said that there can be no waiver of a condition unless in writing; but I should rather put it that the defendants have estopped themselves by their conduct from insisting upon a strict compliance; and the making no reply to the plaintiff when he offered still to supply the proofs if the defendants desired it, should, I think, equally estop them from insisting on the benefit of any defence founded on this condition.[2]

Estoppel of that kind should be called estoppel, although sometimes referred to as "waiver."

> The general doctrine in regard to such conduct on the part of insurance companies can be well applied in this case: The preliminary proof of loss will be excused on the ground of waiver by the insurers, if their conduct is such as to induce delay, or to render its production useless or unavailing, or as to induce in the mind of the insured a belief that no proofs will be required.[3]

For example, if the company indicate that the loss will be "fixed up" without action on the part of the assured, it could not afterwards disappoint the reasonable expectation of the assured.[4] And, generally, the following extracts may be agreed to:

> While one party has time and opportunity to comply with a condition precedent, if the other party does or says anything to put him off his guard, and to induce him to believe that the condition is waived, or that a strict compliance with it will not be insisted on, he is afterwards estopped from claiming non-performance of the condition.[5]

[1] Matthews *v.* Capital, etc., 1902, 91 N. W. 676; 115 Wis. 272.

[2] Morrow *v.* Lancashire, 1899, 26 Ont. App. 177.

[3] Kenton, etc. *v.* Wigginton, 1889, 89 Ky. 336; 12 S. W. 668.

[4] Lake *v.* Farmer's, etc., 1900, 81 N. W. 710; 110 Iowa, 473.

[5] Underwood *v.* Farmer's, etc., 1874, 57 N. Y. 500.

If something be said or done by the other party by which the former is induced to believe that the condition is waived . . . the latter is estopped, etc.[1]

Withholding the policy from the assured, when possession of it is necessary for the preparation of the proofs, will estop the company from taking advantage of failure to send them in.[2]

So it is held that if the company itself undertakes to prepare the proofs, that is a sufficient excuse for inaction by the insured.[3]

And in estimating the validity of proffered excuses for the non-delivery of proofs, the fact that the insured is unfamiliar with business may be considered; for the question always is whether the company's conduct was "calculated to throw him off his guard." [4]

These are all clear classes of estoppel. Some of the judicial opinions so indicate; others erroneously (it is submitted) proceed upon "waiver"; while others confuse the two, as in a previous quotation, and as in the frequently repeated statement that "waiver rests upon estoppel." [5]

An analogous point will be dealt with in the next succeeding chapter.[6]

No Proofs — Denial of Liability

Classification. — The numerous cases as to the effect of a denial of liability by the company (on grounds not asso-

[1] Van Allen *v.* Farmer's, etc., 1877, 10 Hun (N. Y.) 397.

[2] Caldwell *v.* Stadacona, etc., 1883, 11 S. C. Can. 212; Mitchell *v.* London, etc., 1886, 12 Ont. 706; Turley *v.* N. Am., etc., 1840, 25 Wend. 373; Dougherty *v.* Metropolitan, etc., 1896, 3 N. Y. App. Div. 313; 38 N. Y. Supp. 258; Sullivan *v.* Prudential, etc., 1901, 63 N. Y. App. Div. 280; 71 N. Y. Supp. 525; Taylor *v.* Glens Falls, etc., 1902, 32 So. 887; 44 Fla. 273.

[3] American, etc. *v.* Sweetser, 1888, 116 Ind. 370; 19 N. E. 159; Searle *v.* Dwelling-House, etc., 1890, 152 Mass. 263; 25 N. E. 290; Washburn *v.* Merchants, etc., 1900, 81 N. W. 707; 110 Iowa, 423; Strause *v.* Palatine, etc., 1901, 128 N. C. 64; 38 S. E. 256; Germania, etc. *v.* Pitcher, 1902, 64 N. E. 922; 160 Ind. 392.

[4] Thierolf *v.* Universal, etc., 1885, 110 Pa. 37; 30 Atl. 414.

[5] Ervay *v.* Fire Assce., etc., 1903, 119 Iowa, 304; 93 N. W. 290; *Ante*, pp. 31–37.

[6] *Post*, pp. 282–284.

ciated with proofs) upon its defence of non-delivery of proofs, may be classified as follows:

1. Cases relating to denials during the period prescribed for delivery of proofs.

2. Cases relating to denials after the expiration of that period.

1. Denial During the Period. — "Waiver." Authorities are fairly unanimous in declaring that denial of liability by the company, during the period for delivery of proofs, "waives" all objections either to their non-production or to defects in those produced.

> It is universally held, we believe, that the absolute refusal of a company to pay the loss in any event, constitutes a waiver of the right to insist upon a compliance with such provisions.[1]
>
> Denial of responsibility, within the time for making preliminary proofs and before they are made, is the same as a notice to the assured that payment will not be made in any event. It is therefore a waiver of the condition.[2]
>
> Waiver of a condition requiring proof of loss within a certain time may be inferred from such acts and conduct as are inconsistent with the intention to insist upon a strict performance.[3]
>
> The rule would seem to be the same here as in the case of obligations to tender performance of contracts generally. If notice be given in advance that the tender, whether of money or of other performance, will not be accepted, it need not be made. It always excuses the performance of a condition precedent, if it be hindered or waived by the other party.[4]

[1] Ins. Co. *v.* Gracey, 1890, 15 Col. 70; 24 Pac. 577.

[2] Gerling *v.* Agricultural, etc., 1892, 39 W. Va. 703; 20 S. E. 691.

[3] Providence *v.* Wolf, 1907, 168 Ind. 697; 80 N. E. 26.

[4] McManus *v.* Western, etc., 1899, 43 N. Y. App. Div. 559, 48 N. Y. Supp. 820. And see Fire, etc. *v.* Felrath, 1884, 77 Ala. 194; Kansas, etc. *v.* White, 1887, 36 Kan. 760; 14 Pac. 275; Niagara, etc. *v.* Lea, 1889, 73 Tex. 641; 11 S. W. 1024; Millard *v.* Supreme, etc., 1889, 81 Cal. 340; Lumbermen's, etc. *v.* Bell, 1896, 166 Ill. 400; 45 N. E. 130; Cooper *v.* Ins. Co., 1897, 96 Wis. 362; 71 N. W. 606; Hilton *v.* Phœnix, etc., 1898, 92 Me. 272; 42 Atl. 412; Morrow *v.* Lancashire, etc., 1898, 29 Ont. 377; 26 Ont. App. 173; Boorholtz *v.* Marshall, etc., 1899, 109 Ia. 522; 80 N. W. 542; Home, etc. *v.* Mears, 1899, 105 Ky. 323; 49 S. W. 31; Phillips *v.* Benevolent, etc., 1899, 120 Mich. 142; 79 N. W. 1; Home, etc. *v.* Sylvester,

Referring to the rule just stated, one of the text-writers has said:

> On principle this rule is not clear or satisfactory. . . . Simply because the assured is believed to have violated one condition precedent, why should the court permit him to violate with impunity another condition precedent? [1]

The criticism is pertinent against suggestions of "waiver," for it is difficult to see why the assertion of one ground of defence should be held to be a relinquishment [2] of other defences. The policy provides observance of various conditions as prerequisites of liability and action. "Waiver" cannot alter the contract.

DENIAL DURING THE PERIOD — NEW CONTRACT AND ESTOPPEL. As against assertion of new contract or estoppel, the criticism just quoted is inapplicable. By a new contract, a term of the old one may be eliminated. Conduct or language of the insurer indicative of assumption of liability without delivery of proofs, coupled with consequent inaction on the part of the insured, may be sufficient proof of a new agreement by the parties which will modify the old one.[3] And conduct or language of the company calculated to throw the policy-holder off his guard may work an estoppel.[4]

DENIAL DURING THE PERIOD — A USELESS THING. Sometimes both "waiver" and estoppel are repudiated:

1900, 25 Ind. App. 207; 57 N. E. 991; Continental, etc. *v.* Wickham, 1900, 110 Ga. 129; 35 S. E. 287 ("upheld by an unbroken line of authorities"); Germania, etc. *v.* Pitcher, 1902, 160 Ind. 392; 64 N. E. 922; Taylor *v.* Glens Falls, etc., 1902, 32 So. 887; 44 Fla. 273; Fowlie *v.* Ocean, etc., 1902, 4 Ont. L. R. 146; 33 S. C. Can. 253; Lansing *v.* Commercial, etc., 1903, 93 N. W. 757; 4 Neb. 140; Hayes *v.* Continental, etc., 1903, 72 S. W. 135; 98 Mo. App. 410; Ætna, etc. *v.* Bockting, 1906, 39 Ind. App. 586; 79 N. E. 524.

1 Richards on Ins., 3d ed., pp. 179, 180. And see Thompson *v.* Ins. Co., 1881, 104 U. S. 259; Lantz *v.* Vermont, etc., 1891, 139 Pa. 560; 21 Atl. 80; Schmertz *v.* U. S., etc., 1902, 55 C. C. A. 104; 118 Fed. 250.

2 "Waiver" is said to be a relinquishment: *ante*, p 6.

3 *Ante*, pp. 131–137.

4 *Ante*, pp. 142, 220.

> It is not exactly accurate, perhaps, to call it a waiver, or an estoppel either; but it is so called for the sake of brevity. Really, it means that the law never requires a useless thing to be done.[1]

But the law does require people to fulfill their contracts, even though they may have agreed to quite useless, and even absurd stipulations.

Denial During the Period — Election. Election has been suggested as a ground upon which non-delivery of proofs (after the insurer's denial of liability upon other grounds) may be excused.

> We see no reason why such cases should not be put on the ground of election. The company, instead of waiting proofs as a basis for investigation, voluntarily assumed a position that, if maintained, would render it useless to furnish proof; and, as the condition is in the nature of a forfeiture that the courts are disposed to relieve from, if there is any basis for so doing, it seems but reasonable to prevent the company from taking an inconsistent position with reference to the clause thereafter.[2]

The suggestion appears to be that refusal to pay, upon the ground of, say, vacancy of the premises prior to loss, is inconsistent with an objection that, after loss, proofs were not delivered; that, for that reason, the insurer must elect between the two objections; and that the company ought to have waited until the proofs came in. If it had waited, and no proofs came, very clearly the company could have taken both objections. There would be, at that time, no inconsistency between them. And if there be no inconsistency when the two objections exist, how can there be inconsistency if one of them, and merely because one of them, is potential? Moreover, the company, by waiting, would be leaving itself open to the inference of election to continue the policy, notwithstanding the vacancy.[3]

[1] Dezell *v.* Fidelity, etc., 1903, 75 S. W. 1102; 176 Mo. 253.

[2] Germania, etc. *v.* Pitcher, 1902, 160 Ind. 392; 64 N. E. 922.

[3] *Ante*, p. 172.

DENIAL DURING THE PERIOD — OTHER CONSIDERATIONS. Displacement of "waiver" being the prime object of the present work, ascertainment of some principle (besides new contract and estoppel above referred to) upon which production of proofs is rendered unnecessary by a denial of liability might well be left untouched. A few observations, however, are offered. Let us consider, without assuming to pass judgment upon them the following:

1. Tender of performance as affected by refusal to accept.
2. Conditions precedent as affected by some acts of the parties.
3. A rule of convenience.
4. Anticipatory breach of executory contract.

TENDER. The usual assertion that announcement of determination not to accept payment of money or delivery of goods "waives" the necessity for a tender is a very crude method of stating the legal situation. Observe that neither payment nor delivery is a unilateral act — neither is possible to one of the parties, in the absence of co-operation by the other.[1] Suppose, then, that delivery of goods by A to B is a condition precedent to A's enforcement of B's obligations under the contract, and that A tenders delivery and B refuses acceptance, upon what ground can A sue B? He cannot allege performance of the condition precedent (for he did not deliver the goods) and, according to the contract, B, in the absence of performance, is not liable. The ever-handy "waiver" being inappropriate, we say that

[1] There may be hesitation in accepting this statement. Cannot, it may be asked, goods be left at the purchaser's shop or house, or be sent to him through the postoffice? See Hart-Parr Co. *v.* Finley, 1915, 153 N. W. 137 (N. D.). Experiment with payment of money. Can you pay if the other party will not accept it? You may surreptitiously slip the money into his pocket, or smuggle it into his cash box, or deposit it in his bank account, but that is not payment. Can you effect personal service of a writ upon a man if he will not receive it? You can do that which the practice permits in case of refusal to receive, but you cannot deliver to him if he will not accept.

> It is a principle of law that a man shall not avail himself of a non-performance which he has himself occasioned —[1]

that he is estopped from so doing.

That being understood, consider the necessity for tender of performance. There is (we shall say) no specific reference to it in the contract,[2] and there is no law, statutory or other, which makes tender, under all circumstances, a condition precedent to action for non-acceptance. If B be willing to accept delivery, then tender of the goods is necessary. But if B be not willing to accept — if he has announced that he will not accept — then tender is not necessary. Introduction of "waiver" is inappropriate. B "waives" nothing; for under the circumstances, he is entitled to nothing. All that we need say is, that having rendered delivery by A impossible, B

> shall not avail himself of a non-performance which he has himself occasioned.

The application of this to the necessity for delivery of proofs of loss, after an insurance company has denied liability under the policy, is obvious. Remember that the company is alleging that, because of some breach of condition, it has elected to terminate the policy; that the policy no longer exists as a contract between the parties; and that none of its provisions is obligatory upon anybody. The company is saying, therefore, either (1) we will not accept the proofs; or (2) we will receive them, but not as delivered in pursuance of the policy.[3] It is saying that it will not do that which is a necessary part of the delivery of the proofs. In

[1] Addison on Contracts, 1911, p. 146; Jones *v.* Somers, 1903, 204 Pa. 329; 54 Atl. 169.

[2] The contract usually provides for delivery — not for tender when acceptance has been refused.

[3] The company must, at the least, say this latter; for if it accepted delivery in pursuance of the policy, it would be affirming the continued existence of the policy.

other words, it is making performance of the condition precedent to action impossible, and of such non-performance it cannot avail itself.

CONDITIONS PRECEDENT. Reply may be offered to the company's assertion of non-delivery of proofs upon the ground, also, that that which is a condition precedent may, by the action of the parties, cease to have that character.

> I cannot help thinking that the performance of an act may be at one time a condition precedent and not at another. For instance, if I bargain for the purchase of ten horses for a certain sum of money, and the seller delivers only nine, I may say to him, "I will not accept them; my bargain was for ten." But if, instead of so doing, I take the nine horses and use them, then that which was at one time a condition precedent, by my own conduct has become no condition precedent. Therefore the delivery of ten horses was a condition precedent at one time and not at another.[1]

May we say that, by the action of the insurance company and the concurrence of the policy-holder, the delivery of proofs had ceased to be a condition precedent of action?

A RULE OF CONVENIENCE. The courts sometimes assign a rule of convenience as a ground for absolution from the performance of conditions precedent. During an argument, Erle, J., asked:

> Suppose the contract was that the plaintiff should send a ship to a certain port for a cargo, and the defendant should then load one on board; but defendant wrote that he could not furnish a cargo; must the ship be sent, to return empty?[2]

The same question might be asked in the case of a contract to build a ship; and with reference, also, to the less onerous work of preparation and tender of proofs.

[1] White *v.* Beaton, 1861, 7 H. & N. 50. The learned judge evidently had in mind a contract for the delivery of ten specific horses, and the inability of the vendor to deliver the tenth.

[2] Cort *v.* Ambergate, 1851, 17 Q. B. 127.

ANTICIPATORY BREACH OF AN EXECUTORY CONTRACT. There is one more possible ground of reply to the company, namely, that

> The renunciation of a contract by one of the parties before the time for performance has come, discharges the other, if he so choose, and entitles him at once to sue for a breach. A contract is a contract from the time it is made, and not from the time that performance of it is due.[1]

Applying this against an insurance company, may we say that it is alleging that it has terminated the contract; that, by that action, the policy-holder (if he so desire) is discharged from fulfillment of his obligations; and that without performance of stipulated conditions, an action may be brought in payment of the loss? Or would not the reply be that the assured is asserting that the policy is in force, and that he cannot, at the same time, say that its obligations do not bind him.

"WAIVER" NOT THE GROUND OF DECISION. We shall not stay to inquire as to the merits of these four suggested replies to the company's plea of non-delivery of proofs after denial of liability. All that we are at present interested in is the elimination of "waiver."

2. DENIAL AFTER THE PERIOD—NO PROOFS—"WAIVER." If "waiver" be merely an element of confusion when applied to denials of liability during the period prescribed for the delivery of proofs, it can have no better claim to attention when applied to denials after the expiration of the period.[2]

[1] Anson on Contracts, 1906, p. 361. See Hochster *v.* Delatour, 1853, 2 E. & B. 678; Frost *v.* Knight, 1872, L. R. 7 Ex. 111; 41 L. J., Ex. 78; 26 L. T. 77; Braithwaite *v.* Foreign, etc., 1905, 2 K. B. 543; 74 L. J., K. B. 688; 92 L. T. 637. See infra, pp. 278–280.

The principle has been accepted by the U. S. Supreme Court in Roehm *v.* Horst, 1900, 178 U. S. 1, and almost universally by the other American Courts (*Ibid.* p. 13). And see Saunders *v.* McDonough, 1914, 67 So. 591. It has been rejected in Mass.: Porter *v.* Supreme, etc., 1903, 183 Mass. 326.

[2] Ætna, etc. *v.* Bockting, 1906, 39 Ind. App. 586; 79 N. E. 524.

For the situation, in the latter case, is that the company has now a perfect defence upon the ground of non-delivery of proofs, and it has, or it thinks that it has, defence, also, upon some other ground. If, under such circumstances, the company denied liability for non-delivery of proofs, very clearly its other defence — arson for example — would not be eliminated. And no valid reason could be given for the contrary assertion that, by putting forward the defence of arson, it "waived" its defence of non-delivery of proofs. If "waiver" be, as is said, "an intended relinquishment of a known right,"[1] it fails, in such cases, because of absence of intention to relinquish. And if the company did intend to relinquish the defence, but on further consideration adhered to it and pleaded it, would the intention be a sufficient reply to the plea? Probably not. Nevertheless, advocates acting for policy-holders may, if they have faith in "waiver," urge the following:

1. Very many of the cases which declare that denial of liability "waives" proofs make no distinction between denials during, and denials subsequent to, the period.

2. Some cases clearly do apply "waiver" to denials subsequent to expiration of the period.[2]

3. And some declare that denial, even after action brought—denial in the company's pleading—is a "waiver" of proofs.

The authorities as to denials after action are irreconcilable. Some indicate that

> A waiver, to be operative, must take place before an action is brought upon the policy, and, it would seem, before the time for supplying the proofs under the policy has expired.[3]

[1] *Ante*, p. 6.

[2] Owen *v.* Farmer's, etc., 1869, 57 Barb. 518; Pennsylvania, etc. *v.* Dougherty, 1883, 102 Pa. 568; Lebanon, etc. *v.* Erb, 1886, 112 Pa. 149; Kiernan *v.* Dutchess, etc., 1896, 150 N. Y. 190; 44 N. E. 698; Dezell *v.* Fidelity, etc., 1903, 75 S. W., 1102; 176 Mo. 253; Johnson *v.* Bankers, etc., 1915, 151 N. W. 413.

[3] Wood on Fire Ins., § 452; Westchester, etc. *v.* Coverdale, 1899, 9 Kan. App.

While others declare that if, when a company is sued, it pleads a denial of liability upon the policy, it cannot at the same time complain that a provision in the policy providing for proofs of loss has not been complied with.[1]

Possibly it might be urged that pleading a denial of liability is evidence of a previous denial; just as a plea in trover, denying the plaintiff's property, obviates the necessity of proof of demand of the goods and refusal to give them up prior to action — the plea is some evidence of previous refusal. This point has not been raised.

It may well be asked, also, why a denial of liability immediately prior to action (at any time after expiration of the time for filing the proofs) is a "waiver" of the production of proofs within the prescribed period, and a similar, but more formal, denial immediately after action has not a like effect. Is the fact that now the plaintiff's demand is made by writ and the defendant's denial by pleading, a sufficient reason for changing the significance of the denial?

Denial after the Period — No Proofs — Estoppel. Policy-holders can get no comfort from estoppel as a reason for non-delivery of proofs, when the company's denial of liability is subsequent to the period prescribed by the contract; for he cannot say that the company's action after the period prevented his delivery of proofs during the period:

> But the error we find here, which is fatal to the case, is the failure to allege that defendants had denied liability within the sixty days directly succeeding the loss.[2]

Estoppel is, however, frequently upheld upon the following ground:

651; 58 Pac. 1029. And see Whyte *v.* Western, etc., 1875, 22 L. C. Jur. 215; 7 Rev. Leg. 106 (A Privy Council case not elsewhere reported).

[1] See *post*, p. 270.

[2] Continental, etc. *v.* Chance, 1915, 150 Pac. 114. And see Ætna, etc. *v.* Bockting, 1906, 39 Ind. App. 586; 79 N. E. 524.

The doctrine that an insurance company, by putting its refusal to pay the loss upon a definite ground, different from want of preliminary proofs or of defect in their form or substance, waives the right to insist upon the failure to make such proof as a defence to an action on the policy, is in harmony with the elementary principle that a party who places his refusal upon one ground cannot, after action brought, change it to another and different one.[1]

But the point is not well taken, and no analogy can be cited in support of it. A man may refuse to pay a note on one ground, without thereby "waiving," or being estopped, as to any other defence. In a vendor and purchaser case, it was said:

In a very carefully considered case, where this precise question was involved, our court held that a buyer having more than one reason for rejecting goods does not, by assigning one reason, conclusively admit that there is no other, and may justify his refusal to accept the goods on another ground. . . .[2]

And in an insurance case, it was said:

In the opinion in Welsh *v.* London Assurance Corp., 151 Pa. 607, Mitchell, J., in speaking of the denial of liability for specified reasons as a waiver of other defences, says: "The only ground upon which such a result can rest is estoppel. No party is required to name all his reasons at once, or any reason at all, and the assignment of one reason for refusal to pay cannot be a waiver of any other existing reason, unless the other is one which could have been remedied or obviated, and the adversary was so far misled or lulled into security by the silence as to such reason that to enforce it now would be unfair or unjust: Ins. Co. *v.* Brown, 128 Pa. 386. The whole doctrine depends on estoppel, and the essential feature of it is loss or injury to the other party by the act of the party to be estopped. In this respect there is nothing

[1] Ætna *v.* Shryer, 1882, 85 Ind. 362. Approved in Germania *v.* Pitcher, 1902, 160 Ind. 392; 64 N. E. 922. And see Bailey *v.* Hope, etc., 1869, 56 Me. 474; Fire, etc. *v.* Felrath, 1884, 77 Ala. 201; Edwards *v.* Baltimore, etc., 1845, 3 Gill, 186 (Md.); Fowlie *v.* Ocean, etc., 1901, 4 Ont. L. R. 146; 33 S. C. Can. 253; Burns *v.* Freeling, 1903, 98 Mo. App. 267; 71 S. W. 1128; Brink *v.* Hanover, etc., 1880, 80 N. Y. 108.

[2] Woldert, etc. *v.* Pillman, 1915, 176 S. W. 457; 191 Mo. App. 15.

> peculiar about actions upon insurance policies. They stand on the same footing as other litigation.[1]

Notwithstanding this, it is sometimes asserted that

> the company cannot be permitted at the same time to say that the policy was not a valid and existing contract, and claim privileges derived only under the contract.[2]

If that mean merely that, by rules of pleading, two such defences cannot be pleaded together, the point ceases to be one of general interest. In England and elsewhere, it was, at one time, impossible to pay money into court in satisfaction of the alleged cause of action, and at the same time to deny the existence of the cause altogether.

Further discussion as to the effect of denials of liability may be found in the chapter on "Insurance. Time for Commencement of Action." [3]

Defective Proofs Delivered within the Prescribed Period

We have now to consider the various grounds upon which argument can be offered in support of an assertion of liability of an insurer, notwithstanding the existence of defects in proofs delivered within the prescribed period.

[1] Freedman *v.* Providence, etc., 1896, 175 Pa. 360; 34 Atl. 730.

[2] Home, etc. *v.* Fallon, 1895, 45 Neb. 554; 63 N. W. 860. See upon this subject: Westlake *v.* St. Lawrence, 1852, 14 Barb. 206; Ætna, etc. *v.* Simmons, 1896, 49 Neb. 811; 69 N. W. 125; Omaha, etc. *v.* Dierks, 1895, 43 Neb. 473; 61 N. W. 740 (a good review of the cases); St. Louis *v.* Kyle, 1848, 11 Mo. 278; Martin *v.* Bank of Fayetteville, 1902, 131 N. C. 121; 42 S. E. 558; McComas *v.* Covenant, etc., 1874, 56 Mo. 573; Rochester, etc. *v.* Liberty, etc., 1895, 44 Neb. 537; 62 N. W. 877; German, etc. *v.* Kline, 1895, 44 Neb. 395; 62 N. W. 857; Omaha, etc. *v.* Hildebrand, 1898, 74 N. W. 589; 54 Neb. 306; Farmer's, etc. *v.* Frick, 1876, 29 Ohio 466; Dezell *v.* Fidelity, etc., 1903, 75 S. W. 1102; 176 Mo. 253; Atlantic, etc. *v.* Nero, 1914, 66 So. 780; Moran *v.* Knights of Columbus, 1915, 151 Pac. 353; 46 Wash. 397; Schultz *v.* Des Moines, etc., 1915, 153 N. W. 884; 35 S. D. 627; Nat'l Live Stock, etc. *v.* Elliott, 1915, 108 N. E. 784; 60 Ind. App. 112.

If the policy-holder contend that the policy is "a valid and subsisting contract" can he, at the same time, neglect performance of its conditions?

[3] *Post*, p. 278.

ACCEPTANCE. In making reply to defences of defective proofs, the profession appears to have overlooked, to some extent,[1] the fact that defective work may be accepted in satisfaction of work contracted for. The allied doctrines of new contract, and accord and satisfaction, might alternatively be appealed to in such cases. Probably, they themselves stand in need of analytical examination; but there is, at least, a reality and a substantiality about them to which "waiver" is a stranger, and, with them, "waiver" and estoppel ought not to be confused.[2] Examination of the subject is beyond the scope of this work. But suggestion may be offered, that in some cases in which insurers have been held to be estopped by not making objection to defective proofs, acceptance of them might very well have been the ground of decision.

ESTOPPEL. The courts very generally agree that the company must object promptly to defective proofs, *if there be time to correct them;* and, if there be a duty to object, neglect of it may very well estop the company from denial of its liability.

> Good faith required that the company should apprise the assured of any objections entertained, before she lost her rights to supply defects or omissions.[3]
>
> We regard the doctrine as well settled, that where notice and proofs of loss . . . have been made out and delivered to the company in due time, and they are retained by it without objection, the company cannot question . . . their sufficiency.[4]

[1] There are some exceptions: Emden *v.* Augusta, etc., 1815, 12 Mass. 308; Prentice *v.* Knickerbocker, etc., 1897, 77 N. Y. 483; Armstrong *v.* Agricultural, etc., 1892, 130 N. Y. 566; 29 N. E. 991; Ervay *v.* Fire Assce., etc., 1903, 119 Iowa, 304; 93 N. W. 290.

[2] For example, Bishop on Contracts, 1907, p. 332, has the following: "The principle on which in various circumstances a performance, in time or manner differing from the stipulations which are waived, is accorded the same effect as a literal performance is evidently that of estoppel."

[3] Winnesheck, etc. *v.* Schuller, 1871, 60 Ill. 465.

[4] Continental, etc. *v.* Rogers, 1887, 119 Ill. 474; 10 N. E. 242.

Having received notice of the loss, the defendants should have objected if it was not sufficiently formal, or was deficient in the information required by the by-laws.[1]

Very many authorities support these dicta,[2] but not a few of them fail to make the necessary distinction between cases in which the proofs are delivered at such time, prior to the expiration of the prescribed period, as would permit the possibility of correction, and cases in which there could have been no such possibility. The distinction is important.

SPECIFICATION OF OBJECTIONS. Some of the cases, besides affirming the company's obligation to object to defective proofs, declare that the company must specifically point out the nature of its objections. It is said that the general rule is,

> that when the company declines to receive the proofs of loss and to pay it, upon the ground of any insufficiency or informality in such proofs, or because made out of time, as was done in this in-

[1] Bartlett *v.* Union, etc., 1859, 46 Me. 503.

[2] Heath *v.* Franklin, etc., 1848, 55 Mass. 257; Underhill *v.* Agawam, etc., 1850, 60 Mass. 440; Blake *v.* Exchange, 1858, 78 Mass. 265; Lewis *v.* Monmouth, 1864, 52 Me. 499; Post *v.* Ætna, etc., 1864, 43 Barb. 351; Ayres *v.* Hartford, etc., 1864, 17 Iowa, 176; Killips *v.* Putnam, 1871, 28 Wis. 472; Jones *v.* Mechanics, etc., 1872, 36 N. J. L. 29; Basch *v.* Humboldt, 1872, 35 N. J. Law, 429; Patterson *v.* Triumph, 1876, 64 Me. 500; American, etc. *v.* Mahone, 1878, 56 Miss. 180; Mercantile, etc. *v.* Holthano, 1880, 43 Mich. 423; 5 N. W. 642; Rumsey *v.* Phœnix, 1880, 1 Fed. 396; 17 Blatch. 527; Ætna, etc. *v.* Shryer, 1882, 85 Ind. 362; Fire, etc. *v.* Felrath, 1884, 77 Ala. 194; Welsh *v.* London, etc., 1892, 151 Pa. St. 607; 25 Atl. 142; DeVan *v.* Commercial, etc., 1895, 36 N. Y. Supp. 931; 51 N. E. 1090; Hanover, etc. *v.* Shrader, 1895, 11 Tex. C. A. 255; 31 S. W. 1100; Alston *v.* Phœnix, etc., 1896, 100 Ga. 287; 27 S. E. 981; National, etc. *v.* Whitacre, 1896, 43 N. E. 905; 15 Ind. App. 506; Angler *v.* Western, etc., 1897, 10 S. D. 82 (The S. D. statute makes the distinction above referred to); Cooper *v.* Ins. Co., 1897, 96 Wis. 362; 71 N. W. 606; Cummins *v.* German-Am., etc., 1900, 197 Pa. St. 61; 46 Atl. 902; Braymer *v.* Commercial, 1901, 199 Pa. 259; 48 Atl. 972; Taylor *v.* Glens Falls, etc., 1902, 32 So. 887; 44 Fla. 273; Bingell *v.* Royal, etc., 1913, 240 Pa. 412; 87 Atl. 955; Alezunas *v.* Grainte, etc., 1913, 88 Atl. 413; 111 Me. 171; Carpenter *v.* Modern, etc., 1913, 142 N. W. 411; Linglebach *v.* Theresa, etc., 1913, 154 Wis. 595; 143 N. W. 688; Oklahoma *v.* Wagester, 1913, 132 Pac. 1071; 38 Okla. 52; Edwards *v.* Baltimore, etc., 1845, 3 Gill. (Md.) 186; Badger *v.* Glens Falls, etc., 1880, 49 Wis. 395.

stance, it shall, in its communication to the assured, state the grounds of such refusal on its part, as the same are then known or are believed to exist by the officers or agents having charge of the business.[1]

Where there are defects in the proofs of loss, whether formal, substantial, or, indeed, in any respect, which could have been supplied, if specific objections had been made thereto by the underwriters, a failure on their part to object to the proofs upon that ground, or to point out the specific defect, or to call for the information omitted within a reasonable time, is considered a waiver, however defective, informal, or insufficient, such proofs may be.[2]

It was the duty of the company on the receipt of the proofs to return them if they were objectionable, and point out the particular defects.[3]

And where a set of proofs was returned as

unsatisfactory and incomplete, in that it does not set forth as required by section 10 of the printed conditions of the policy, etc.,

and a copy of section 10 was enclosed, it was held that the objection was not sufficiently explicit.[4] But another case is substantially to the contrary effect, and is the more acceptable authority.[5] And a carefully prepared opinion in a New York case ought to be considered.[6]

[1] O'Connor *v.* Hartford, etc., 1872, 31 Wis. 165. And see Miller's, etc. *v.* Jackson, 1895, 60 Ill. App. 224; Fidelity, etc. *v.* Sadau, 1915, 178 S. W. 559; Niagara, etc. *v.* Layne, 1915, 172 S. W. 1090; 162 Ky. 665.

[2] Wood on Ins., 2d ed., § 456; approved in Northern *v.* Samuels, 1895, 33 S. W. 239; 11 Tex. App. 417.

[3] Universal, etc. *v.* Block, 1 Atl. 523; 109 Pa. 535. And see O'Connor *v.* Hartford, etc., 1872, 31 Wis. 165; American, etc. *v.* Mahone, 1878, 56 Miss. 182; Myers, etc. *v.* Council Bluffs, etc., 1887, 72 Iowa, 176; 33 N. W. 453; Armstrong *v.* Agricultural, etc., 1890, 130 N. Y. 565; 29 N. E. 991; Western, etc. *v.* Richardson, 1894, 40 Neb. 1; 58 N. W. 597; Tomuschat *v.* North British, etc., 1914, 92 Atl. 329; 77 N. H. 388; Wakely *v.* Sun Ins., etc., 1914, 92 Atl. 136; 246 Pa. 268.

[4] Davis Shoe Co. *v.* Kittanning, etc., 1890, 138 Pa. St. 73. And see Schmurr *v.* State, etc., 1896, 30 Or. 29; 46 Pac. 363.

[5] Gauche *v.* London, etc., 1881, 10 Fed. 347; 4 Woods 102.

[6] Kimball *v.* Hamilton, etc., 1861, 8 Bosw. (N. Y.) 495; 21 N. Y. Supp. 6.

Upon general principles, the company might, possibly, be held to be estopped from raising, after expiration of the period for delivering proofs, objections of which it was previously aware. It might be argued that seeing the mistake into which the assured had fallen, the company was under duty to advise him of it.[1] But while, a good deal of authority for such a proposition can be cited, analogy would appear to lead to a contrary conclusion. For example, if a tenant, desiring to avail himself of a right of renewal, serve an insufficient notice, it has never been considered that the landlord is under obligation to suggest amendment of it.

If the company has not inspected the proofs, and if it has not become aware of defects in them, at such a time as would have enabled corrections to be made, argument upon the ground of estoppel would be more difficult. There can be no duty on the part of the company to supervise the work of the insurer. On the other hand, retention without examination might be thought to be evidence of indifference and consequent acceptance; and means of knowledge, when there is a duty to inquire, may be held to be equivalent to knowledge.[2]

It would be difficult to hold that an insurance company is under obligation to inform the executors of a deceased policy-holder that non-payment, within a few days, of an overdue premium will render the policy voidable.[3]

Denial of Liability. Denial by the insurer, within the prescribed period, of all liability under the policy, upon grounds other than the non-delivery of proofs, as a sufficient reply to a plea of their non-delivery, has already been dealt with; and we have seen that, by such denial, the company may have rendered unnecessary the delivery of the proofs.[4]

[1] Ewart on Estoppel, pp. 28–67. [2] *Ante*, p. 82.

[3] Simpson *v.* Accident, etc., 1857, 2 C. B., N. S. 257; 26 L. J., C. P. 289. And see Ewart on Estoppel, pp. 66, 67.

[4] *Ante*, pp. 259–270.

Other reasons apply to cases in which, after defective proofs have been delivered, the company denies liability upon other grounds. For such action, having a tendency to induce belief in the company's satisfaction with the documents as delivered, it might be held (1) either to estop the company from raising objections to them, or (2) to furnish ground for the assertion that the company had accepted the documents as sufficient.

In a case relating to the law of vendor and purchaser, it was said:

> If the vendor refuses to sign (the conveyance) for specific causes, and omits to mention other causes which he rightfully might have urged, and which if urged the other party would have acted upon and remedied, he will be considered as waiving such other causes, unless the circumstances show it was not so understood . . . . Waiver in this respect is founded on estoppel *in pais*. It presupposes that if the matter had been mentioned as an objection, it would have been obviated by the other party.[1]

Subject to a protest that if there be estoppel, "waiver" (whatever it is) need not be founded upon it, the dictum is satisfactory.

DEFECTS IN NOTICE OF LOSS. The same principles apply to defective notices of loss:

> A failure to give notice within the time required stands upon a different ground from the failure to give the notice in due form. The latter defect may be remedied by a new and more accurate form; but the former, if insisted upon by the insurers, is irremediable. It may, indeed, be waived, but it would be reasonable to require a different kind of evidence from that which ought to be satisfactory in cases of a mere defect in form. The silence of the insurers upon a mere defect of form might be very injurious to the assured, since if the defect were pointed out to him, he might at once supply the deficiency and save himself from loss. A failure to give the notice in due time, on the contrary, leaves the

[1] Burns *v.* Freeling, 1903, 71 S. W. 1128 (Kan.). And see Todd *v.* Haggart, 1827, Moody & Mal. 128; Gerrish *v.* Norris, 1851, 9 Cush. 170.

> insured entirely at the mercy of the insurers; and to point out to him the fact will not, in the least, aid him to remedy the defect. The omission to point it out to him is therefore no wrong, or prejudice, or want of good faith towards him, nor is the insurer under any legal obligation to do so.[1]

This statement of the law has been approved by the Supreme Court of Canada,[2] and, with the substitution of election for " waiver," may be regarded as substantially correct, both as to notice of loss and proofs of loss.

[1] May on Ins., § 464, paraphrasing language used in Patrick *v.* Farmer's, etc., 1862, 43 N. H. 623.

[2] Accident, etc. *v.* Young, 1892, 20 Can. S. C. 284. See also Edwards *v.* Baltimore, etc., 1845, 3 Gill (Md.) 176; St. Louis, etc. *v.* Kyle, 1848, 11 Mo. 278; London, etc. *v.* Siwy, 1903, 35 Ind. App. 340; 66 N. E. 481.

CHAPTER XV

INSURANCE

Time for Commencement of Action

Stipulations Valid. A stipulation in a policy prescribing the period within which an action must be brought is not invalid upon grounds of public policy.[1] And it is said that a time-limitation

> is of the essence of the contract in conditions of this kind, and there is no power in the court to dispense with the condition, or excuse the non-performance of it.[2]

" Waiver." Theoretically, the courts so hold, but, practically they often pay little heed to time-limitations. Forfeiture and " waiver," here as elsewhere, are supposed to conciliate theory and practice. It is said that

> a 12 months statute of limitation, although assented to by the parties, operates as a forfeiture. It is therefore to be strictly construed.[3]
>
> Slight evidence of waiver, as in other cases of forfeiture, will be sufficient to defeat its application.[4]

[1] Peoria, etc. *v.* Whitehill, 1861, 25 Ill. 466; Garrettson *v.* Merchants, etc., 1901, 86 N. W. 32; 114 Iowa 17.

[2] Owen *v.* Farmers, etc., 1869, 57 Barb. 520.

[3] Kenton *v.* Downs, 1890, 13 S. W. 882; 90 Ky. 236; Weir *v.* Ins. Co., 4 L. R. Ir. 680.

[4] Ripley *v.* Ætna, etc., 1859, 29 Barb. 552. Approved in Gulf, etc. *v.* Travick, 1891, 15 S. W. 568; 8 Tex. 270; Burlington, etc. *v.* Tobey, 1895, 30 S. W. 1111; 10 Tex. C. A. 425.

And it is said that where the delivery of proofs of loss has been "waived," any time-limitations dating from delivery will also be "waived."

> A waiver of the proof is a waiver of the condition that payment is not to be made till a limited time after the proof, so that, in such case, suit may be brought at once upon denial of the liability.[1]

That "waiver" (if anything, a unilateral act) cannot vary the terms of a contract — that it cannot reduce, extend, or eliminate a period of time fixed by the parties for performance of their obligations — has been sufficiently shown in a previous chapter.[2] One agreement may be superseded by another. Or the case may be one of unexercised election to terminate the agreement. Or the facts may be sufficient to prove estoppel in favor of the defaulter. But one term of a contract can be no more susceptible of annihilation by "waiver" than are the other terms, and, consequently, the contract as a whole. What has been already said will not here be repeated. Consideration will be confined to a few points which are somewhat peculiar to the law of insurance.

DENIAL OF LIABILITY. Many cases have declared that denial by an insurance company of liability under its policy is a "waiver" of the time-limitation, and enables the policyholder to sue when he pleases[3] upon the ground that

> The renunciation of a contract by one of the parties before the time for performance has commenced discharges the other, if he so choose, and entitles him at once to sue for a breach.[4]

This rule, unacceptable enough in itself, can have no application to an action for a loss under a policy of insurance.

[1] May on Ins., vol. 2, § 469. Approved in Phœnix, etc. *v.* Center, etc., 1895, 31 S. W. 446; 10 Tex. C. A. 535.

[2] *Ante*, pp. 131–142.

[3] Snowden *v.* Kittaning, etc., 1888, 122 Pa. 502; 15 Atl. 22; Phœnix *v.* Center, 1895, 31 S. W. 446; 10 Tex. C. A. 535.

[4] Anson on Contracts, 1906, 361. And see *ante*, p. 266.

Cockburn, C. J., is said to have supplied the best support of the doctrine when he declared that

> The promisee has an inchoate right to the performance of the bargain, which becomes complete when the time for performance has arrived. In the meantime he has a right to have the contract kept open as a subsisting and effective contract.[1]

But if that be true, the action ought to be not for non-performance of (we may say) the September contractual activity, but for damages for the July repudiation. And perhaps the best that can be said for the rule (now widely supported[2]) is,

> that it is for the common benefit of both parties that the contract shall be taken to be broken as to all its incidents including non-performance at the appointed time . . . the eventual non-performance may, therefore, by anticipation, be treated as a cause of action.[3]

RENUNCIATION OR REFUSAL TO PERFORM. Sufficient distinction has not been made between renunciation of a contract and a refusal to perform its obligations — between an assertion that because of fraud (for example) no obligation attached, and a mere refusal to pay or to do. Part of the rule appears to be, that

> if the promisee will not accept the renunciation, and continues to insist upon performance, the contract remains in existence for the benefit, and at the risk, of both parties.[4]

That is easily understood — one party denies obligation, and the other may assent and cancel, or he may wait and sue. For example, a man promises that he will, after his

[1] Frost *v.* Knight, 1872, L. R. 7 Ex. p. 112; 41 L. J., Ex. 78; 26 L. T. 77. And see Anson on Contracts, 1906, pp. 360, 1.

[2] Dingley *v.* Oler, 1886, 117 U. S. 490; Roehm *v.* Horst, 1900, 178 U. S. 18; Donati *v.* Cleveland, 1915, 221 Fed. 168; 137 C. C. A. 68; Hart-Parr Co. *v.* Finley, 1915, 153 N. W. 137.

[3] Frost *v.* Knight, *supra.*

[4] Anson on Contracts, 1906, 362; based on Frost *v.* Knight, *supra.*

father's death, marry a certain woman; during his father's lifetime, he declares that he will not marry her; and the woman may elect either to cancel the contract, or to await the date for performance and then sue for damages. But it was under precisely those circumstances that it was held in Frost *v.* Knight[1] that the woman might treat the declaration as an anticipatory non-performance and bring her action for damages during the father's lifetime. She elected neither to cancel, nor to maintain and wait. She was permitted to sue, as if she had maintained, at the anticipatory time, as if she had cancelled.

Promissory Notes. If the decision just referred to be sound, there appears to be no good reason why it should not be applied to promissory notes — a maker denies liability and declares that he will not pay when the note falls due, with the result that he may be sued at once. But the courts will not so agree, and when an insurance company argued that it could not be sued before the date specified in the policy and urged the note-analogy, the court said:

> The parallel is not good. The latter is wholly a unilateral contract, with rights and liabilities fixed and determined, and without anything for adjustment, and without occasion for act of waiver by either party. To change the liability requires a new promise, not a denial or waiver. The decisions have all been in harmony with the views herein expressed.[2]

In later cases, this decision has been approved of, and in one of them the court said that the principle had been

> upheld by an unbroken line of American authorities.[3]

The Supreme Court of the United States has distinguished the cases in this way:

> We think it obvious that both as to renunciation after commencement of performance and renunciation before the time for per-

[1] *Supra.* [2] Cobb *v.* Ins. Co., 1873, 11 Kan. 93.
[3] Continental, etc. *v.* Wickham, 1899, 110 Ga. 129; 35 S. E. 287.

formance has arrived, money contracts, pure and simple, stand on a different footing from executory contracts for the purchase and sale of goods.[1]

The court did not, however, explain the difference, and it is somewhat difficult to formulate anything quite satisfactory. But, in any case, the distinction does not help us in the present inquiry, for a policy of insurance is a money contract.

Doctrine Qualified. In a carefully considered opinion, an Illinois court said:

> From all the authorities, we deduce the rule that where, and only where, a limitation by contract is an existing and available defence at the time the company denies liability on other grounds and ignores such limitation, it is waived and cannot afterwards be relied upon as a defence.[2]

For example, if the stipulation were that no action should be brought after twelve months from loss, and if within that time the company should deny liability, the time-limit would not be "waived" — because, at the date of the denial, the limitation was not an available defence. But if the denial were made after the expiry of the twelve months, when the defence was available, the assertion of the former defence would be a " waiver " of the latter, if not mentioned. And so also if the stipulation were that no action should be brought before three months after the loss, and within that period the company denied liability on other grounds, the limitation would be " waived " — because, at the date of the denial, the defence was available.

But this rule — that when a company has two defences it must assert both — appears to have rather irregular application. If a company has one defence on the ground of arson and another on the time-limitation clause, assertion

[1] Roehm *v.* Horst, 1900, 178 U. S., p. 18.

[2] Hansell-Elcock, etc. *v.* Frankfort, etc., 1913, 177 Ill. App. 500.

of the arson defence is said to be a "waiver" of the defence as to time; but no court has suggested that if the company were to say to the policy-holder that his time for action had expired, the company would thereby have "waived" its defence of arson.

When the denial is made during (say) the three months after the loss (within which no action may be brought) the right of the policy-holder to bring immediate action has been upheld upon the ground that the reason for the stipulation for delay was to enable the company (1) to investigate, and (2) to provide the money; and, if liability be denied, neither of these reasons can exist. But the question would still remain whether the clause must fall with the reasons which induced the parties to agree to it, and an affirmative answer would be difficult. No one has suggested the establishment of a general rule of that kind.

When the denial of liability is made after the expiration of the period within which, according to the contract, an action may be brought, acceptance of the doctrine is still more difficult. The company now, we may say, believes that it has two perfect defences, arson and contractual limitation, and the decisions indicate that if the company mentions arson without the limitation, the limitation has vanished from the contract. For that, at all events, no support can be found in assertion as to the reasons which actuated the parties in framing their agreement.

ESTOPPEL. If "waiver" cannot be a sufficient reply to a plea of a contractual time-limitation, what is to be said as to estoppel? This, first, that we must keep the two things well distinguished. For "waiver" (if it be anything) is a unilateral act, whereas for estoppel there must have been action, or inaction, by the estoppel-asserter consequent upon the conduct of the estoppel-denier. Nevertheless, the latest writer on the law of insurance has placed the following under the heading "Waiver of Limitation:"

The policy provision being in derogation of the general statute of limitation, the courts are not slow in holding the company estopped from insisting upon it, where the promise or conduct of the company has induced the delay.[1]

Observing necessary distinction, we say that conduct which induces the insured not to commence proceedings during the period prescribed by the contract, although it fall short of proof of a new contract, may estop the insurer from setting up defence upon the ground of delay.

If the delay to bring suit is a result to which the company mainly contributed, by holding out hopes of an amicable adjustment, the company cannot be permitted to take advantage of the delay under the limitation clause of the policy.[2]

A course of conduct on the part of the defendant, or representations of its officers, which would give reasonable grounds upon which plaintiff did in fact base the belief that his claim would be settled, would estop the defendant to set up the limitation provided by the policy.[3]

Where an insurance company shall, by fraud or by holding out reasonable hopes of an adjustment, deter a party assured . . . from commencing his suit, he honestly confiding in the pretences and promises of the insurer, the condition would be no bar.[4]

It has been held that mere pendency of negotiations for settlement, or interviews respecting adjustment, would not

[1] Richards on Insurance, p. 457.

[2] Martin *v.* Jersey, etc., 44 N. J. Law, 273. Approved in Burlington, etc. *v.* Tobey, 1895, 30 S. W. 1111; 10 Tex. C. A. 425. And see Ames *v.* New York, etc., 1865, 14 N. Y. 253; Home Ins. Co. *v.* Myer, 1879, 93 Ill. 271; Mutual, etc. *v.* Tolbert, 1895, 33 S.W. 296; Union, etc. *v.* Phillips, 1900, 101 Fed. 33; 41 C. C. A. 263.

[3] Mickey *v.* Burlington, etc., 35 Iowa, 175. And see Grant *v.* Lexington, etc., 1854, 5 Ind. 23; Hipwell *v.* Knight, 1833, 1 Y. & C. Ex. 418; Ames *v.* New York, etc., 1856, 14 N. Y. 253; Brady *v.* Western, etc., 1867, 17 U. C., C. P. 597; Farmer's etc. *v.* Chestnut, 1869, 50 Ill. 111; First Nat'l., etc. *v.* Goff, 1872, 31 Wis. 77; Little *v.* Phœnix, etc., 1877, 123 Mass. 380; Hughes *v.* Metropolitan, etc., 1877, 1 C. P. D. 135; 46 L. J., C. P. 583; 36 L. T. 932; 2 A. C. 439; St. Paul, etc. *v.* McGregor, 1885, 63 Tex. 399; Horst *v.* London, etc., 1889, 73 Tex. 67; 11 S. W. 148; Mutual, etc. *v.* Tolbert, 1895, 33 S. W. 295.

[4] Peoria, etc. *v.* Whitehill, 1861, 25 Ill. 466. Approved in Derrick *v.* Lamar, etc., 1874, 74 Ill. 404; Home *v.* Myer, 93 Ill. 271; Allemania, etc. *v.* Peck, 133 Ill. 220; 24 N. E. 538.

deprive the company of the benefit of the time limit.[1] While upon the other hand, it is said

> a positive act of the defendant intended to induce postponement is not necessary. Silence on the subject in the midst of negotiations for settlement during the year, however intended, was held by the General Term to be competent evidence to go to the jury, and, if competent, its weight was to be determined by them. The court, especially to aid a forfeiture, and a very harsh one too, will not scrutinize very closely their verdict on such a point.[2]

FURTHER CONSIDERATION. " Waiver " of the delivery by a policy-holder of proofs of loss, by denial of liability upon other grounds, has been discussed in a previous chapter [3] and some observations pertinent to the subject now in hand may be found there.

[1] McFarland *v.* Peabody, etc., 1873, 6 W. Va. 425; Gooden *v.* Amoskeag, etc., 1849, 20 N. H. 73.

[2] Ripley *v.* Ætna Ins. Co. 1859, 29 Barb. 552.

[3] *Ante*, pp. 259–270.

CHAPTER XVI

INSURANCE

"Waiver" of the "No-Waiver" Clauses

Courts *v.* Companies. Little risk would be assumed, were we to say that if, instead of policies providing that (under certain circumstances) they should be "void," the draughtsmen had always written "voidable at the election of the company," the customary "no-waiver" clauses would never have come into existence. Not observing the meaning of the word which they had put in their contracts, the companies (upon the happening of prohibited events) became accustomed to declare that the policies had been forfeited — meaning terminated — when in reality nothing had happened to them. The courts, not perceiving that that assertion was quite erroneous, answered forfeiture with "waiver." The companies replied with their "no-waiver" clauses. And the courts rejoined with "waiver of no-waiver," and said that, in any case, the no-waiver clauses applied (1) to conditions of liability only, and not to conditions of action, such as those relating to notices and proofs of loss,[1] and (2)

[1] Washburn, etc. *v.* Merchants, etc., 1900, 110 Iowa 423; 81 N. W. 707. But see Northern, etc. *v.* Grand View, etc., 1901, 183 U. S. 327; 101 Fed. 77.

not to those conditions which relate to the inception of the contract.

> Until the contract is consummated, the company has no rights which are susceptible of waiver, nor can any condition be properly said to be modified or stricken from a policy until there is a policy.[1]

It is all very unreal.

CLASSIFICATION. The clauses are of three kinds, and a few words must be devoted to each of them.

1. Clauses in which it is agreed that there shall be "no waiver" except in a particular way — for example, by writing, or by endorsement on the policy.

2. Clauses in which it is agreed that no agent of the company shall have power to "waive."

3. Clauses in which it is agreed that certain specified acts shall not be "waivers."

Let us look at the law as laid down in the cases, and afterwards make such criticism of it as may seem to be necessary.

1. No Waiver Except in a Particular Way

> THE AUTHORITIES. Parties to contracts cannot disable themselves from making any contracts allowed by law in any mode the law allows contracts to be made. A written contract may be changed by parol, and a parol one changed by a writing, despite any provisions in the contracts to the contrary.[2]
>
> One who has agreed that he will only contract by writing . . . does not preclude himself from making a parol bargain to change it, and there is no more force in an agreement in writing not to agree by parol, than in a parol agreement not to agree in writing.[3]

[1] Continental, etc. *v.* Ruckman, 1889, 127 Ill. 373. And see McAllister *v.* New England, etc., 1869, 101 Mass. 558; Sears *v.* Agricultural, etc., 1882, 32 U. C., C. P. 600; Wood *v.* American, etc., 1896, 149 N. Y. 382; 44 N. E. 80.

[2] Ins. Co. *v.* Norwood, 16 C. C. A. 136; 69 Fed. 71. Approved in McElroy *v.* British, etc., 1899, 94 Fed. 990; 36 C. C. A. 615. And see Murphy *v.* Royal, etc., 1899, 52 La. Ann. 775; 27 So. 143; Metropolitan Life *v.* Johnson, 1911, 49 Ind. App. 233; 94 N. E. 785.

[3] Ins. Co. *v.* Earle, 33 Mich. 143. Approved in Copeland *v.* Hewett, 1902, 53 Atl. 37; 96 Me. 525.

A contracting party cannot so tie his own hands, so restrict his own legal capacity for future action, that he has not the power, even with the assent of the other party, to bind or obligate himself by his further action or agreement, contrary to the terms of the written contract, Westchester *v.* Earle, 33 Mich. 143. This is self-evident.[1]

There can be no more force in an agreement in writing not to agree by parol, than in a parol agreement not to agree in writing. Every such agreement is ended by the new one which contradicts it.[2]

CLAUSES NUGATORY. Clauses of the kind under consideration are, therefore, practically nugatory.[3] Even legislatures cannot deprive themselves of authority to exercise their powers. And an insurance company cannot, by agreement, preclude itself from entering into subsequent agreements, or being bound by subsequent acts. Many cases apply this view to provisions that there shall be no "waiver" unless in writing;[4] or unless by indorsement on the policy;[5] or by some particular officer.[6]

[1] Lamberton *v.* Connecticut, etc., 1888, 39 Minn. 131; 39 N. W. 76. See also Thompson *v.* Traders, etc., 1902, 68 S. W. 889; 169 Mo. 12; Ross-Langford *v.* Mercantile, 1902, 71 S. W. 720; 97 Mo. App. 79; United States, etc. *v.* Lesser, 1900, 126 Ala. 568; 28 So. 646; Palmer *v.* St. Paul, 1878, 44 Wis. 201.

[2] Westchester, etc. *v.* Earle, 33 Mich. 143. Approved in Home, etc. *v.* Gibson, 1894, 72 Miss. 58.

[3] Smalldone *v.* President, etc., 1867, 44 N. Y. Supp. 201.

[4] Beebe *v.* Ohio, etc., 1892, 93 Mich. 514; 53 N. W. 818; Smalldone *v.* President, 1867, 44 N. Y. Supp. 201; Northern *v.* Grand View, etc., 1900, 41 C. C. A. 207; 101 Fed. 80; 183 U. S. 321; 22 S. C. 133; Copeland *v.* Hewitt, 1902, 53 Atl. 36; 96 Me. 525; Orient, etc. *v.* McKnight, 1902, 96 Ill. App. 525; 64 N. E. 339; Ross-Langford *v.* Mercantile, etc., 1902, 71 S. W. 720; 97 Mo. App. 79; Morrow *v.* Lancashire, 1899, 26 Ont. App. 179.

The above are insurance cases. Roe *v.* Harrison, 1788, 2 T. R. 425, deals with a similar provision in a lease.

[5] Palmer *v.* St. Paul, etc., 1878, 44 Wis. 201; Lamberton *v.* Connecticut, etc., 1888, 39 Minn. 129; 39 N. W. 76; McFetridge *v.* American, etc., 1895, 90 Wis. 138; 62 N. W. 938; Northam *v.* International, etc., 1899, 45 N. Y. App. D. 177; 61 N. Y. Supp. 45; Stage *v.* Home, etc., 1902, 76 N. Y. App. Div. 509; 78 N. Y. Supp. 555; Home *v.* Nichols, 1903, 72 S. W. 440. But see Quinlan *v.* Prov., etc. 133 N. Y. 356; 31 N. E. 31.

[6] United States, etc. *v.* Lesser, 1900, 28 So. 646; 126 Ala. 568; Phœnix, etc. *v.* Caldwell, 1900, 58 N. E. 314; 85 Ill. App. 104; Continental, etc. *v.* Norris, 1902,

> It has been so many times decided that although a policy of insurance contains a stipulation that nothing less than a written agreement indorsed on the policy will suffice to establish a waiver, yet it is admissible to show, by parol testimony, a waiver by acts *in pais*, that it is scarcely necessary to refer to the authorities.[1]

The non-waiver clauses can themselves be "waived."[2]

WAIVER OF PROVISION OF CHARTER. Assertion (as in a Massachusett's case[3]) that a company can "waive" the provisions of its own charter has an unattractive sound. Can a company, by "waiver," render itself liable to pay, if its charter declare that, under circumstances which have happened, the policy shall be "void?" Not, if *void* mean cancelled or terminated. But all difficulty disappears if we interpret the charter as declaring that the policy shall be void at the election of the company. In that case the company becomes liable not by "waiving" the provisions of its charter, but by exercising the election which it gives.

2. CLAUSES IN WHICH IT IS AGREED THAT NO AGENT OF THE COMPANY SHALL HAVE POWER TO "WAIVE"

A CURIOUS CLAUSE. Put in the form of an agreement, this a rather curious clause. It assumes that the authority which a principal may, at any future time, choose to give to his agent may be regulated in advance by a contract between the principal and somebody else; and that such a contract will prevent the principal, even with the assent of the "somebody else," doing through an agent that which he might do himself. It would be absurd to contend, that because of

30 Tex. C. A. 299; 70 S. W. 769. And see Chapman *v.* Delaware, etc., 1883, 23 N. B. 121.

[1] Mix *v.* Royal, etc., 1895, 169 Pa. 639; 32 Atl. 460.

[2] Union, etc. *v.* Whetzel, 1902, 29 Ind. App. 658; 65 N. E. 15.

[3] Clark *v.* New England, etc., 1850, 60 Mass. 342. A company may "waive" the provisions of its own by-laws: Supreme, etc. *v.* Volkert, 1900, 25 Ind. App. 627; 57 N. E. 203.

such a clause in a policy, the company would be powerless to give express authority to one of its officers to "waive" conditions. Could it not authorize its officers to pay the claim (something of a "waiver"), even though all the conditions had been broken?

In the form of an agreement, or in any other form, such a clause may very well be a notification to the assured, that no agent of the company has, at present, authority to "waive."[1] But such a notification is of course not worth giving if it be untrue — that is if the agent actually has, at the moment, authority to "waive." The authorities generally support the view that while the clause in question is notice to the assured of the limitation of the agent's authority, yet, that notwithstanding such notice, an agent may "waive," if in reality he has authority to do so.[2]

Clause as an Agreement. It is sometimes said that a stipulation, to the effect that an agent has no authority to "waive," is an agreement, and that the courts cannot alter it.[3] That is quite true, but it may be altered by the parties. They agreed (we may say) that the company would not act through an agent; and afterwards, with the assent of the policy-holder, the company did so act.

For example, an insurance company promises (agrees) that it will not "waive" a provision for nullity of the policy upon default in payment; default happens; what is the situation?

[1] Knickerbocker, etc. *v.* Norton, 1877, 96 U. S. 234; Phœnix *v.* Doster, 1882, 106 U. S. 34; U. S., etc. *v.* Lesser, 1900, 126 Ala. 568; 28 So. 646; Murphy *v.* Royal, etc., 1899, 52 La. Ann. 775; 27 So. 143.

[2] Gould *v.* Dwelling House, etc., 1892, 90 Mich. 302; 51 N. W. 455; New York, etc. *v.* Fletcher, 1885, 117 U. S. 530; Nixon *v.* Travellers, etc., 1901, 65 Pac. 195; 25 Wash. 254; Sheldon *v.* Parker, 1902, 92 N. W. 923; 66 Neb. 610; Weed *v.* London, etc., 1889, 116 N. Y. 117; 22 N. E. 229; McElroy *v.* British, etc., 1899, 94 Fed. 998; 36 C. C. A. 615; Provident, etc. *v.* Oliver, 1899, 22 Tex. Civ. App. 8; 53 S. W. 594; Phœnix, etc. *v.* Caldwell, 1900, 85 Ill. App. 104; 58 N. E. 314; United States, etc. *v.* Lesser, 1900, 126 Ala. 568; 28 So. 646; Wolf *v.* Dwelling House, 1900, 86 Mo. App. 580; Ross-Langford *v.* Mercantile, etc., 1902, 97 Mo. App. 71; 71 S. W. 720.

[3] Waynesboro, etc. *v.* Conover, 1881, 98 Pa. 384.

Can it accept the premium when offered? If so it can "waive" the default. And if the company promises that no agent of the company shall "waive" default; and default happens, cannot the company authorize an agent to accept a premium?

3. Clauses in Which It Is Agreed That Certain Specified Acts Shall Not Be "Waivers"

Apart from the paradoxical character of an agreement which provides that a "waiver" shall not be a "waiver," there seems to be no good reason (from a forfeiture and "waiver" point of view) for doubting that the parties may agree that certain acts shall not be "waivers"; for that may be but giving a specific character to an otherwise equivocal act.[1] The following clause of the Rhode Island statutory policy [2] may be defended upon that ground:

> This company shall not be held to have waived any power or condition of this policy, or any forfeiture thereof, by any requirement, act, or proceeding, on its part, relating to the appraisal, or to any examination herein provided for.[3]

Such acts being equivocal, the policy gives to them an agreed character.

> An adjustment does not necessarily imply liability, and accordingly it may be made under a reservation as to the question of liability.[4]

Election. So far, we have been using the language of the courts, namely the language of forfeiture and "waiver." And we must now observe that all difficulties associated

[1] Phœnix, etc. *v.* Fleming, 1898, 65 Ark. 54; 44 S. W. 464.

[2] Gen. Laws, c. 183, s. 5.

[3] Fournier *v.* German, 1901, 23 R. I. 36; 49 Atl. 98. Bishop *v.* Agricultural, etc., 1892, 130 N. Y. 488; 29 N. E. 844; Corson *v.* Anchor, etc., 1901, 85 N. W. 806; 113 Iowa 641.

[4] Whipple *v.* Ins. Co., 1875, 11 R. I. 139. Approved in Fournier *v.* German, etc., 1901, 49 Atl. 97; 23 R. I. 36.

with the " no-waiver " clauses disappear with recognition of the fact that they are aimed at that which does not exist. For, as breach of a condition does not work a forfeiture, so there is nothing to " waive "; and stipulation, therefore, prohibitive of " waiver " of forfeiture is useless.

A breach gives the company a right to elect whether to continue or to terminate the policy. " Waiver " can have no relation to the permitted election. And in future, we may see, in better drawn policies, some " non-election " clauses — some provision that no agent of the company shall have power to elect; that certain acts shall not be deemed to be evidence of election; and so on.

INDEX

INDEX

PRINTED AT
THE HARVARD UNIVERSITY PRESS
CAMBRIDGE, MASS., U. S. A.